MAKING SOCIOLOGICAL SENSE

FIRST EDITION

MAKING SOCIOLOGICAL SENSE

EDITED BY C. CANDACE COFFMAN

cognella®

SAN DIEGO

Bassim Hamadeh, CEO and Publisher
Mazin Hassan, Acquisitions Editor
Kaela Martin, Project Editor
Berenice Quirnio, Associate Production Editor
Jackie Bignotti, Production Artist
Michael Skinner, Licensing Coordinator
Natalie Piccotti, Director of Marketing
Kassie Graves, Vice President of Editorial
Jamie Giganti, Director of Academic Publishing

CONTENTS

PREFACE

The materials available to teach Introduction to Sociology are vast. However, many of the books out there share the traits of being very costly and far too much reading for today's students. I have taught at the university level for more than 15 years and have had the opportunity to teach students at elite private schools, research universities, and community colleges. In all of these settings, I had students who struggled to get through a week's reading. I also always had at least some students who did not purchase the course materials because they were too costly. In creating this anthology, I sought to build something that was accessible financially and that students would actually read. We may want them to read six articles a week or a 70-page textbook chapter a week, but it just isn't realistic to think that they will.

In selecting articles for this anthology, I have attempted to broadly cover the work in the field of sociology. It is also an attempt to present sociology as a science that is research based and rooted in social theory. Exposure to original works by classic theorists and research articles by modern sociologists is key to understanding sociology as a field. Many of these articles are part of larger works, which the reading will sometimes refer to. It was not possible to cut all of these references without leaving the piece "choppy," so some of these statements stand and hopefully will not be too distracting to the reader.

The articles are arranged by sections: a first section that introduces the sociological perspective, a second framing systems of stratification, and a third that focuses on social institutions. The sociological perspective section contains a classic work by C. Wright Mills and a more modern work that looks at how consumption is part of society. The second section has articles that deal with gender stratification, economic inequality, and race hierarchies. The final section has an article on male menopause, which could be linked to discussions of health or aging; an article on social networks and health; Lareau's work on parenting styles and social class; an article that examines how systems of inequality affect our education systems; a critique of capitalism; and an article that connects religion and children's support of their aging parents. This last section is categorized as focusing on social institutions. The articles can be used to focus on different aspects of society. So, for example, the article on male menopause could be assigned in a section covering health or in a section of your course focusing on gender. This both provides flexibility for different instructors' use of the book and, hopefully, highlights that few aspects of studying people in society are about just one thing.

Each article has key terms and guiding questions the student should have in mind as he or she reads the article. There is always a question asking the student to state the main point of the article—something students often come away from an article unable to do. The questions are meant to guide the student as he or she reads, to help him or her be more focused and attentive. There is also a question asking the student to think about how the article might apply to his or her everyday life.

INTRODUCTION

Welcome to the world of sociology. In this science, we examine all the ways in which people are affected by living in a society. The term "society" encompasses several things. It means people, living together in groups, whose behavior is patterned. Think about how you behave when you go into a coffee shop: you go to the counter, you order your coffee, you find a seat—by yourself or with others. You might work on your computer (I am currently writing this in a coffee shop), visit with friends, or maybe even read a book. Most everything I have mentioned here is patterned, from the use of space to what you consume, how you consume it, and what you do in this space. You are in a "coffee shop" as a socially structured space with **norms** and expectations for what you will do there. If you went to a bar or tap room, would you follow the same behavior and do the same things? What about if you were at your place of worship? Different social spaces have different expectations for behavior. This is just one example among many of how we follow patterns for our day-to-day behavior. These patterns are one part of what we mean when we use the term "society."

Society also includes larger social structures that help meet the needs of people and of society itself. This includes things like an economic system and a political system as well as less obvious structures such as gender and ethnicity. We all occupy places in these systems. You have a gender and one or more ethnic identities. You have a position in the economic structure (for many reading this, this position is that of a college student). Each of these positions is called a **status**. Each status has expectations for behavior associated with it, which we refer to as **roles**.

THE ORGANIZATION OF THIS BOOK

This book seeks to introduce the reader to the field of sociology through exposure to the work of sociologists. It is broken into three sections: one orienting the reader to the sociological perspective, one that looks at major systems of inequality that are major forces in our society, and finally, one looking at institutions in society. Institutions are social structures that have specific roles or functions: for example, the education system and the healthcare system. These institutions intersect with other broad systems and structures in our society. Your instructor might emphasize one or another aspect of these connections.

Questions are presented at the beginning of each article to help you be focused in your reading. Read through them, set them aside, and then give the article a careful read-through. Then go back and answer the questions—most likely reviewing the article again as you do so.

Each article has a question asking you what the main point of the article is. This is sometimes the most challenging question for students. As you are reading the article, take notes. (I recommend you do this by hand, with a pen or pencil and a notebook. Try it—it works.) In your note taking, first ask yourself: What is the topic of the article? Once you have an idea what the topic is, as you read (or after you have read the article through entirely once), ask yourself: Is the author trying to convince me of something about the topic? Is he or she taking a position? Is the author arguing against things that might have been already said about the topic? And finally, after you have read the article, imagine you want to tell someone about what you just read, in one sentence.

LEARNING OUTCOMES

Following successful completion of the readings and exercises in the book, the student should be able to:

- Articulate the sociological perspective and its contribution to the understanding of human behavior and society

- Describe the way systems of stratification such as race, gender, and class affect our daily lives and greatly affect one's life chances (i.e., how likely one is to be successful, healthy, and happy)

- Explain how institutions such as education and health are affected by macro-level social factors (such as race, class, and gender) and micro-level factors (such as connections to other people)

- Apply sociological concepts to their daily lives and understanding of the world

SECTION I

A SOCIOLOGICAL PERSPECTIVE

Sociology is the study of people. Many disciplines study people. History, economics, medicine—these are all the study of people. So what is it about sociology that makes it different? What makes it a unique field? What, then, is a sociological perspective?

In sociology, we study people *in society*. We are interested in how being in a group, living in a larger social structure, influences everything from the "nitty-gritty" day-to-day behavior and interactions of people to the larger opportunities and constraints they face in life. How likely are you to get an education, get a good job, have a long and healthy life? Aspects of the social structure—things like your social class at birth, your race, your gender, and your sexual orientation—affect these outcomes.

Your day-to-day interactions with people, this "nitty-gritty" daily life, are also affected by where you are in the social structure. The position you hold in the social structure as an individual is called a **status**. These statuses have associated **roles**: things you do, or are expected to do, because you occupy a particular status. We all hold multiple statuses, including our genders, our occupations (at least one of yours is probably a student if you are reading this book), and our positions in our families (brother, sister, son, daughter). In your status as a son or daughter, your roles include things like being reasonably obedient to your parents.

Later, as an adult child of elderly parents, your role will include making sure your parents are well cared for in their old age.

So these role expectations affect how we think about ourselves (Are you proud of how you treat your parents?), what we do with our time (Did you spend part of your weekend mowing your widowed mother's lawn?), and how we want others to see us (Would it cause you shame if you weren't able to help out your elderly mother? If she suffered neglect because you live too far away to help her yourself or you were unable to pay for her to be in a high-quality assisted living facility?).

Other statuses affect what Goffman called the "presentation of self" (Erving Goffman, *The Presentation of Self in Everyday Life* [New York: Anchor Books, 1959]). Think about what clothing you choose to wear on a given day. Is it part of how you express your gender identity? Does your clothing selection differ based on whether you are going to school, work, or your place of worship? These different locations link to different social statuses you hold, which you negotiate and express in different ways.

So, sociologists examine how being part of large social structures (such as the economy and class structure) affects peoples' likelihood of doing well or not doing well (something we refer to as "life chances"). Taking this perspective is referred to as **macro-level** analysis. The level of analysis that looks at how we negotiate our day-to-day lives and social interactions is the **micro-level** perspective.

The sociological perspective then, is the examination of how being in a society affects human behavior, identity, and life chances. In the first reading in this section, "Psychology and Social Science" by C. Wright Mills, Mills lays out the contrasting features of a sociological perspective and a psychological perspective, which he refers to as the **sociological imagination.**

Another major factor in the study of society and the people who live in it is culture. Culture encompasses many things, most particularly ideas and beliefs people learn growing up in a society that are shared among members of the group.

The second reading in this section, "Theories of Food and the Social Meanings of Coffee" by Catherine M. Tucker, examines how something that seems very basic—the food and drink we use to nourish our bodies—exists within a web of social and cultural meaning. What we consume and who we consume it with is part of how we express and negotiate our social status. This article in particular looks at how coffee consumption is part of social class.

CHAPTER 1

PSYCHOLOGY AND SOCIAL SCIENCE

Consider the following questions as you read this section.

QUESTIONS TO CONSIDER

1   How does Mills say we are to understand the biography of the individual? What ought we pay attention to? How does Mills say the sociological perspective differs from the psychological one?

2   How do you usually think about your life? Things that happen to you? How might this explanation shift if you apply the sociological perspective?

3   What is the main point of the article?

KEY TERMS

the sociological imagination

PSYCHOLOGY AND SOCIAL SCIENCE

BY C. WRIGHT MILLS

S ocial scientists want to understand not only social structure and history; they want to understand the varieties of individual men and women that are historically selected and formed by the social structures in which they live. The biographies of these people cannot be understood without reference to the historical structures in which are organized the milieux of their everyday lives. It is now possible to trace the meanings of historic transformations not only for individual ways of life but for the very characters of a variety of human beings. As the history-making unit, the nation-state is also the unit within which types of men and women are formed: it is the man-making unit. That is one reason why struggle between nations and between blocs of nations is also struggle over the types of human beings that will eventually prevail; that is why culture and politics are now so intimately related, and that is why there is such need and such demand for the sociological imagination. The problems of social and historical psychology are in many ways the most intriguing that we can today confront. For it is in this area, it happens, that the major intellectual traditions of our time, in fact of Western civilization, have now come to a most exciting confluence.

There is no end to arguments about the relations between "psychology" and "the social sciences." Most of the arguments have been formal attempts to integrate a variety of ideas about "the individual" and "the group." No doubt they are all useful, in some way to somebody; fortunately, in our attempt to formulate the tasks of social science, they need not concern us. For however psychologists may define their field of work, the economist and the sociologist, the political scientist, the anthropologist and the historian, in their studies of human society, must make assumptions about "human nature" and as well, by their studies, imply a variety of conceptions of man. These assumptions and implications now usually fall into the borderline area of "social psychology."

Interest in this area has increased because, like history, psychology is so fundamental to work in social sciences that insofar as psychologists have not turned to the problems involved, social scientists have become their own psychologists. Economists, long the most formalized of social scientists, have become aware that the old "economic man," hedonistic and calculating, can no longer be assumed as the psychological foundations of an adequate study of economic institutions. Within anthropology there has grown up a strong interest in "personality and culture"; within sociology as well as psychology, "social psychology" is now a busy field of study. Psychiatry—the most problematic field of both medicine and social study—has become a confusion of perspectives, drawn from virtually all social, biological, and psychological fields of study.

In reaction to these intellectual developments, some psychologists have taken up a variety of work in "social psychology," others have attempted, in a variety of ways, to redefine psychology so as to retain a field of study apart from obviously social factors, and some have confined their activities to work in human physiology. I do not wish to examine here the academic specialties within psychology—a field now greatly torn and split—much less to judge them.

There is one style of psychological reflection which has not usually been taken up explicitly by academic psychologists but which nonetheless has exerted influence upon them, as well as upon our entire intellectual life. In psychoanalysis, and especially in the work of Freud himself, the problem of the nature of human nature is stated within the broadest of frameworks. In brief, during the last generation, two and one-half steps forward have been taken by the less rigid of the psychoanalysts.

First, the physiology of the individual organism was transcended, and there began the study of those little family circles in which such dreadful melodramas occurred. Freud may be said to have discovered from an unexpected viewpoint—the medical— the analysis of the individual in his parental family. Of course, the "influence" of the family upon man had been noticed; what was new was that as a social institution it became, in Freud's view, intrinsic to the inner character and life-fate of the individual.

Second, the social element in the lens of psychoanalysis was greatly broadened, especially by what may be called sociological work on the superego. In America, to the psychoanalytic tradition was joined one having quite different sources, which came to early flower in the social behaviorism of George H. Mead. But then a limitation or a hesitancy set in. The small-scale setting of "interpersonal relations" is now clearly seen; the broader context in which these relations themselves, and hence the individual himself, are situated has not been. There are, of course, exceptions, notably

Erich Fromm who has related economic and religious institutions and traced out their meaning for types of individuals. One reason for the general hesitancy is the limited social role of the analyst; his work and his perspective are professionally tied to the individual patient; the problems of which he is aware and of which he can readily become aware, under the specialized conditions of his practice, are limited and limiting. Unfortunately, psychoanalysis has not become a firm and integral part of academic research.[1]

The next step forward in psychoanalytic studies is to do fully for other institutional areas what Freud began to do so magnificently for kinship institutions of a selected type. What is needed is the idea of social structure as a composition of institutional orders, each of which we must study psychologically as Freud studied certain kinship institutions. The psychiatry, the actual therapy of "interpersonal" relations, has already begun to raise questions about a troublesome central point: the tendency to anchor values and norms in the supposed needs of the individuals *per se*. For if the individual's very nature cannot be understood without close reference to social reality, then we must analyze it in such reference. And such analysis includes not only the locating of the individual, as a biographical entity, within various interpersonal milieux—but the locating of these milieux within their social structure.

On the basis of developments in psychoanalysis, as well as in social psychology as a whole, it is now possible to state briefly the psychological concerns of the social sciences. I list here, in the barest of summary, only those propositions which I take as the most fruitful hunches, or, at the least, as legitimate assumptions on the part of the working social scientist.[2]

(1) The external biography of an individual cannot be adequately understood without references to the institutions within which it is enacted. For this biography consists of acquiring, of dropping, of modifying, in a very intimate way, of moving from one role to another. One is a child in a certain kind of family, one is a playmate in a certain kind of child's group; a student, a workman, a foreman, a general, a mother. Much of human life consists of playing such roles within specific institutions. To understand the biography of an individual, we must understand the significance and meaning of the roles he has played and does play; to understand these roles we must understand the institutions of which they are a part.

(2) But the view of man as a social creature enables us to go much deeper than merely viewing the external biography as a sequence of social roles. Such a view requires us to understand the most internal and "psychological" features of man: in particular, his self-image and his conscience and indeed the very growth of his mind. It may well be that the most radical discovery within recent psychology, psychoanalysis, and social science is the discovery of how so many of the most intimate features of the person are socially patterned and even implanted. Within the quite broad limits of the

glandular and nervous apparatus, the emotions of fear and hatred and love and rage, in all their varieties, must be understood in close and continual reference to the social biography and the social context in which they are experienced and expressed. Within the quite broad limits of the physiology of the sense organs, our very perception of the physical world, the colors we discriminate, the smells we become aware of, the noises we hear, are socially patterned and socially limited. The motivations of men, and even the varying extents to which various types of men are typically aware of them, are to be understood in terms of the vocabularies of motive that prevail in a society and of social changes and confusions among such vocabularies.

(3) The biography and the character of the individual cannot be understood merely in terms of milieux, and certainly not entirely in terms of early milieux—those of the infant and the child. Adequate understanding requires the setting of these milieux, both earlier and later, in their structural framework, taking into account any transformations of this framework that may occur within the span of the individual's lifetime.

The understanding of social structure and of structural changes as they bear upon more intimate milieux enables us to understand the causes of individual conduct, feelings, and limitations on self-awareness, which men in specific milieux cannot themselves detect. The test of an adequate conception of any type of man cannot rest upon whether individuals of this type find it pleasantly in line with their own self-images. Often, in fact, it is because they live only in certain milieux that men do not and cannot be expected to know the causes of their condition and the limits of their selfhood. Groups of men who have truly adequate views of themselves and of their own social positions are indeed rare. To assume the contrary, as is often done by virtue of the very methods used by some social scientists, is to assume a degree of rational self-consciousness and self-knowledge that not even eighteenth century psychologists would allow. Max Weber's idea of "The Puritan Man," of his motives and of his function within religious and economic institutions, enables us to understand him better than he understood himself: Weber's use of the notion of structure enabled him to transcend "the individual's" own awareness of himself and his milieux.

The relevance of earlier experience, "the weight" of childhood, in the psychology of adult character is itself relative to the type of childhood and the type of social biography that prevail in various given societies. It is, for example, now quite apparent that the role of "the father" in the building of a personality must be stated within the limits of specific types of fathers and specific types of families, and in terms of the place such families occupy within the social structure of which these families are a part.

(4) The idea of social structure cannot be built up only from ideas or from facts about a specific series of individuals, their reactions to their milieux. Attempts to explain social and historical events, economics and political, religious, and military institutions, on the basis of psychological theories about "the individual" often rest

upon the assumption that society is nothing but a great scatter of individuals and that, accordingly, if we know all about these "atoms" we can in some way add up the information and thus know about society. It is not a fruitful assumption. In fact, we cannot even know what is most elemental about "the individual" by any psychological study of him as a socially isolated creature. Except in the abstract building of models, which of course may be useful, the economist cannot assume The Economic Man; nor can the psychiatrist of family life (and practically all psychiatrists are, in fact, specialists of this one social area) assume the classical Oedipal Man. For just as the structural relations of economic and political roles are now often decisive for understanding the economic conduct of individuals, so are the great changes, since Victorian fatherhood, in the roles within the family and in the family's location as an institution within modern societies.

(5) The principle of historical specificity holds for psychology as well as for the social sciences. Even quite intimate features of man's inner life are best formulated as problems within specific historical contexts. To realize that this is an entirely reasonable assumption, one has only to reflect for a moment upon the wide variety of men and women that is displayed in the course of human history. Psychologists, as well as social scientists, should indeed think well before finishing any sentences the subject of which is "man."

The human variety is such that no "elemental" psychologies, no theory of "instincts," no principles of "basic human nature" of which we know, enable us to account for the enormous human variety of types and individuals. Anything that can be asserted about man apart from what is inherent in the social-historical realities of human life will refer mainly to the quite wide biological limits and potentialities of the human species. Within these limits and rising out of these potentialities, such a panorama of human types confronts us that to attempt to explain it in terms of a theory of "basic human nature" is to confine human history itself in some arid little cage of concepts about "human nature"—as often as not constructed from some precise and irrelevant trivialities about mice in a maze.

The very idea of some "human nature" common to man as man is a violation of the social and historical specificity that careful work in the human studies requires; at the very least, it is an abstraction that social students have not earned the right to make. Surely we ought occasionally to remember that in truth we do not know much about man, and that all the knowledge we do have does not entirely remove the element of mystery that surrounds his variety as it is revealed in history and in biography. Sometimes we do want to wallow in that mystery, to feel that we are, after all, a part of it, and perhaps we should; but being men of the West, we will inevitably also study the human variety, which for us means removing the mystery from our view of it. In doing so, let us not forget what it is we are studying and how little we know of man, of history, of biography, and of the societies of which we are at once creators and creatures. Realizing this, perhaps we should be at once more careful and less pretentious about the methods we would employ when we get down to our work.

NOTES

1 Another major reason for the tendency to apotheosize "interpersonal relations" is the sponge-like quality and limitations of the word "culture," in terms of which much of the social in man's depths has been recognized and asserted. In contrast with social structure, the concept "culture" is one of the spongiest words in social science, although, perhaps for that reason, in the hands of an expert, enormously useful. In practice, the concept "culture" is more often a loose reference to social milieux plus "tradition" than an adequate idea of social structure.

2 For detailed discussion of the point of view expressed here, see Gerth and Mills, *Character and Social Structure* (New York: Harcourt, Brace, 1953).

CHAPTER 2

THEORIES OF FOOD AND THE SOCIAL MEANING OF COFFEE

Consider the following questions as you read this article.

QUESTIONS TO CONSIDER

1   What binaries did Lévi-Strauss state there were for foods? What does he link this to?

2   How is coffee linked to social class? Do you think your social class affects your choices of food and drink?

3   What is the main point of the article?

KEY TERMS

the raw and the cooked
commodity fetishism

THEORIES OF FOOD AND THE SOCIAL MEANING OF COFFEE

BY CATHERINE M. TUCKER

> Food is always about more than simply what fills the stomach.
>
> (Rouse and Hoskins 2004: 226)

Food has always been of interest to social scientists, but for many years, the study of food remained on the edges of scholarly theories and debates. Since the 1950s, however, food has become an increasingly pertinent topic for scholars studying globalization, cultural identity, and social change (Mintz and Du Bois 2002). Coffee, in particular, offers interesting opportunities for study because of its relationships to global markets as well as group and national identities, and it is a political commodity with great economic importance. Coffee is the second most valuable commodity traded on world markets (although in times of economic crisis, it occasionally falls to third place). The world's most valuable commodity is petroleum, our premier source of energy for transportation. Petroleum and its derivatives find their way into innumerable goods used in all facets of our lives—plastics, electronics, carpets, building materials, clothing, furniture, machinery, pesticides, and many chemical products. When compared with petroleum, coffee seems misplaced as a major generator of international trade dollars.

Coffee provides little nutritional benefit, and it is not a major component in any industrial product other than itself. While coffee can serve as a useful stimulant, a number of the world's coffee drinkers prefer decaffeinated coffees or prepare weak coffee to reduce caffeine content. Moreover, coffee is only one of many sources of caffeine, including tea, chocolate, sodas, diet aids, analgesics, and caffeine tablets. Therefore coffee's economic value, prevalence, and popularity must derive from more than its nutritional, medical, or stimulating qualities. In part, coffee is valuable because it is consumed by large numbers of people who live in places far from its points of origin. But more important, coffee's popularity and economic importance trace to its social utility and associated meanings and values. We drink coffee for many reasons beyond caffeine; like many things we eat, coffee evokes feelings and communicates values unrelated to nutritional content.

SOCIAL IMPLICATIONS OF FOOD

Food exists within complex webs of social relationships. Food provides nutrition for physical sustenance, but it also serves to support social and cultural survival. Food-sharing builds relationships within families and groups; food exchanges with people outside immediate social circles can help build social networks and develop political alliances (Bryant et al. 2003). From birth, the food we eat becomes associated with family, home, and shared experiences that go beyond meals. Our favorite "comfort food" is often a simple dish from childhood; its comfort derives not from novelty or elegance but from deep familiarity and often associations with love and security. A cup of coffee with milk and sugar signifies relaxation for me; it reminds me of the hours I spent talking with friends in graduate school while sipping coffee with free refills. We know we belong where we eat familiar foods in the company of people who share similar memories and experiences, and inviting people to share our meals can be a sign of friendship, or sometimes more. For example, inviting a boyfriend or girlfriend over for dinner with the family can imply that the relationship may be more than a transitory affection.

Food selection and preparation can communicate social skills, shared values, and cultural knowledge, which can be particularly important for women who are usually responsible for food preparation. Among African American women who convert to Islam, food selection and preparation can become empowering religious practices as they follow dietary principles while expressing their perspectives on the historical, symbolic, political, and cultural dimensions of African American "soul foods" (Rouse and Hoskins 2004). Across ethnic and religious backgrounds, bridal gift registries in the USA often include a coffee maker for soon-to-be married couples. Coffee-making may be seen as a necessary skill, depending on one's cultural background. One of my friends, Halima, is from Egypt but, due to her family circumstances, she grew up without learning how to make coffee. When Halima came to the USA as a young bride, she met an Egyptian woman who owned a coffee shop. Halima confided that she did not know how to make coffee, and the shop owner pulled her into the kitchen to teach her. An hour later, Halima knew how to make coffee, and had absorbed a cultural lesson as well: if she wanted to have a long and happy marriage, she needed to be able to make good Egyptian coffee.

Each coffee-consuming society tends have a dominant way to prepare coffee, even when there may be other options. In the USA, filtered coffee is the default form. In Mexico, Central America, and Scandinavia, boiled coffee dominated for many years. Instant coffee has become typical for many parts of South America. Thick boiled coffee, served in tiny cups, remains popular in the Middle East. Each brew carries its own consistency and range of flavors that seem "right" to the people who drink it; when offered a different brew, it may barely seem like coffee at all.

Acceptance or rejection of coffee, or any food, offered to guests may be seen as accepting or rejecting an offer of friendship. Guests who wish to develop friendly relationships with their hosts usually attempt to eat everything put before them, however unfamiliar or personally problematic. During my first fieldwork as a young anthropologist, I worked with a team of researchers in the highlands of Peru. While on an early visit to a family in the community, I was offered a plate of fried sheep's blood. They purchased the blood from the slaughterhouse because they could not afford meat. I had never eaten anything like it; reddish brown globules slid in grease around the plate and tasted like salty rust. I wanted very much to gain their trust and friendship, so I ate it with as much relish as I could muster. My introduction as a teenager to traditionally prepared Colombian coffee did not prove much easier; my hosts served me thick coffee, complete with the grounds, in a demitasse cup dosed liberally with sugar. I sipped it politely, but despite the small quantity, I felt a jolt of energy and did not get much sleep that night. I didn't care for fried blood or traditional Colombian coffee, but in accepting my hosts' gift of food without question, I symbolically accepted them and opened a door to friendship.

RAW, COOKED, OR ROTTEN? PERCEPTIONS OF FOOD, NATURE, AND CULTURE

The meanings and values ascribed to foods may relate to ways that the human mind interprets and categorizes the world. Lévi-Strauss, a renowned French anthropologist, proposed that foods fall into one of three broad categories: "raw," "cooked," or "rotted." By collecting information on myths and food beliefs around the world, he argued that while societies vary in how they interpret the meanings of food, they still deal with dualities such as raw/cooked, raw/rotted, and cooked/rotted, which symbolize and echo other oppositions: nature/culture, good/bad, edible/inedible, self/other, desirable/repulsive. Raw foods are "natural," "unprocessed," and "wild"; they often require some kind of preparation, such as washing, peeling, and cutting to be deemed edible. Cooked foods have been transformed through roasting, boiling, or smoking to become "civilized." Societies tend to regard roasting, boiling, or smoking as having different levels of prestige. Among Western societies, roasting tends to have higher prestige than boiling. The relative status of these forms of cooking varies across history and people (Lévi-Strauss 1983, 2008). There is no universal way to ascertain a food's position in a cultural system of meaningful oppositions and dualities. Instead, it is necessary to understand a people's perspectives and experiences.

The way society categorizes a food reflects its prestige, usefulness, and potential risks, which reflect historical, political, and economic processes, and preferences whose roots may be long forgotten. Perceptions of food risks emerge because of the ways that society links potentially edible substances to social values and experiences. In the USA, edible food discarded by restaurants and groceries becomes "rotted" the moment it hits the dumpster. Insects are considered to be inedible in western society because they are associated with filth and decay (they are "raw" or "rotten"), but in most of the world, people recognize certain insects as delicious and nourishing foods (Bryant et al. 2003). A given food may take on multiple meanings as people negotiate its social values, political meanings, and symbolic representations. The television show "Fear Factor" played upon Western distastes by challenging contestants to do unpleasant things, such as eating insects while competing for monetary prizes. Contestants who chose to eat the insects symbolically and physically transformed the inedible ("raw" or "rotten") to the edible, defying one social norm in order to fulfill another social norm: willingness to sacrifice for monetary gain. In forcing contestants to choose between social norms, the show compelled the audience to question where their preferences and priorities lay. Can something repulsive be made tolerable by the possibility of enrichment (and fleeting fame)? Few Westerners found the answers simple. Lévi-Strauss's perspective helps us to understand that the dilemma emerges from Western perceptions of underlying oppositions. For someone from an insect-eating society, there would be no opposition or repulsion, and no dilemma.

BREWING UP AN EDIBLE AND MEANINGFUL COMMODITY

Coffee does not present moral conundrums for most drinkers, but how does society interpret coffee? Clearly, coffee is "cooked." It has been roasted, ground, and mixed with water by some means—boiling, percolating, filtering, pressing, or steaming under pressure. In this sense, coffee is a complex culinary creation. Yet coffee is also represented as something "natural," "wild," and uncivilized in Western society, because of its associations with exotic origins and dangerous diseases that medical science does not understand well. The perceived risks of coffee led certain religions to ban it and some physicians to warn against it, while the perceived benefits of coffee resulted in the creation of coffee breaks.

Lévi-Strauss suggested that different social meanings map consistently to different types of food preparation: the high prestige activities involve greater patience, more complex technology and resources, or greater skill to carry out well (Lévi-Strauss 1983). Espresso drinks carry the highest social prestige for coffee preparation; it requires special machinery and training to create a perfect shot of espresso, a fine latte, or a cappuccino. People who prefer these drinks may be perceived as more ambitious or wealthy than those who drink regular coffee; thus coffee can be a marker of socioeconomic class.

Yet because a shot of espresso or a cappuccino is within the economic grasp of nearly everyone, people may choose to consume these drinks not only out of enjoyment, but also to appear affluent, discriminating, or tasteful. Similarly, people of wealth may choose regular coffee in part to signal humility, lack of pretention, a connection to modest origins, or shared values with the middle and lower classes. The choice of coffee can thus signal membership in or identification with a social class, but it can also be used to transcend, contradict, or undermine social class divisions. The malleability of coffee to send many messages is part of what makes it so appealing to people of many social backgrounds.

Coffee is also subject to a multitude of opinions because people's experiences and reactions to it vary. The current multiplicity of meanings associated with coffee has emerged (or re-emerged) since the 1980s. Between 1960 and 1988, the percentage of coffee drinkers in the USA fell gradually from 74 percent to 50 percent (Roseberry 1996). Small coffee roasters and shop owners realized that they needed to expand their clientele, and attract young people who had grown up preferring soft drinks. Meanwhile, transnational food corporations that dominate coffee markets (Nestlé, General Foods, Sara Lee, Philip Morris, Proctor and Gamble) depended on their diversified business interests to protect them from declining coffee sales. The big companies' decisions to produce successively cheaper and therefore less flavorful coffee between the 1960s and 1980s most likely contributed to falling demand. Independent entrepreneurs took advantage of the lack of good coffee to draw clients who appreciated quality, flavor, and variety (Roseberry 1996).

COFFEE, IDENTITY, AND MEANING IN THE USA

In the USA, "regular" coffee typically means filtered or percolated coffee. But why coffee instead of tea? American preference for coffee emerged through specific historical events leading up to the Revolutionary War, but it endures because social values and national identity became linked to coffee drinking. In other places, tea, *mate*, or *qat* gained these meaningful linkages. Coffee, however, is unusual as a global commodity because food preferences usually arise when sources are nearby. Tea is native to Asia, where the majority of the world's tea drinkers reside. *Qat*, a popular beverage in the Middle East, grows natively in the region, as does cacao (chocolate) in Mexico, where hot chocolate emerged prehistorically as a favorite elite beverage. *Yerba mate* from local bushes remains a more popular drink in Uruguay and Argentina than coffee, which can be had from nearby Brazil. Instead, most of the world's coffee drinkers live half a world away from the people who produce coffee. Increasing recognition in the USA of coffee's origins now influences people's choices.

Coffee drinkers can choose fair trade, organic, and shade-grown coffees because they appreciate high quality coffee. Or they may see their choice, and their willingness to spend a bit more, as a way of showing solidarity with coffee growers, countering some of the inequities of the profit-driven global economy, and supporting environmental sustainability (Jaffee 2007). "Yuppies" who favor gourmet coffee may also be longing for a more genteel past before mass consumption, and endeavoring to reconstruct a more wholesome era by favoring whole-bean coffees, gourmet shops featuring antique coffee grinders, and diversity in coffee varietals and roasts (Roseberry 1996). Choosing fair trade or other specialty coffees can symbolize resistance to the dominant society. Within punk culture, the choice of fair trade and organic coffee symbolized opposition to capitalism, and rejection of a society characterized by profound social inequities (Clark 2004). In the past 20 years, fair trade and specialty coffees have become the fastest growing segment of the global coffee market. The success of these coffees in many "niche" markets reflects associations with social values and meanings held dear by people across a range of social groups and political perspectives.

The diversity of meanings associated with types of coffee is reinforced by the contrasts in public spaces in which coffee is consumed. Social meanings of place and space intersect with social class and individual identity. Upscale coffee shops contrast with working-class delicatessens; barbershops with coffee pots in waiting areas create an entirely different social space than elegant hair-styling salons with espresso makers in the foyer, even if both provide a similar service. Coffee is an equalizer as well as a marker of difference. Its omnipresence suggests cultural consensus, but it can also be an object of contention. Ironically, the cheapest, least flavorful coffee is associated with some of the world's wealthiest multinational conglomerates, while high quality coffee is associated with independent entrepreneurs, local cooperatives, small coffee shops, and not-for-profit environmental and social justice organizations.

COFFEE AND FETISHISM OF COMMODITIES

Through systems of production and distribution, our choices of food can transform the Earth, and may degrade or conserve the soil and water upon which we depend for sustenance. One of the results of the modern agroindustrial complex has been to separate people from food production. Many things that we consume, including coffee, come prepared and packaged in ways that utterly disguise or contain very little of its original content. A package of hamburger carries no element that implies a cow; a can of ground coffee represents nothing of the bush and cherry of its origins. Some prepared foodstuffs have more to do with laboratory processes and chemical additives than agricultural fields and pastures (Pollan 2008). Instant coffee derives from an industrial process of dehydrating or freeze-drying brewed coffee made from inferior beans, to form a powder that dissolves easily in water. While convenient, the resulting beverage offers a flavor barely reminiscent of fresh-brewed coffee, with less caffeine and a more bitter taste. Marx described this profound separation of the consumer from the producer, and the utter transformation of a final product from the original form, as "fetishism of commodities" (Marx 1978: 319–29). When coffee drinkers consume their brew without knowledge or concern for its origins, they deny their connections to any troubling truth of how it came to their table. Because coffee is produced far away from the majority of its consumers, it has been particularly vulnerable to these separations. But the growth in fair trade and specialty coffees is an attempt to re-connect consumers with producers. The Slow Food and local food movements that are spreading through Europe, the USA, Canada, and Japan in recent years reveal increasing awareness among consumers that they have lost ties to the producers of their food. This awareness has triggered a commitment to rebuild those linkages. The efforts present a humble challenge to the dominance of impersonal global markets, and have created opportunities to renegotiate the culturally specific and globally relevant significance of coffee and many other foods.

Coffee's popularity, however, can only be understood in relationship to global markets. While its origins precede the development of the modern world system, the use of coffee as a beverage apparently emerged not long before the time that European vessels began exploring the globe. Thereafter, the history of coffee becomes inseparable from the history of colonialism, imperialism and the rise of global capitalism. To comprehend the economic, social, and cultural significance of coffee, we must explore its history.

[...]

REFERENCES

Bryant, C.A., K.M. DeWalt, A. Courtney, and J. Schwartz. 2003. *The Cultural Feast: An Introduction to Food and Society.* Belmont, CA: Thomson Wadsworth.

Clark, D. 2004. "The Raw and the Rotten: Punk Cuisine." *Ethnology 43*: 19–31.

Jaffee, D. 2007. *Brewing Justice: Fair Trade Coffee, Sustainability, and Survival.* Berkeley: University of California Press.

Lévi-Strauss, C. 1983. *The Raw and the Cooked: Mythologiques Vol. I.* Chicago: University of Chicago Press.

———. 2008. "The Culinary Triangle." Pp. 36–43 in *Food and Culture: A Reader,* 2nd edition, eds. C. Counihan and P. Van Esterik. New York: Routledge.

Marx, K. 1978. Capital, Volume One. Pp. 294–439 in *The Marx-Engels Reader,* ed. R.C. Tucker. New York: W.W. Norton.

Mintz, S.W., and C.M. Du Bois. 2002. "The Anthropology of Food and Eating." *Annual Review of Anthropology 31*: 99–119.

Pollan, M. 2008. *In Defense of Food: An Eater's Manifesto.* New York: Penguin.

Roseberry, W. 1996. "The Rise of Yuppie Coffees and the Reimagination of Class in the United States." *American Anthropologist 98*: 762–75.

Rouse, C., and J. Hoskins. 2004. "Purity, Soul Food, and Sunni Islam: Explorations at the Intersection of Consumption and Resistance." *Cultural Anthropology 19*: 226–49.

SECTION II

STRUCTURES OF CONSTRAINT AND OPPORTUNITY

One of the aspects of social structure that is of utmost importance but that can be difficult to "see" is the systems of inequality we live within. Every society has valued resources. In most—if not all—societies, there is not equal access to these resources for all people in the society. Prestige, or social value, is also not equally shared among all members of society. Not surprisingly, levels of access to resources and levels of access to prestige tend to be interrelated. The major systems of stratification to be discussed in this section are race, class, and gender.

RACE

The term "race" is a tricky one. It is something we believe in, but it doesn't really exist, and it has a major effect on your life opportunities. So, we believe people can be grouped according to skin color into biologically differentiated subgroups. In actual fact, the only biological difference among these supposed subgroups is skin color, and the boundaries of those are not really existence.[1] So in this sense, race isn't real.

---

1 The American Anthropological Association website provides an excellent resource for exploring the topic of race. See http://www.understandingrace.org/.

The way that race is real is socially. The race concept grew out of interactions among people globally in which people of one so-called "race" colonized, enslaved, and committed genocide against people of other so-called "races." Mostly, we are talking about northern Europeans ("whites") conquering and enslaving "nonwhites," but other groups have behaved similarly. In the early colonial United States, we had the establishment of hierarchies of race, with whites controlling more power and resources and nonwhites having less power, less access to resources, and less personal freedom. The article on white privilege looks at how today, though we no longer have legal racism, racial inequality—one people being marked as different, as not really belonging—can play out in some very subtle ways and have very real consequences.

CLASS

Your social class is in part determined by your position in the economic structure: the type of work you do and the income that you earn. This further connects with your education level, the income and wealth of the family you were born into, the neighborhood you live in, and your social connections to other people. The article in this section, "How Inequality Wrecks Everything We Care About" by Chuck Collins, looks at how an increase in economic stratification is having negative effects on our society as a whole.

GENDER

It is obvious that there are biological—physical and genetic—differences between males and females. Gender is less obvious. As people in a society, we express and "perform" our maleness and femaleness through how we dress and how we carry ourselves (sit, stand, walk, talk). It is also your experience of yourself as male or female. And while gender is related to sex, it isn't entirely determined by it.

Gender develops through a socialization process. In general, socialization refers to how one grows up in a society and learns to be a person in the society: how one learns the culture and norms and how to occupy social statuses and perform social roles. One of the things we learn is to "be" our gender. There can be many agents of socialization in a young person's life. The article by Michael A. Messner, "'They're Different—and They're Born Different': Engendering the Kids," looks at how youth baseball and softball coaches view and interact with boys and girls. The attitudes of influential people in young peoples' lives can affect their self-concepts—their socialization as males or females.

CHAPTER 3

THEY'RE DIFFERENT— AND THEY'RE BORN DIFFERENT

Consider the following questions as you read this chapter.

QUESTIONS TO CONSIDER

1   What are the three threads Messner found in his research? Explain each and give an example.

2   Did you play sports as a child? Do you now? After reading this article, do you think your gender may have affected how you were treated? Expectations of your abilities?

3   What is the main point of the article?

KEY TERMS

soft essentialism

THEY'RE DIFFERENT— AND THEY'RE BORN DIFFERENT

ENGENDERING THE KIDS

BY MICHAEL A. MESSNER

The fields are wet on this cool, sunny day in late-January. Suzel and I cut back and forth from the Arroyo, where the boys' baseball tryouts are taking place, to the Orange Grove softball field, the site of the girls' tryouts. Both events are structured similarly, but they differ in some striking ways. The boys' tryout has a serious and formal feel to it. Milling around behind the backstop, the parents joke with each other and talk about how their sons (and they) are nervous about the tryout. Everybody knows that each boy's performance today is being scrutinized and is consequential. One of the parents tells me that he took his son to the batting cages early this morning to get him warmed up for this event; I realize—too late—that I should have done this for Sasha too, to give him an edge. Near the edge of the infield, in short right field, roughly a dozen managers, all men, sit in folding lawn chairs, holding clipboards, chatting with each other. Each boy wears a large number on his chest so that the managers can identify him. When it's his turn, the boy's name and number are announced over the P.A. system, after which the boy steps to the plate and swings at three or four pitches from a pitching machine. Before the final pitch, the coach who is running the machine yells to the boy, "Okay, run the bases on this next one." Whether the kid hits the ball or not, he runs the bases. Next, the boy fields three grounders from the shortstop position and throws to first; he then runs to the outfield and fields three fly balls hit by a machine, and then he's done. The managers in the chairs say nothing to the kids before, during, or after the tryout. But the notes they are taking on how well or poorly each boy hit, ran, fielded, and threw are the data they will use to place the boys in different leagues and teams in the upcoming draft.

At Orange Grove, there is a similar scene. People stand around talking and waiting as individual girls take their turn at the plate, then field and throw a few balls. As at the Arroyo, the managers (mostly men, but I see two women among them) are sitting, and a few are standing, as they write notes on clipboards. One difference here is that the pitching is being delivered "live," not by a machine. The man who is pitching is running a fairly constant monologue, giving tips and encouragement to each girl who steps to the plate. "Okay, Sweetie, watch the ball and hit it." In fact, he seems to call each girl who steps to the plate "Sweetie." There's another man standing near the plate who is giving lots of one-on-one instruction to each girl on her batting stance and swinging mechanics. The girls we are watching here are roughly the same age as the boys we had watched earlier at the Arroyo; however, the tone of the event is very different. The boys' tryout seemed impersonal, very formal. The coaches seemed to assume that the boys knew exactly what to do, and they just sat back and judged the boys' performances. The girls' tryout has a more informal feel to it, and the coaches' interactions with the girls are more directly warm, helpful, and sometimes (from my point of view) condescending in their tone.

Underlying the "everyone plays" philosophy at the heart of AYSO and Little League Baseball/Softball is the assumption that there are benefits for kids—healthy exercise, social development, building self-confidence, and having fun—that every kid has a right to. Every single coach we interviewed said that there was value in sports participation for kids. Doug Berger was happy that his daughter had played many years of soccer: "As my daughter gets older, I appreciate more and more the physical health it's given her. I mean, she's in great shape—she does cross country, she does track—you know, she does all these other things that she probably wouldn't have done if she hadn't have played soccer, because I don't think she was a natural athlete, and it gave her confidence." Pam Burke saw these kinds of benefits as her son's birthright and had decided to coach his soccer team after her son experienced a "horrible" coach: "I said, I am not going to have him turned away from competing in community soccer because he is not the star of the team. There is a place for everyone in AYSO. You don't have to be the star. And everyone should be able to play and have fun, and enjoy it and get better, and learn something, make a friend, and so for that reason I coached his team."

The enthusiasm that volunteer coaches have for the benefits of sports should not surprise us. A 2008 national survey indicated that 95 percent of parents in the United States agree that participation in youth sports raises kids' self-esteem, and a vast majority of adults expect educational, social, and health benefits to accrue to their athletic children.[1] And this parental support for kids playing sports is no longer reserved just for boys. Parents today overwhelmingly agree that sports participation is good for their daughters, too. But my research reveals some striking differences in how boys and girls are viewed and treated by adult volunteer coaches. As the vignette that opens this chapter illustrates, boys and girls can be engaged in a similar activity—in this case, a beginning-of-the-season tryout—on the very same day and yet have very different experiences. Here, as is usually the case in organized youth sports, the kids were sex-segregated, and in this case they had been tracked into playing different sports—boys displaying their baseball skills on one field, girls their softball skills on another. And though the content of the activity was very similar, the adults in charge shaped the informal dynamics of the activity quite differently. After watching these sorts of scenes, and especially after analyzing the coaches' responses to interview questions that got them directly talking about kids, coaches, and gender, I came to see tensions and contradictions between the commitment to equal access to sports for all kids that most adults espouse, on the one hand, and the fact that many adults think about, talk about, and treat boys and girls in quite different ways, on the other hand.

Parents today understand that in the not-too-distant past sports was considered to be just for boys.[2] As such, the institution of sport created categorical differences between women and men that helped to buttress ideologies of male superiority and power and female inferiority and submission. This belief in naturally occurring categorical difference between the sexes—what I call "hard essentialism"—provided the ideological foundation for the ideal post–World War II middle-class family, with a male breadwinner and female homemaker/mother. Today, youth sports can no longer support people's simplistic beliefs in categorical sex difference. In fact, it seems to have become common sense that sports are for boys *and* for girls. The adults in my study uniformly applauded girls' participation in sports, and many spoke of the advantages they think will accrue to girls who play. Soccer coach Al Evans, for instance, saw sports participation for his daughter as a kind of inoculation against sexist dangers that girls and young women face in daily life: "I'm like the original Title IX dad. I so believe, you know, whether my girls are good at it or not, I want her to play, because it's, like, all the things you're fighting against—young women, you know, the billboards, the this, the that, the sexuality of everything, I mean *all* of that. Sports is our like anti-drug program, ultimately." Whether such expectations about the wide-ranging benefits of sports for girls are fully realistic or not, parents' support for girls playing sports makes it far more difficult today for them to hold to simplistic, categorical views of natural sex difference. Girls' and women's massive movement into sport over the past thirty years has made sport a realm of contested gender relations.[3] Participants within such a contested terrain are forced to deal with built-in contradictions. This was reflected in my interviews with youth coaches.

When asked to reflect on whether or how it mattered for boys to be coached by men or by women, and girls to be coached by men or by women, most coaches meandered and often struggled to weave a coherent narrative. I found it fascinating that these thoughtful and articulate people could be so clear-thinking and plainspoken about nearly everything, but when it came to questions about kids, coaches, and gender, there was a great deal of confusion, hemming and hawing, and contradiction in their statements. It often seemed to me that I was hearing them struggling on the spot to weave together a coherent narrative on gender, using threads of thought that clashed with one another. In disentangling these complicated narratives, I have identified three threads that coaches variously wove into their talk about coaches, kids, and gender:

> *Equality.* This view sees social equality between boys and girls, and between women and men, as desirable. The more moderate version of this thread expresses support for girls' participation in sports. The more consciously feminist purveyors of this view see sport as a way for girls to become empowered in a sexist society, and they advocate for more women coaches to help empower girls and to challenge boys' sexist assumptions about women. On its own, the Equality Thread has trouble supporting adults' narratives of children and sport, because sex-segregated sports, divisions of labor in families and workplaces, and essentialist beliefs continue to undercut a full-on commitment to the ideal of social equality.

> *Natural Difference.* Adults who use this thread narrate boys and girls, men and women, as naturally "hard-wired" to be different. In its extreme form, this view sees two binary, categorically different sexes (men are from Mars, women are from Venus) who have traits that (ideally) complement each other—like Yin and Yang, instrumental and expressive, breadwinner and homemaker. By itself, the

categorical "hard essentialism" of the Natural Difference Thread can no longer hold up to form a coherent narrative on kids and gender, as it has been challenged by feminist ideals of equality and by empirical evidence that shows that when girls and women play sports, many of them are stronger, faster, and more skilled than many boys and men.[4]

Equity-with-Difference. This thread, a narrative attempt to negotiate the tensions between feminist beliefs in social equality and essentialist beliefs in natural difference, posits girls and boys as separate and different but favors equal opportunities for all kids. I will spend the majority of this chapter discussing the nuances of this thread, and I will show that there are common asymmetries in the ways that adults negotiate the tensions between these two principles when talking about boys or talking about girls. The result is an ascendant gender ideology that I call "soft essentialism."

Though most of the coaches draw on elements of each of these three threads, they don't use them equally. A few use far more of the Equality Thread to weave their narrative of coaches, kids, and gender. A few draw more on the Natural Difference Thread. Most coaches use a bit of each of these first two threads, woven together with a large spool of the Equity-with-Difference Thread, to create the narrative fabric of soft essentialism. In this chapter, I will draw mostly from interviews to illustrate how the tensions within and between coaches' narratives about kids and gender reveal emergent contradictions and tensions in contemporary gender relations, both inside and outside organized sports.

"YOU CAN DO ANYTHING A GUY CAN DO": THE EQUALITY THREAD

It is an accomplishment of feminism that, in roughly three decades, we have changed the ways we think about, talk about, and organize youth sports. A moderate form of the Equality Thread of coaches' narratives about gender was expressed by many coaches as support for girls' opportunities to play sports, and by some as a desire for more "balance" in the number of women and men coaches. A few coaches, more often women than men, spoke of gender and youth sports in more overtly feminist terms.

I would define a "feminist" sensibility, in the most general sense, as incorporating three beliefs: first, that sex-segregated institutional arrangements, buttressed by sexist beliefs (and sometimes violence), have systematically harmed and disadvantaged girls and women, while privileging men; second, that the narrow definitions of masculinity that boys are encouraged to adopt in order to compete for a share of patriarchal privilege tend to harm boys and men, narrowing their range of emotional expressivity and damaging their health and relationships; and third, that we should commit ourselves to individual and collective actions that change these arrangements, to move toward social equality that empowers girls and women and more fully humanizes boys and men. Coaches who wove strong strands of the Equality Thread into their narratives tended to invoke one or more of the following three themes: the importance of adult female role-modeling for girls; women coaches as better able to understand and meet the particular needs of girls; and women coaches as helping to generate respect for women from both girls and boys.

ROLE-MODELING FOR GIRLS

Isabel Bacad saw her work as a soccer coach as part of a mission to empower girls to play sports, and to become coaches later in life: "I think it tells them that I can coach—*women* can coach—it's not just the men that can coach sports, and it may push them to continue with the sport or maybe coaching later on too. If they see that other women are coaching, yeah, they can do it too." Joan Ring says that she gets support from other mothers for being a strong female role model for girls: "The mothers—they all say, 'I'm so glad my daughter got you 'cause she needs a role model like you.' And people in the community come up to me: 'Well, maybe my daughter can be on your team, with a woman coach; we've never had one of those.' "

For Pam Burke, being a role model for girls hits close to home. Burke had been a "tomboy" as a young girl, and had experienced the enjoyment of athletic participation but also the pain of being "ostracized and shunned" by both boys and girls during adolescence:

> I think that it is very important for girls to have female role models
> in athletics, and there aren't many. I remember when I was growing
> up, I was a tomboy. And for many years I was accepted by the boys,
> because I could compete—you know, out in the streets, in the
> playground, in school. Um, but not by the girls; they didn't want the
> rough-and-tumble girl in their group. But at some point the boys
> couldn't be seen with the girls—we couldn't be playing together.

And so—that was kind of a tough place to be, as a girl who wants to play sports—when the boys start turning away and saying, "Uhhh, this is just for boys." 'Cause you are kind of ostracized—at least when I was a kid, I was, you know, *shunned,* by both groups for a while.

Now, as a mother and a girls' soccer coach, Pam Burke is motivated in part by a desire to create a positive, affirming space where athletically oriented girls feel fully accepted:

> I had [a] little girl on my All-Star team, and she—she reminded me of me. She was a tomboy: she wore boys' clothes, she had a boys' haircut, and her mom told me that year, she had a horrible, horrible year at school. Because that was the year that the boys started rejecting her. And the girls didn't want her. And she didn't want to be with the girls anyway. She wanted to play sports; she didn't want to, you know, sit and talk about going to mall and braiding your hair and whatever. And she was thankful—her mom was coming to me, to thank me for—showing that it was okay, to be in sports, even as a women, a mother. You know, you don't have to be a *man* to be in sports. You can be a woman, you can be a girl, and still be in sports and still be accepted. And she said her daughter really benefited from having a woman coach, so that was part of my motivation for coaching my daughter's team.

Doug Berger, too, thinks it would be beneficial to have more women coaches as role models, not just to empower girls in sports, but in other aspects of life, too: "My daughter, from a very early age, we kind of instilled in her that you can do anything a guy can do, and she was a cheerleader in junior high school, but she also played soccer and she was good in academics, and it was very important to us that she did all of it, and not just, you know, just get one side or the other. And her coaches in cross-country are female, her coach in soccer is female, and I think it's good for her to have that role model." Berger saw female adult role models in sports as important to his daughter's understanding that she "can do anything a guy can do," and his words invoke an image of a gender-divided social world, to which he wanted his daughter to have full access: having his daughter play sports was part of a hope that she not "just get one side or the other." This idea, that women coaches in sports can help girls to broaden their outlook and their possibilities in life, is a common aspect of the Equality Thread in parents' narratives about their daughters.

MEN COACHES CAN'T OR DON'T GIVE GIRLS WHAT THEY NEED

Some coaches said that they favor having more women coaches for girls because women better understand the particular kinds of problems and constraints that girls face in a sexist society. Pam Burke said, "I think there is a quality or characteristic about women that men often lack or fail to demonstrate, and that is the emotional aspect of supporting their players. I often see men not doing that, and I don't think they do it to be malicious and I'm not saying they are mean to their players, but sometimes they fail to support them emotionally … . I don't know if as a rule men are willing to do that, and I think women are." Some of the men coaches spoke of an "awkwardness" in talking about "certain topics" with the girls on their teams. Soccer coach Lenn Molina said he sometimes uses his team mom to talk to the girls:

> I know with men it's kinda hard for [the girls] to relate, and it's hard for *me* to relate to the girls sometimes, and that's why I have a team mom. I go, "Uh, could you?" and she's like, "Sure, I'll help you with this situation." Sometimes it's emotional, sometimes it's—it's physical, sometimes it's, "Well, I don't wanna talk to the coach; coach is a guy"—where they don't wanna tell me, because it's something personal, and they'll go to their own peers first, they always do that, but if they had a female coach, they might open up more.

Molina's description of the girls' needs to talk about "personal" matters, and his acknowledgement that "Sometimes it's emotional, sometimes it's—it's physical" speaks to the awkwardness that some male coaches feel in teaching or counseling girl players, beyond the technicalities of the game. Part of this awkwardness that some men feel with girls has to do with a particular form of gendered surveillance that men commonly experience.

We spoke with soccer coaches about the Safe Haven Certification course that AYSO requires all coaches to take in order to ensure the kids' emotional and physical health and safety. Much of this course focuses on things that coaches should know to avoid any possible hint of inappropriate sexual contact or relations with the kids. Some coaches saw the course as "mostly common sense," and a few saw it as a "total waste of time." Most of the coaches we spoke with recognized the need to be cognizant of this danger when adults work with kids. As soccer coach Al Evans said, "I think that it's a legitimate concern, you know—I've done a lot of research on, like, child molestation and stuff like that—it's bad. I mean, it's like half the women in the United States don't even make it to eighteen without being molested or raped, I mean, it's, like, atrocious, right? So, I mean, all this stuff's very real to me. It's just, it's just living in the modern world." However, most men coaches recognized how the general climate of distrust of men who work with kids has led them to limit their interactions with the kids in ways that make them "safe" from suspicion but that also severely constrain their ability to interact in an emotionally supportive way. Ironically, it seems to be that the men coaches who are most aware of the emotional needs of the kids are the ones who feel most constrained by the context. Soccer coach Dave Chadwick said that his male cousin one time had a formal complaint filed against him by a parent, who accused him of "inappropriately touching" a boy on his team. The boy had been lying down on the field injured and crying, and the coach had knelt next to him, "in front of probably fifty parents and thirty kids," and was "kind of holding the ankle and just kind of touching down by the shoe, and then he went by the knee and kind of was touching to see if everything was okay. Basically, kind of checking and seeing where did it hurt and was this child going to be able to continue." Chadwick said that this incident, and the general feeling of scrutiny, has led him to be very careful and limited in his emotional and physical interactions with the girls on his team:

> In Safe Haven, it's almost like you have to build a concrete fortress around ya and just—and I understand the liability issues, but there comes a point to where—there was a girl who was five or six years old and it was the morning of the opening day, where they walk around the track and the teams introduce and they wave to the parents in the stands, and this little girl, this little Jenny, she came running up and just grabbed my legs so tight. I mean, she wouldn't let go. It was like, "I need you right now. I need to be hugged." And it's like, I'm sorry, I'm a hugger and—you know, times like that, I mean, *I can't*. When my girls would come up to me and sometimes they get hurt, sometimes they get—all different emotions … . I think it's a connection. It's kind of an emotional connection. It's at times a physical connection.

Especially when the situation calls for "a physical connection," Chadwick and other male coaches said that they deploy conscious strategies:

> You know, I'll high-five, or I'll, you know, touch girls on the top or give them a little headlock around the head. I'm very careful … . It's an issue, and it scares the hell out of all of the coaches. I mean, we're all living in fear. It is a problem. In terms of being with girls,

my general policy has been that if I'm dealing with kids that are eight and under, I'm gonna hug 'em. They come up to me, they've hurt themselves, they fell and got a little booboo on their knee and they come runnin' over to me and they hug me, I'm not gonna turn 'em away. I make it open in front of the whole field, protect myself as much as I can. As the kids get older, I'm more careful. It's head, sometimes hand on the shoulder, on the side of the head, high five, top of the head—very, very, very careful. It sucks.

This practice of patting kids on the tops of their heads (mentioned by several of the men coaches) as a substitute for hugging, is reminiscent of the strategies used by male elementary school teachers studied by the sociologist Paul Sargent. Male teachers, Sargent said, may be privileged in some ways, compared with their female counterparts who far outnumber them, but they are aware of being under constant suspicion and scrutiny as potential child molesters, and they respond by never allowing a child to sit on their laps, giving head pats instead of hugs, and never being alone with a child.[5]

Though suspicion and scrutiny of men may explain some of the male coaches' emotional distance from their players, and some of their awkwardness in talking with girls about "personal" issues, it is likely also grounded in men's having been raised as emotionally stunted, "normal" boys who have had their capacity for empathy systematically suppressed.[6] Some men coaches' lack of emotional support for their players can extend to sexist (albeit unintended) damage inflicted on girls. A woman soccer coach e-mailed me a few months after I had interviewed her, appalled by the following story about her daughter Meryl's male coach's incompetence and insensitivity to girls' common body issues:

> Meryl has a male coach in GU10. At the first mini-practice, she is the oldest and twice as tall as the others in this two-year grouping. She is muscular and bigger. The coach has coached his sons in the past, 12 yr. old and 15. He tells the little girls, "Do a toe kick." This is something that from day one, you try to school out of kids. That is not how you kick in soccer. When I comment, in shock, he has this, "these are little girls" reply—"this is all they can do." Even though some of them have been in the AYSO Under-six and Under-eight divisions in the past. We break and meet in a circle some time later. He looks down at Meryl and says, "When you are finished this season your legs will look like hers," and he points out a little girl half Meryl's height and size. COMPARING IN FRONT OF THE GROUP! Then he says, "They will be pure muscle." I assume he is trying to

recover. The following day before the first practice I take him aside and tell him that with girls it is not a good idea to comment about their bodies. Meryl is particularly self-conscious about her body and her legs (she doesn't like to wear shorts even). I assumed that he slipped up, but instead he said that he had no idea that what he said might be offensive and he took my comment well. I, of course, was outraged (inside). It may be incorrect to assume that women are more sensitive to these female cultural issues on body image, problems with anorexia, etc. in our society.

Reflected in this story is the mother's recognition of the kinds of issues that girls and young women face in a world that teaches them to be ultra-critical of their own bodies, and of how this self-surveillance can contribute to eating disorders and related health problems. Cognizant parents hope that sports will help their daughters develop healthy habits and positive body images, but this mother's story suggests that an insensitive male coach's words can possibly undo this positive potentiality in sports, and she wonders whether women coaches might be more "sensitive to these female cultural issues on body image."[7]

WOMEN COACHES TEACH GIRLS AND BOYS TO RESPECT WOMEN

Rosa Ramirez does not think it's particularly important for boys to be coached by men. To the contrary, she thinks it's "a bad thing" that so many kids assume that women should just be team moms, and she would like to see more women coaching girls and boys. Jessica Torres agrees: "Oh yeah, definitely, I think a lot of kids would like to see their moms out there. You know, I think it would add a little bit of heightened respect for the woman, you know. Because they're used to seeing them in a homemaker role or just—you know, not that women don't work nowadays, but it's just not in that athletic role, you know. I think it would give them a newfound respect for women in general." Norma Delgado also said that she thinks it's important for more women to coach boys: "I would love more, yeah, I think that's important. I think it breaks gender stereotypes. I think it's important for boys to see women outside of the tradition of the roles [like] the team mom that they're used to seeing them in. I think that they don't realize that a lot of women have a competitive fire that can inspire them as much if not more than the dads who are yelling at them, you know. I think it'll go a long way to, you know, perceiving women in terms of equal … for boys to see women coaching boys."

A small number of the men also went beyond simply saying it's desirable to have "balance" between women and men. For instance, Bill Munson said that his ideal for AYSO would be "to have half women and half men coaching," because, "I think it's real good for boys to see women in a coaching experience, and frankly I think it's good for girls to see women in a coaching experience—for all kids to see moms or wives or women in a role of leadership, particularly in athletics, where you know historically women have not been." And one of the more stridently feminist statements on this topic was made by soccer coach Carlos Ruiz, who said that it's important for there to be women coaching girls and boys:

> I think that social positions for boys and girls are still different in our society. I think there are things that happen in society that are much more destructive of girls, especially at this age, from beginning about age ten to about age twenty that have very serious consequences. So to have them experience their own power as women, I think, is helpful to have strong women in their lives that are not their mothers.
>
> [Do you think it's important for boys to be coached by women?]
>
> Yes, I do. I think that the benefits would be that they stop associating all women that they know with the women's portrayal in mass culture or even the role of their own mother in their own lives, and that they broaden their experience of who women are in society. And that that could be achieved by having a strong, a good female coach.

"THEY'RE JUST DIFFERENT": THE NATURAL DIFFERENCE THREAD

Coaches' essentialism—their belief in natural differences between boys and girls—tends to run up against their commitment to equality for girls and boys. And, as I shall show, it tends to be stronger when they are talking about boys than when they are talking about girls. When asked whether there are good reasons for boys to be coached by men, soccer coach Michael Ortiz said yes, especially for older boys:

> At U10, because the level of play is a lot more rigorous, the kids are a lot more demanding—you're starting to get some prepubescent

boys here and, just the energy level and that type of thing … . I think the boys respect more a male figure at that point. I've noticed it particularly for some of the players that have single moms. I think boys need interaction with men. There's some studies that have been in England showing that boys who become homosexuals tend to have a very poor relationship with their father between the critical ages of three or four years old and seven. So, I think there's a real important time to have a good role model, whether it's a father or coach or whatever at that point in time. Beyond that, I think there are certain things that you need to teach boys, and I think men can model that. Um, I don't think that women, because we're wired differently, you know, can. I think women have something to offer boys. I don't necessarily think that it has to be a coach. It could be a Cub Scout leader or whatever that could provide a female influence, but I think at some point I think there needs to be a male interaction.

Ortiz's statement shows some of the common strains in conservative essentialist thought about gender. He believes that women and men are "wired differently," but this hard-wiring is clearly not enough, in his mind, to ensure that boys become properly masculine and heterosexual. At the heart of his argument is the belief that boys and girls need "appropriate modeling of womanliness and manliness, you know, femininity and masculinity," and that one way to model this is through coaching. When asked if he thought it was good for girls to have women coaches, his response revealed a common way that gender essentialism is played out in adults' narratives about youth sports:

Um … is it important? I know that there's a lot of dads that coach soccer for girls and that's fine. Because again, you need appropriate modeling of womanliness and manliness, you know, femininity and masculinity, I think, regardless of whether you have boys or girls. I want my daughter to know how a man should act appropriately as well as I want my sons.

Put simply, despite the presence of girls in sports—which he supports—Ortiz still views adult leadership in sport as a primarily male realm, a place where men can model "appropriate" forms of masculinity for boys *and* for girls. Thus, while it's okay for women to coach girls, it's not necessary. But it *is* necessary for men to coach boys, in order to model masculinity and to prevent homosexuality. Albert Riley, who coaches girls' softball, held a similar view:

I think it's much more important for men to coach boys than it would be for women to coach boys. Again the respect issue, and I just think from a perspective of a dad, like a dad with a son or whatever, um, you know, moms are so important in the growing up and the maturing process and all that, [but] I just don't think that they would get the response as a coach of boys that a man would get from boys.

As we have seen, most women coaches do not complain of a lack of respect from kids, but they do feel pressure from parents, especially from fathers. And it's fathers' essentialist views—especially as they relate to their sons—that help to create and maintain the glass ceiling on women coaches in boys' sports, especially baseball. Joan Ring said, "Well, my experience in general is that parents are happier to have a female coach coach girls than they are to have a female coach coach boys." And Barbara Jones said that a woman coach has to deal with the parent who thinks, "Who's this woman coaching my son?" Indeed, George Starr told me a story, his voice betraying his incredulous disapproval, of a man who did not want his son coached by a woman:

A couple of years ago, there was this lady moved to town, and she volunteered to coach a Little League team. She had experience, so I backed her, and she was approved by the board. That year we were having trouble getting enough coaches, and I had tried and tried to get Kirk Babcock to coach, but he said no, he'd rather not coach that year; he'd rather just run the league. Well, come draft day, Kirk's son is drafted by this lady. Immediately, Kirk announces that he's decided to coach, and takes his son off her team. He just didn't want his son to be coached by a woman.

Somewhat ironically, coaches' narratives about girls sometimes served as a basis for arguing for the value of women coaches. For instance, Albert Riley—probably among the least "feminist" coaches we interviewed—sees value in having more women coaches, especially as girls get older and go through puberty. When asked if he thinks it is important for women to coach girls teams, he replied:

I do. I do. I wish more did, and I wish more qualified women would step up and take that on, because I think it would be better, be-cause, you know, girls can relate to women better. I mean, I had a situation this year where my [male] coach and I are playing catch and all of a sudden these girls are talking about a girl at school [whose] period started. And now they're all talking about this. I said, "G-Girls, Coach Seth and I don't need to hear this stuff!" [*He laughs.*] And what do they do?—Next thing you know they're all around one of the moms who's my scorekeeper, talking about it, you know. And those types of things [women] can relate to, you know, and if a girl's having a prob—an issue or something.

THE EQUITY-WITH-DIFFERENCE THREAD

How do adult coaches simultaneously make sense of their belief in natural differences between the sexes and their commitment to equality for girls and boys? How are these apparently contradictory beliefs woven together in their narratives about kids and sports? Several themes emerged from the interviews that can be seen as ways that adults attempted to navigate the complicated terrain of thinking and talking about kids and gender in this era of increasing opportunities for girls. First, most coaches believe that it is necessary to have sex-segregated sports for boys and girls because of what they assume to be the natural differences between the sexes. Second, rather than talking about "equality" for women and men coaches, many spoke of favoring a "mix" of women and men that would benefit kids by providing them with the different traits they assumed men and women bring to coaching. Third, many coaches talk (approvingly) about how sports participation can stretch girls *away* from their presumably softer and cooperative nature and *toward* more individualistic, competitive, and aggressive traits that will benefit them, while assuming (often implicitly) that playing sports is already fully consistent with boys' aggressive and competitive natures. And fourth, many coaches view boys as having a singular simple natural essence, yet seem also to assume that they are vulnerable to feminization if they are not hardened by the leadership of adult men.

SEX-SEGREGATED SPORTS

In 1973, when Little League Baseball was fighting their legal battles to exclude girls from baseball, LLB president Dr. Creighton J. Hale, who held a Ph.D. in physiology, drew on biological arguments to make the case against girls' inclusion. "There are differences between the male and female, in spite of the trend now to say there aren't any differences," he argued, adding that boys had more muscle fibers and "power units" that made them faster and stronger than girls. It is indicative of the sea-change brought about by girls' movement into sport that by the year 2001, this same Dr. Hale had changed his views. He now says that girls' inclusion in sports is "one of the best things that's happened," and he speaks proudly of one of his granddaughters in Ohio: "This year she became the first girl ever selected to play on the Little League [Baseball] tournament team there." Referring to his own transformation, he wryly adds, "What goes around comes around."[8] Like many adults interviewed in my study, Dr. Hale no longer holds categorically essentialist views that would bar girls from playing certain sports. And it's notable that he, like many men of his generation, has had his eyes opened not so much by medical science, but by seeing with his own eyes how his daughters' or granddaughters' athletic abilities blossomed, once they were given the opportunity to play.

While girls' movement into sports has challenged essentialist assumptions, most adults still seem to believe that sports should be sex-segregated. This continued sex-segregation of kids' sports creates a context within which essentialism can still be constructed, albeit in a somewhat different form. One common way that youth sports coaches bridged their belief in opportunities for girls with their belief in natural difference was to talk less often in terms of *equality* (a condition within which boys and girls are fully equal in status, rights, and opportunities), and more in terms of *equity* (a condition within which every individual is treated fairly and impartially). For many people, the idea of treating girls "fairly" coexists straightforwardly with the idea that their essential difference from boys requires that they be separated into different sports activities. As we have seen, AYSO separates girls and boys from the very youngest ages, while Little League allows sex-integrated T-ball for the youngest kids but then herds kids onto separate gendered paths—boys to baseball, girls to softball.

The United States long ago broke away from the "separate but equal" idea that underlay race relations during the Jim Crow era, acknowledging ultimately that separate schools, drinking fountains, restaurants, buses, and other public facilities are inherently *unequal*. By contrast, most advocates of gender equity in sports in the United States have explicitly argued for *equitable but separate* athletic funding, leagues, and facilities for girls and women. Recently, though, political scientist Eileen McDonagh and journalist Laura Pappano have argued provocatively that there is no good reason for our routine separation of girls' and boys' sports, and that this institutionalized sex-segregation disadvantages girls and women—in short, they argue that "separate is not equal in sports."[9] What are the implications of the ways that we routinely sex-segregate children's sports? How do adults balance this separation of boys' and girls' sports activities against their commitment to equity for all kids? Though nearly all of the coaches seem implicitly to accept sex-segregation, some ask critical questions about it. Soccer coach Kathi Ralston brings a feminist sensibility to her criticism of sex-segregation in Little League, while also neatly weaving together her belief in natural difference with her commitment to equity for girls and boys. Boys and girls are just different, she says, but at the same time, she wants opportunities opened up to them that offer them a range of choices:

> The thing I find very funny is, Why is there softball? I mean, it's a sexist sport. Can't girls play baseball? Or why can't boys play softball? It's just sort of a random thing—I guess they thought girls needed a softer ball, and it's a slower and safer game. Why don't they have a girls' Little League [Baseball], you know? It seems like softball was just invented as a dumbed-down baseball. I don't think you would ever hear of a boy playing softball … . I have to say, having had daughters and having had a son, it's made me throw up my arms and say, "Whatever. They're different—and they're *born* different." [But] I think that instead of drawing this line, that boys can only do this and girls only that, we need to draw a path that's broad enough so that they can all do whatever they want.

What Ralston is expressing is a rejection of categorical separation of boys and girls in favor of an opening of choices to kids, and this belief exists alongside her essentialist belief that "They're different, and they're *born* different." Soccer coach Nikki Lopez also favors doing away with sex-segregated sports for kids, because she thinks it would make girls better athletes:

> There probably are a lot of people that don't agree with me: I think the girls and the boys should play together. I know a lot of AYSO regions do play the girls and boys together under-6. But girls would be much better athletes, and I don't think that it would bring the boys down if they play together. I mean our girls play together with the boys at school at recess and in both soccer and basketball. I've seen them play basketball; they beat the boys all day long. I just think overall that women would be much better athletes, much more competitive athletes, and I don't think that it would do any harm to the boys, it won't bring them down a level, if they played together.

Most coaches, however, disagree with Ralston and Lopez, and believe it's best for girls and boys to have separate leagues. Soccer coach Barbara Jones, for instance, fears that putting the kids together might disadvantage the girls, perhaps driving them away from playing sports: "I like it when they're separate. I like having the girls and boys separate. There used to be co-ed at the under-6. But I think it's nice for the girls to have their own teams. You know, I think that you might find a different dynamic—I think you'd find different issues. I think you'd find the coaching was different for the girls than for the boys on the same team. Or the treatment was different. So, to me, I like having them separated."

As Jones's words suggest, the question of what's best for kids—sex-segregated or integrated teams—is complicated, even from a feminist perspective. If one is interested in giving boys experiences that will counter the kinds of sexist attitudes and assumptions that they commonly develop in male-only sports, then one would likely favor co-ed sports. The more boys can learn, early on, that will allow them to fully respect girls' and women's full range of abilities, the better off they will be in their future relationships with women—as classmates, co-workers, bosses, and family members. However, if one is thinking of girls' interests, this seems a more complicated question. As Barbara Jones suggested, she fears that, especially given the fact that coaching is still so dominated by men, sex-integrated teams might create "different issues … different treatment" that might alienate girls, pushing them out of sports and thus denying them the many benefits of sports participation. Perhaps a good middle ground at this historical moment would be to do both—to have all-girls' leagues as an option, alongside fully integrated leagues.[10] For the moment, though, the vast majority of kids do play in sex-segregated sports, and this leaves few opportunities for essentialist assumptions to be fully contested. I have written elsewhere of the valuable lessons that young boys can learn when they see with their own eyes that the girls they are playing sports with are every bit as skilled as the boys are.[11] But kids older than age five or six rarely if ever get a chance to play organized co-ed sports. After T-ball, most girls are channeled into playing softball, but they retain a legal right to play Little League Baseball, and occasionally during my years of field research I saw a baseball team with a girl on it. What kind of impact does this have on kids' and adults' assumptions about gender? Consider the following field note, taken during a 13–14-year-olds Little League Baseball game:

> It's a playoff game, with everything at stake. The winner goes on to play another game; the loser is done for the season. Tight game, late innings; you can feel the tension in the air with every pitch. James hits a sharp grounder down the third base line, just fair. Their third baseman darts quickly to her right, backhands the ball well behind the bag, her momentum carrying her into foul territory. She plants her right foot and makes the long throw, a laser to first base, just nipping the runner. A very tough play on this full-sized field. What's remarkable to me is that nobody in the dugout (or behind me in the stands) remarks that it was the only girl on either team

that made this play. A kid in our dugout just says, "Damn. Great play!" and the game goes on.

What struck me about this moment was just how unremarkable it was that the kid who made this "great play" was the only girl on the field. Perhaps since the boys had already been through many seasons where there was a girl here, a girl there playing baseball with them, it was simply no big deal that a girl had made such a good play. Does this kind of moment in some fundamental way challenge essentialist ideas the boys might otherwise be learning through sex-segregated sports? I can't answer this question definitively, as I did not interview the kids. But what I can say is that the boys on both teams, and the adults in the stands—some of whom had earlier that same day watched their daughters play softball—saw this girl make that nice stop and the perfect throw. The mere presence of a highly skilled girl competing effectively with the boys creates a different dynamic that makes the creation of hard, categorical essentialism less likely. On the other hand, perhaps this moment was unremarkable precisely because the girl who made this great play is *not* viewed as representing the category "girls." Rather, perhaps the girl is a single "token," who instead of challenging assumptions of natural differences between the sexes becomes a kind of "honorary," or "fictive," boy, like the girls who cross gender boundaries in Barrie Thorne's classic study of children and gender on grade school playgrounds?[12] Despite the occasional girl "crosser" into boys' sports, the dominant fact about how we structure kids' sports is (near) categorical sex-segregation.

A "MIX" OF WOMEN AND MEN IS GOOD FOR KIDS

A second way that adults bridge a belief in equality with a belief in natural difference is to talk not about creating equal opportunities for women coaches, but to speak in somewhat more vague terms of the benefits of there being "balance," or a "mix" of women and men, in coaching youth sports. Soccer coach Dave Chadwick said: "I don't think there has to be one gender or another [coaching the kids] necessarily. It'd be nice if there were a balance, I guess." Soccer coach Terri Patrick sees boys and girls as having a different, probably biologically based, essence, but he likes the idea that men and women coaches can bring unique and complementary traits to coaching:

> I think men and women contribute some very similar things and some very different things. I think men obviously have been raised

to be more competitive, women have been raised to be more cooperative—whether that's an inherent, um, genetic difference, I kind of tend to believe that it is. I tend to believe the way that we have evolved as humans have created some inherent gender differences in the way we approach life. There are differences in our brains in the way that they work.

These essentialist ideas, however, do not lead Patrick to conclude that girls should be excluded from sports, or that kids are better suited having men coaches. Instead, she states that with a "mix" of women and men in coaching, kids will benefit from exposure to the range of attributes that men and women bring to the field:

I think women, for boys, will teach them that soccer is a team sport. I think they approach the sport differently, and approach team sports differently, as a cooperative team effort, which is what gets you the results. Men's approach is that it's a competitive thing, and I think they tend to reward superstars more then they do a team effort. [So] I think it's equally important for boys and girls—it's nice for girls to see a woman as a role model; it's nice for boys to see a woman as a role model. I think it's better for the kids to see a mix.

Many coaches spoke of this "mix" or "balance" between women and men in ways that revealed a certain asymmetry in their thinking about boys and girls. For instance, soccer coach Don Clark said that having more women coaches and more male elementary school teachers is desirable because both boys and girls "just crave that balance, that additional dimension of humanity":

I'm traditional in a lot of my views, but not nearly as much as maybe my father or my grandfather, and I really think that there needs to be fluidity between the genders. I think that's very important—the kind of more-fluid nature between the genders in lots of aspects of life. And I think the more young boys and young girls are exposed to both male and female coaches and politicians and parenting and parenting styles, I think it just leads to a better, more multidimensional, probably stronger adult in the future.

As Clark's words clearly indicate, his view may in some ways echo a "traditional" essentialism, but this is not his father's or his grandfather's essentialism. It is an essentialism that recognizes the contemporary blurring (though surely not obliteration) of boundaries between men's and women's separate worlds, and the "fluid nature" of those who move across those boundaries. As he continued to speak, however, his views of boys' and girls' differences suggest that he sees them fitting differently within this world:

> There's a different—girls are very competitive and can be very competitive, but their approach to a lot of sports is different than boys and I think—I think it's probably more pure. I mean, you know, sometimes guys can get so doggone *focused*—myself included— that it's just, it becomes like this *laser,* and I think female athletes see a bigger field a lot of times, see a bigger dynamic, see a more fluid give-and-take situation than boys.

As with other coaches we interviewed, it seems that the "fluidity between the genders" that Clark sees really relates more to the girls than to the boys. The images he invokes suggests girls are "more fluid" and are able to "see a bigger field," while boys are relatively fixed, "focused … like this *laser.*" This idea, that girls are flexibly able to move across a broad social field, whereas boys are rigidly focused to a particular path, is a theme that came up time and again in the interviews with coaches. In fact, the more I listened to the coaches—both men and women—the more I concluded that feminism has given adults a clear vocabulary with which to talk about girls' lives as a *socially contextualized field of choices.* By contrast, we still don't have very sophisticated ways of thinking about boys, beyond assuming that everything they do is driven by "testosterone" and by their natural predisposition to be active, aggressive, and competitive.

SPORTS STRETCH GIRLS AND ARE NATURAL TO BOYS

Many of the parents who held essentialist views of boys and girls saw sports participation as a way for girls to learn more conventionally masculine traits that would benefit them in public life. These adults seemed to see boys' aggressive and competitive traits as a simple expression of nature, played out within (but not constructed by) sports, while girls were viewed as malleable, their softer natures reformable through sports participation. Research on children and families has shown, in fact, that parents tend to push sons to conform to culturally valued conceptions of masculinity more strongly than they push their daughters to conform narrowly to feminine traits. Parents also tend to reward boys more than girls for gender conformity.[13] This gender asymmetry reflects the longstanding cultural valuation of masculinity and the devaluation of femininity: it's acceptable to many parents—even highly valued—for girls to adopt some masculine traits—to become "tomboys" and to strive for educational and career success;[14] but the boy who values or displays culturally defined "feminine" traits is still too often stigmatized, ridiculed, viewed as a failure. This asymmetry has likely been amplified as contemporary professional-class families have increasingly absorbed feminist-inspired ideals of girls and women having access to public life. For example, Gilbert Morales, who has coached both girls and boys at various age-levels, suggested that sports participation creates aggressive traits in girls that make them more like boys:

> They're very, very different in style … . The girls tend to form a team much easier than boys. Boys seem to have a much more competitive streak in them and a much more aggressive streak in them than the girls do—sometimes to the detriment of the team. They are individuals playing together, not a team working together, which I think is one of the significant differences that I've seen between the boys' team and the girls'. I think that changes a little bit as the girls get older and become more trained or conditioned into behaving in a more aggressive manner—the girls 19-and-under, 16-and-under teams were much more similar to the boys' teams in terms of aggressive behavior, in terms of the way they played the game—even in the showboating and even in some of the taunting that can occur, like when they would make a nice tackle and knock somebody down, glaring at the player on the ground. So, over time, girls who would have been aggressive, to some extent, and competitive, to some extent, I think learn to be more so. And I think what happens is, as they grow older, those who are willing to be like that—be more similar to boys, I think—stay in the sport. And I think that's where the similarities—they become more similar. So, I think as that happens, as they get older, I think the differences tend to get a little bit more blurred.

Morales, like many coaches we interviewed, assumes that girls are naturally cooperative and group-oriented, but he concludes that with athletic experiences, they can become aggressively competitive individuals, "more similar to the boys." Boys, though, are still viewed categorically by Morales, whose unspoken assumption seems to be that boys are naturally aggressive individualists, and that this essential nature is played out in sports. Boys and girls become more similar, "the differences … a little bit more blurred," when girls play sports and become more like boys. These sorts of assumptions made me think about my own two sons, who are very different from each other. My younger son Sasha, whom I have mentioned in this book, enjoys sports, plays baseball and runs cross-country. My older son Miles, now eighteen years old, never took to organized sports, having dropped out of AYSO and Little League by the time he was eight or nine years old. Miles was the kind of kid who, when the soccer ball came within striking distance, would not automatically go after it; instead he'd hesitate, until another, more aggressive boy went after the ball, and then he'd just move along with the pack of kids, rarely touching the ball. His gentleness and lack of aggressiveness—traits which, incidentally, I see as major attributes that make him a kind and good person—did not serve him well in sports. So, like many boys who don't fit the mold, he opted out of sports early on, thus avoiding the discomfort or even public humiliation that so many boys face as marginal or poor athletes.[15] Coaches' narratives rarely recognize this kind of range among boys, tending instead to assume that all boys have a natural affinity with sports. This assumption—especially when compared with the common view of girls as flexible, complex, and fluid—speaks volumes to our one-dimensional and still largely unreconstructed views of boys.

BOYS NEED MALE COACHES

Adults' common view of boys as destined by their nature to compete in public life seems almost to occur by default, as they just don't seem to think that much about boys and gender. Baseball coach Mitch Flores said that it was fine for girls to be coached by either men or women, but when we asked him about whether it mattered for men to coach boys, he seemed stunned by the question:

> Men to coach boys? My, I never even gave that a thought. I—I, um, that seems—it seemed pretty natural. There aren't—there are no women coaching boys' baseball or men's baseball.
>
> [Do you think it's good for boys to see women as coaches?]
>
> Um. I don't think, I don't know, I don't—I don't know. I wouldn't …

When we asked soccer coach Mark Daly what he thought about women coaching girls, he replied quickly and clearly: "I think it is good for the girls to see girls as coaches—I think it is important to see women, in coaching roles, 'cause it does teach them that [sports] doesn't all just stop. I mean could be a life long thing." But when asked what he thought about women coaching boys, he said, "Um, and for the guys I—I really don't have an opinion. I mean, I—I never had any female coaches, but I never thought about it, um, I just never thought about it."

Many coaches—men and women—struggled similarly to find words to talk about boys and gender. Soccer coach Al Evans, when asked if it was important for boys to be coached by women or by men, confessed confusion and ambivalence:

> I don't know, uh, I don't get—um, I think I really don't know. I mean I'm really of two minds. In one sense, there's all of that, you know, they learn how to behave like men kind of blah-blah-blah, but you know girls don't learn how to behave like men by watching. I don't know, there's such a debate about that going on in everything I've read that I—I'm still not of a mind on it. I think in the final analysis, for instance, uh, I—I really don't know. I suspect that it probably doesn't make much difference. I think that there—there—oh boy, I don't know. See I really am—I'm completely conflicted.

His confusion and ambivalence about boys and gender, however, contrasted sharply with his sense of clarity about whether it matters for girls to have women coaches:

> Uh, that I'm a little more clear about. I think at some point, because of, like, self-esteem issues and stuff like that, I think it is. I think that when my daughters are able to coach it'll be important for them to coach. I do think that for women one of the components is to have someone that they can look up to, and that's a motivator, that's a cool thing. So it's important.

Many coaches similarly struggled and stumbled around to weave a coherent narrative about boys and gender, and eventually many settled into one or more of the three following themes that are familiar in cultural discourse: boys—especially older boys—respect men's leadership and respond better to men's voices than to women's; boys need to be toughened by men; boys need men in their lives because of the predominance of women in their lives as teachers and mothers (especially in single-parent families). I will illustrate these three themes briefly below, but I want first to note an irony here. On the one hand, adults' narratives tend to view boys as driven by a fairly straightforward natural drive to be competitive, individualist actors in sports and other aspects of public life. But on the other hand, underlying these essentialist constructions of boys are vaguely articulated fears that boys are vulnerable, that they may fail to develop into proper men without adult male role-modeling and leadership.

These fears of the instability of boys' and men's "nature" reflect long-standing "fears of social feminization" of boys, especially prevalent among middle-class fathers.[16]

Soccer coach Barbara Jones says that as long as they were in the younger age brackets, she was certain that it was a good thing for her to have coached both her two sons' and her daughter's soccer teams: "I like being their coach so I can make sure they're not with a guy who's gonna just win at all costs. So, I think for me, I'm contributing to them: a coach who will emphasize all the right things. And I also think it's good for them to see, you know, a mom able—*their* mom is able to coach their team. It's not just dads. Women can do it, too. And I think, in those very subtle ways, they will carry that throughout their life." Jones believes that as the girls get older, it's fine to have either women or men coaches: "Either one would be effective. If they're good, they're gonna be effective—it doesn't matter what their gender is." However, as the boys get to about age eleven or twelve, she's no longer certain what's best, and as she spoke about older boys, it seemed that her feminist sensibilities were wrestling with her hunch that perhaps there's something "instinctual" about older boys needing men coaches:

> That's kind of when they start getting a little bit more rowdy, a little bit more physical and I almost wonder if at that age they need sort of a more physical threat—like a man's bigger, louder voice, or some instinctual kind of thing. And I almost kind of wondered whether about that age is when should they have a male coach to just even, kind of—you know what I mean? Right about that eleven-twelve age. But, on the other hand, then I think, 'I don't know.' I'm not sure about that, actually. I'm still sort of figuring out whether it's important to have a man when they're like eleven-twelve years old. But, on the other hand, I was considering coaching [my son], and I think I could have done it. So, I have mixed feeling about that.

Gilbert Morales, a divorced father, articulates his fears about boys primarily within a discourse of contemporary family breakdown. He thinks it's good role-modeling for girls to have women coaches, but thinks that boys benefit from having men coaches, because contemporary family changes create a breakdown of what he sees as complementary male and female family roles: "I think that in the non-nuclear family now, with a lot of single parents—I think it's difficult for children to get modeling for both male and female roles. And I think that is creating possibly some conflicts in the future where it's gonna be a bunch of individuals living together, not a cooperative effort, because now both the male and the female have to assume responsibilities for what would have been traditional opposite-gender roles." Many coaches who said that boys need men, like Little League coach Nina Ramos, couched their narrative in a similar discourse of family breakdown: "I think guys, boys, need that [male] figure in their life, you know, because there's a lot more divorces and they just don't have that fatherly figure, and I think that helps out." Though herself living in an intact family, Nancy Morrison spoke of the boys' problems in single-parent families almost as though it was hearsay: "I happen to hear, like, parents—like, single parents, for example—if there's a single mom with a son, she is really counting on her son having a male coach to kind of have an influence in his life. Especially if the father is deceased or not around." And Pam Burke first noted the relative stability of families in South Pasadena, but then broadened her analysis to thinking about the general lack of adult male role models in boys' lives: "Although this is a pretty *stable*, kind of *family-oriented* community, there are still boys that have no dads at home, and I think that it is important for them to have male role models, too. And if they don't have a dad at home, 90 per cent of the elementary school teachers are women, you know."

In this context of a perceived absence of adult males in boys' lives, many people see male coaches as surrogates for missing fathers. Soccer coach Eric Caldwell suspects that boys already receive more than ample "mothering" from adult women, and need more men in their lives:

> I have a tendency to say [that it's more important] for men to coach boys than it is that women coach girls. I just kind of have a feeling that boys get so much mothering that its part of their normal activity from their teachers and moms that they need the boy-to-boy time that they are going to get with a male coach. My son has had, I think, two women coaches, and I don't know if they were extremely good or extremely bad, they were just regular coaches. Very talented women, but I kind of had a feeling that they would have maybe benefited a little bit more if they would have had a male coach. You know, like I said, I want that coach to be a little bit of a drill sergeant. The boys get the drill sergeant from the mom and the teacher occasionally, and I think they need the time off from the women drill sergeants and they need a man drill sergeant. So I want them to not only experience the drill sergeant mentality from me and from my wife and from their teacher, but also from another source, which would be a male coach.

It's not only men who feel that boys need male coaches. Shelley Parsons coaches her son's soccer team, but as he has started to get a bit older, "I've been telling my husband, 'You know, I'd like to turn this over to you.' [*She laughs.*] I said, 'I really think [their son] needs you to coach him.' I don't know why I think that, but I really think that at a certain age boys really need a guy. Not that I'm inferior, but I think that that when boys get older, I think they're more influenced by males. I think it has to do with male dominance that—that low voice, you know. I think boys as they get older respond better to a male. That's my own thinking. So I may turn this over to him next year." This assumption about older boys' needs for men—held by many men and some of the women we interviewed—is another component of the age-based "glass ceiling" on women coaches, which I discussed in chapter 3.

What exactly is it that adults believe boys can get from men that they don't get from women? Mark Daly, who has coached both girls' and boys' soccer, says that boys respond well when he yells at them: "The under-19 boys, we had practice last night, and you know I found myself yelling at a couple of them. Whereas when I coached the high school girls, I never—I won't say never, but almost never—scream at them. That's just, I find that they kinda of go into themselves and its kind of, uh, it doesn't work out. Whereas the guys you can yell at him, tell him that he's going to do fifty laps and, and they don't hate you. There's no problem, do you know what I mean?" Mitch Flores has coached both girls' softball and boys' baseball, and he takes a "very different approach" to coaching them:

> When I coached boys baseball, it was totally, it was a total different style. The boys are a little more rough around the edges, and you can talk to them a certain way and they take it and it just rolls right off 'em, but the girls, no way. I'm boisterous, I have a deep, big voice; I can yell at a kid across [the field]. I had some nine-year-olds on the team and I did "*Come on*," you know, and you see the little girls' faces and you're thinking, I hurt this little girl's feelings. I'm sorry, you know: "Are you all right?" And they're standing there and they're quivering, and you're going, "Oh my gosh," and it, but it's a different, it's a different style.

As these coaches' statements show, and as the vignette that opens this chapter illustrates, coaches tend to treat boys and girls differently. To the extent to which they are conscious of this different treatment, they believe it to be a reasoned response to the different natures of boys and girls. Research on kids and gender suggests, however, that the coaches' behaviors are in fact helping to *construct* these differences. Mark Daly's and Mitch Flores's belief that when a coach yells at boys, "there's no problem," that "it just rolls right off 'em," is based on an assumption that boys are emotionally invulnerable, compared with the emotional vulnerability that seems so visible in girls. What they do not recognize, perhaps, is the many years of gender socialization that nine-year-old boys have already endured—from families, peers, popular culture, and sport—that has taught these boys to hide or repress their emotional and physical pain and not to show their vulnerabilities. Rather than simply responding to some natural ability that boys have to "take it," coaches who yell at boys are simply adding another layer to what psychologist William Pollack calls "the hardening of boys."[17] Adults—more often men, but sometimes women as well—too often use emotional separation, shame, and fear to toughen boys in ways that prepare them for the cutthroat competition of public life but that simultaneously stunt their ability to engage in the kinds of mutual intimacy that is the foundation of close relationships and happy family lives. My observations and interviews suggest that fathers are often openly approving of instances where their sons are toughened by other men. When we asked Tony Barnett if there might be some value in women coaching boys, he leapt from thinking about AYSO, which he coaches, to high school football: "Particularly in a sport like football that's so demanding, that's so hard, there's something about, uh, the sort of, the male authority, to have your kid be yelled at by some man who's not your father, that's part of growing up."

In my years of observing boys playing baseball, I've noticed that in the younger age-groups, when a boy gets slightly injured, strikes out, or gets yelled at by a coach for a bad play, he will get visibly upset. Some of these younger boys cry—often privately, pulling their caps over their faces in the dugout—and the other boys and coaches usually don't look at or speak to them, respectfully giving them private space to express feelings that are not considered fully appropriate. With the older boys—especially by age eleven or twelve—these tears and displays of vulnerability are few and far between. Instead, boys' most common response to injuries, to making a bad play, or to getting criticized by the coach, is a short burst of anger—like a thrown helmet after a strikeout—followed by a posture of sullen, determined silence in the dugout.[18] The hardening of boys teaches them to transform any feelings of hurt, pain, or sorrow into the more "appropriately masculine" expressions of contained anger or stoic silence.

To what end do we continue to toughen boys? I believe that we toughen boys because we continue to assume that they are destined for public lives, with jobs and careers, and that their most important responsibility in families will be primarily as breadwinners. Will Solomon, who is very supportive of women coaches and who agrees with the more general idea of gender equality, nevertheless seems to see the value of sport for his sons as partly in the realm of socialization that will toughen them for future competition in a public world of men. For that reason, he said, it's good for his sons to have male coaches, "because part of it is that whole learning how to deal with the other guys. There are guys' ways of dealing with other guys. Now that doesn't mean you shouldn't know [also] some of the more sort of sensitive ways to deal with it. But you gotta also learn how to, you know, talk trash and do all that. Uh, it's—it's just one more piece of survival. And I think there's another side to it too, which is kids have to learn how to deal with assholes growing up. And I think that a good piece of that are things like sports coaches and shop teachers, you know [*laughs*]."

Coaches consistently stated that boys and girls are very different emotionally and interpersonally. Alan Lindgren noted, "Girls are a lot more complex, [while] the boys tend to be—if you go to a boys' game, its very quiet—you can hear a pin drop almost, you know there's just—there's just not much going on ... . With the boys it's—it's *subtler*—they don't really push back very much, they just kinda do it. They keep their thoughts more to themselves, I think." This discourse on emotional differences between girls and boys seems to a certain extent to be institutionalized in youth sports. Little League coach Ted Miller says that he has read articles on coaching that say that when coaching boys, "male coaches can, you know, come up and grab the face mask and shake 'em and yell at 'em, '*Rah-rah!*' " But Miller has learned from these articles that girls "don't seem to respond to that very well, the yelling and screaming." These kinds of comparisons are based on real observations by coaches who work closely with boys and with girls, and most likely they do reflect some real differences. However, the question we should ask is to what extent the coaches' different treatment of boys and girls simply serves as an add-on to differences that have been socially constructed through a myriad of gendering processes that shape boys and girls at deeply emotional levels. In turn, the coaches' actions and discourse about kids serves to *naturalize* these differences, thus helping to reestablish an ideology of gender essentialism.

THE EMERGENCE OF SOFT ESSENTIALISM

Research by sociologist Emily Kane shows that parents are much more supportive of gender nonconformity among young girls than among young boys. Moreover, Kane found that heterosexual fathers are more likely to strongly enforce gender conformity in their sons than are mothers or gay fathers.[19] To put it a different way, fathers tend to enforce a harder essentialism, while mothers tend toward a softer essentialism. And this contemporary essentialism is harder when it comes to boys, and softer, more flexible when it comes to girls. Boys, it seems, are more defined in parents' views by their presumed nature. Driven by testosterone and genes, boys are seen as fairly simple creatures, "hard-wired" to think, act, and respond competitively and aggressively. Girls, by contrast, are viewed as complex, able when given the proper opportunities to combine their supposedly natural nurturant and affective traits with more competitive goal-oriented and aggressive traits.

This idea that boys are defined by their nature, while girls are complex and malleable within shifting social contexts, seems to be an interesting inversion of a long-standing tendency to define women as close to nature and men as aligned with culture. In a highly influential 1974 article entitled "Is Female to Male As Nature Is to Culture?" anthropologist Sherry Ortner wrote that "woman's body seems to doom her to mere reproduction of life; the male, in contrast, lacking natural creative functions, must (or has the opportunity to) assert his creativity externally, 'artificially,' through the medium of technology and symbols. In so doing, he creates relatively lasting, eternal, transcendental objects, while the woman creates only perishables—human beings."[20] Through much of the nineteenth and twentieth centuries, this association of women with "nature" and men with "culture" justified a gender-dichotomized world that confined women to the domestic, private sphere of supportive and procreative activities, while viewing the public world as men's domain.[21]

It is perhaps the hallmark of the contemporary emergence of soft essentialism that boys and men are now seen as defined by their biology—"all that testosterone"—while girls and women, when given a range of opportunities, are seen as capable of exercising "choice." This view of girls allows for us to imagine them as adult women straddling two worlds—the world of family, home, and hearth, where their true nature presumably draws them, and the public world of education, sports, and work, which they will have a right to choose to participate in, or to opt out of. By contrast, this view of boys continues to see the competitive public world of sports, work, and careers as their natural destiny. Since their inflexible biology presumably predisposes men to the public world, they are not viewed as able to "choose" alternative (especially stigmatized, feminine) paths.[22] Ironically, fears that their sons just may "fail" to develop properly lead many adults to engage in (or at least tolerate) a "hardening" and "toughening" of boys that makes it difficult for boys to develop their full emotional potential (empathy, caretaking skills, etc.), something they will need in order to become healthy adults, good partners, and effective parents. Unchallenged, this socially constructed emotional deficit in boys will leave the responsibility on women's shoulders to, through their "choices," straddle both the public world and that of domestic labor. Clearly, essentialism is alive and well in the ways that we think about children. But this is not our grandparents' essentialism. It is an emergent, "soft" essentialism that accommodates the reality of girls' and women's presence in sports, and in public life more generally. The ideology of soft essentialism views girls as "pre-choice," while positioning boys as "pre-career."

Youth sports is an ideal site for the construction of soft essentialism. As an institution that's premised on making visible people's bodily abilities and limitations, sport, more that most other institutions (the military is perhaps equivalent), has historically created and conveyed cultural assumptions and values about essential differences between women and men. Though clearly contested by girls' and women's movement into sport, this is still a place where essentialism is constructed through sex-segregated bodily practices. And there is plenty of evidence that most adults are not only "comfortable" with thinking of boys and girls as naturally different—they in fact revel in the pleasure of shared talk about the ways that girls and boys differ. We live in an era of dramatic changes in gender relations, in education, families, workplaces, and professions—changes that may be confusing and disconcerting to many, resulting in what sociologist Barbara Risman calls "gender vertigo."[23] Given this turbulence in gender relations, perhaps people look for places that reaffirm comfortable ideas of natural difference. As sex-segregation breaks down or disappears in many areas of social life, perhaps the institutional homes of essentialism, because of the psychological security and pleasures it brings, tend to migrate to particular social sites, like youth sports, where continued sex-segregation of bodily practices makes gender difference particularly salient. Perhaps contemporary youth sports, rather than being a context in which gender inequalities and differences are challenged and changed, has instead become a kind of "gender comfort zone," with soft essentialism as its main ideological product.

NOTES

1 This same survey found that families in which kids play one or two organized team sports report higher levels of family happiness than do families of kids who do not play sports. Interestingly, this family happiness benefit seems to reverse itself—dramatically so in single-parent families—when kids play on three, four, or more teams (see Sabo and Veliz 2008).

2 This is not to say that girls and women did not play sports before the 1970s. In fact, there was a boom of female athletic participation that corresponded with the "first wave" of feminism, in the first two decades of the twentieth century. Following a backlash against feminism and female athletics in the 1930s, however, girls' and women's sports were either eliminated or ghettoized. Although working-class communities, and especially those made up of African Americans, continued in some ways to support women's sports through the middle decades of the twentieth century, white middle- and upper-class women no longer played organized sports in great numbers (the exception being some very limited programs within women's colleges) (see Cahn 1994).

3 By the mid-1980s, this idea of sport as a terrain of contested gender meanings was well established in the scholarly literature. See Messner 1988; Willis 1983.

4 In a highly influential article, Mary Jo Kane argues that women's participation in sport has exploded the idea of a natural gender binary and has instead revealed that men's and women's bodily capacities are scattered on a "continuum of difference" (M. Kane 1995; see also Lorber 1993).

5 Sargent 2001.

6 I have written elsewhere about the implications of the socialization of boys, and of institutions, like sport, that systematically teach boys (and reward them) for suppressing their capacity for empathy for self and others (see Messner 2002, chapter 2).

7 Though research suggests that girls generally experience bodily empowerment through their experiences in sport, girls in certain elite-level sports sometimes experience the opposite. Journalist Joan Ryan's research on girls in gymnastics and figure skating revealed frightening stories of eating disorders and injuries, too often enforced by emotionally abusive coaches whose only aim was to create champions (see Ryan 1996).

8 Van Auken and Van Auken 2001, 148.

9 McDonagh and Pappano 2008. Similarly, political scientist Jennifer Ring argues that girls have been denied the opportunity to play baseball because the sport has been a key locus in the United States for the construction of a masculine national identity: "When it was evident that girls and women *could* play and *wanted* to play, their history with the sport was denied and ignored and they were ushered into a 'separate but equal' sport that could be more readily reconciled with femininity without undermining the manliness of American national identity" (Ring 2008).

10 If we fully supported girls to play on integrated teams with boys while maintaining parallel girls-only leagues, it could create some of the same sorts of dynamics that led eventually to the disappearance of baseball's Negro Leagues, after the integration of Major League Baseball in 1947. Rodney Fort and Joel Maxcy argue that "the unabashed talent raiding by MLB killed African American Baseball a couple of years after integration began.... Competitive baseball was lost to countless thousands of fans throughout the South and Midwest, profitable businesses were lost to African American and White AAB team owners, and hundreds of African American players were denied a 'big league' livelihood as the result of integration" (2001, 35; see also Lanctot 2004). Though girls' youth sports are not a profit-generating business, like the professional Negro Leagues were, it is reasonable to expect that the rapid sex-integration of youth sports might result in a similar "talent drain" from all-girls' leagues as most of the most talented and motivated girl athletes gravitate to the integrated leagues. With the all-girls' leagues consisting mostly of the less athletically talented or less-motivated girls, it is an open question whether or in what manner these girls-only leagues would survive.

11 See Messner 2002, 142–46.

12 See Thorne 1993.

13 See Adams and Coltrane 2005; Lytton and Romney 1991.

14 To be sure, especially starting with the age of puberty, and stretching through adulthood, girls and women still find that they are subjected to a double standard. It's okay to express "masculine" traits of competitive individualism and goal-orientation, but a woman will also often be judged negatively if she's seen as less than "feminine."

15 This is certainly not a new insight. A good deal of feminist-inspired writing by men about sports—much of it personal, autobiographical, or journalistic, rather than scholarly—blossomed in the 1970s and early 1980s. And much of this work focused on the pain and humiliation that nonathletic boys had experienced in organized sports and physical education. For the first important collection of these works, see Sabo and Runfola 1980.

16 See Kimmel 1987, in which he argues that urbanization and changes in the organization of middle-class work led, during the turn of the twentieth century, to fears of social feminization and a "crisis of masculinity." The rise of organized sports among educated elite white men was one response to this crisis of middle-class masculinity (see Messner 1992).

17 See Pollack 1999.

18 The common silence in the dugout that surrounds an individual boy's sadness or pain may in one way be seen as a masculine form of collective respect and caretaking: since it's not acceptable to cry, the group gives the boy space to do it, looks away, and does not thus shame him for it. On the other hand, Sherri Grasmuck concluded from her research with boys' Little League Baseball that teams that had a boy who did "emotion work" in the dugout—empathizing with teammates who were upset or injured, staying positive when one or more teammates get down about losing a game—that these teams tended to be more cohesive and thus more successful (see Grasmuck 2005). In my son Sasha's last three years or so of Little League, I was frequently proud of him when, in the dugout, he would play this kind of empathetic, upbeat sort of role for his team, in the face of often more highly skilled boys' anger at their own failures. Coaches can model this kind of emotional caretaking behavior for boys, but in my experience they rarely do.

19 Kane 2006.

20 Ortner 1974, 75. This historical inversion of the gendered nature/culture dichotomy does not imply an inversion of the hierarchical ordering of male over female; to the contrary, I am suggesting that since the definition of men's narrow nature seems to predestine them for competition in public life, it continues to leave domestic-care work for women. Feminism is, in part, a claim by women not to be defined in terms of their natural bodies, but instead to be part of and to help to shape culture. The contemporary equation of girls and women as complex and able to make choices is a partial incorporation of feminism that has broadened women's ability to participate in public life. However, since it leaves boys and men largely untouched, this view ultimately leaves women to deal with the constraints of bridging public and domestic life. When they "choose" to not coach, to become team moms, to opt out of full-time careers and shift their energies toward domestic life,

this choice then reaffirms the idea that their "nature" as nurturers and caretakers has pulled them back—but now, not because they are forced to do so, as was the case for the post–World War II college-educated women in Betty Friedan's *Feminine Mystique*, who were forced to be mothers/housewives; today's professional-class women move toward the domestic sphere because they supposedly *choose* to.

21 Historically, this gendered separation of public versus domestic spheres for men and women was a dominant part of the ideology that supported modern versions of patriarchy. However, it has never been an absolute empirical "fact" that social life was so divided in "Western" industrial or post-industrial nations. In the United States, working-class women and poor women of color were present in the paid labor force in huge numbers from the outset of industrialization and even during times of backlash against women's public lives, like during the post–World War II era (see Sharistanian 1987).

22 Sociologist Martha McCaughey argues convincingly that misunderstood evolutionary ideas are now circulating as an essentialist ideology (about men, but not so much about women) that she calls "the Caveman Mystique . . . that sense of one's manhood as inherently productive, protective, aggressive, and heterosexual" (McCaughey 2008, 23). According to McCaughey, the Caveman Mystique has become a "grand narrative, a totalizing theory explaining men's experiences as though all men act and feel the same way, and as though the ideas of Western science provide a universal truth about those actions and feelings" (17).

23 Risman 1998.

REFERENCES

Acker, Joan. 1990. Hierarchies, jobs, bodies: A theory of gendered organizations. *Gender & Society* 4:139–58.
———. 2006. Inequality regimes: Gender, class, and race in organizations. *Gender & Society* 20:441–64.
Acosta, R. Vivien, and Linda Jean Carpenter. 2000. *Women in intercollegiate sport: A longitudinal study—Twenty-three year update.* Brooklyn, NY: Brooklyn College.
Adam, Michele, and Scott Coltrane. 2005. Boys and men in families: The domestic production of gender, power, and privilege. In *Handbook of studies on men and masculinities,* ed. Michael S. Kimmel, Jeff Hearn, and R. W. Connell, 230–48. Thousand Oaks, CA: Sage Publications.
Baca Zinn, Maxine, D. Stanley Eitzen, and Barbara Wells. 2008. *Diversity in families.* 8th ed. Boston: Allyn & Bacon.
Berlage, Gai Ingham. 1994. *Women in baseball: The forgotten history.* Westport, CT: Greenwood.
Bettie, Julie. 2003. *Women without class: Girls, race, and identity.* Berkeley: University of California Press.
Bird, Joyce. 1996. Welcome to the men's club: Homosociality and the maintenance of hegemonic masculinity. *Gender & Society* 10:120–32.
Blackstone, Amy Maria. 2004. Sociability, work, and gender. *Equal Opportunities International* 23:29–44.
Blau, Francine D., Mary C. Brinton, and David B. Grusky, eds. 2006. *The declining significance of gender?* New York: Russell Sage Foundation.

Bourdieu, Pierre, and Loic J. D. Wacquant. 1992. *An invitation to reflexive sociology.* Chicago: University of Chicago Press.

Boyle, Maree, and Jim McKay. 1995. You leave your troubles at the gate: A case study of the exploitation of older women's labor and "leisure" in sport. *Gender & Society* 9:556–76.

Britton, Dana. 2000. The epistemology of the gendered organization. *Gender & Society* 14: 418–34.

Cahn, Susan. 1994.h *Coming on strong: Gender and sexuality in twentieth-century women's sport.* New York: The Free Press.

Carpenter, Linda Jean, and Vivien R. Acosta. 2008. Women in intercollegiate sport: A longitudinal, national study—Thirty-one year update, 1977–2008. http://webpages.charter.net/womeninsport/2008%20 Summary%20Final.pdf.

Chafetz, Janet Saltzman, and Joseph A. Kotarba. 1995. Son worshipers: The role of Little League mothers in recreating gender." *Studies in Symbolic Interaction* 18:217–41.

———. 1999. Little League mothers and the reproduction of gender. In *Inside Sports,* ed. Jay Coakley and Peter Donnelly, 46–54. London: Routledge.

Charles, Maria, and David B. Grusky. 2004. *Occupational ghettos: The worldwide segregation of women and men.* Stanford, CA: Stanford University Press.

Coakley, Jay. 2002. Using sports to control deviance and violence among youths: Let's be critical and cautious. In *Paradoxes of youth and sport,* ed. Margaret Gatz, Michael A. Messner, and Sandra Ball Rokeach, 13–30. Albany, NY: State University of New York Press.

———. 2006. The good father: Parental expectations and youth sports. *Leisure Studies* 25:153–63.

Collins, Patricia Hill. 1990. *Black feminist thought: Knowledge, consciousness, and the politics of empowerment.* Boston: Unwin-Hyman.

Coltrane, Scott. 1996. *Family man: Fatherhood, housework, and gender equity.* New York: Oxford University Press.

Connell, Raewyn W. 1987. *Gender and power: Society, the person, and sexual politics.* Stanford, CA: Stanford University Press.

———. 2006. Glass ceilings or gendered institutions? Mapping the gender regimes of public sector workers. *Public Administration Review* 66:837–49.

Connell, Raewyn W., and James W. Messerschmidt. 2005. Hegemonic masculinity: Rethinking the concept. *Gender & Society* 19:829–59.

Coontz, Stephanie. 1992. *The way we never were: American families and the nostalgia trap.* New York: Basic Books.

Correll, Shelley J. 2007. Getting a job: Is there a motherhood penalty? *American Journal of Sociology* 112:1297–1338.

Craig, Lyn. 2006. Does father care mean father share? A comparison of how mothers and fathers in intact families spend time with children. *Gender & Society* 20:259–81.

Curry, Timothy. 1991. Fraternal bonding in the locker room: Pro-feminist analysis of talk about competition and women. *Sociology of Sport Journal* 8:119–35.

———. 2000. Booze and bar fights: A journey to the dark side of college athletics. In *Masculinities, gender relations, and sport,* ed. Jim McKay, Donald F. Sabo, and Michael A. Messner, 162–75. Thousand Oaks, CA: Sage Publications.

Daniels, Arlene Kaplan. 1985. Invisible work. *Social Problems* 34:363–74.

———. 1987. Good times and good works: The place of sociability in the work of women volunteers. *Social Problems* 32:403–15.

De Lench, Brooke. 2006. *Home team advantage: The critical role of mothers in youth sports.* New York: HarperCollins.

Deutsch, Francine M. 2007. Undoing gender. *Gender & Society* 21:106–27.

Drago, Robert, Lynn Henninghausen, Jacqueline Rogers, Teresa Vescio, and Kai Dawn Stauffer. 2005. Final report for CAGE: The coaching and gender equity project. Funded by the National Collegiate Athletic Association, the National Association of Collegiate Women Athletics Administrators, and the Commission for Women and Athletics of the Pennsylvania State University. Available for download (Word document) at http://lsir.la.psu.edu/workfam/CAGE.htm.

Dreier, Peter, and Beth Steckler. 2007. Not just for the gentry. *The American Prospect*, January–February, A12–A15.

Dworkin, Shari L. 2001. "Holding back": Negotiating a glass ceiling on women's muscular strength. *Sociological Perspectives* 44:333–50.

Eitzen, D. Stanley, and George H. Sage. 2008. *Sociology of North American sport*. 8th ed. Boulder, CO: Paradigm Publishers.

Eliasoph, Nina. 1998. *Avoiding politics: How Americans produce apathy in everyday life*. Cambridge: Cambridge University Press.

England, Paula. 2006. Toward gender equality: Progress and bottlenecks. In *The declining significance of gender?* ed. Francine D. Blau, Mary C. Brinton, and David B. Grusky, 245–64. New York: Russell Sage Foundation.

Enloe, Cynthia H. 2004. *The curious feminist: Searching for women in a new age of empire*. Berkeley: University of California Press.

Ferguson, Ann Arnett. 2000. *Bad boys: Public schools in the making of black masculinity*. Ann Arbor: University of Michigan Press.

Fine, Gary Alan. 1987. *With the boys: Little League Baseball and preadolescent culture*. Chicago: University of Chicago Press.

Fort, Rodney, and Joel Maxcy. 2001. The demise of African American baseball leagues: A rival league explanation." *Journal of Sports Economics* 2:35–49.

Friedan, Betty. 1963. *The feminine mystique*. New York: Dell.

Glassner, Barry. 1999. *The culture of fear*. New York: Basic Books.

Glazier, Bill. 2003. AYSO Celebrates Community Spirit at Opening Day Event. *South Pasadena Review*, September 17, 2003, 2.

Grasmuck, Sherri. 2005. *Protecting home: Class, race, and masculinity in boys' baseball*. New Brunswick, NJ: Rutgers University Press.

Gregorich, Barbara. 1993. *Women at play: The story of women in baseball*. San Diego: Harcourt, Brace & Co.

Hamilton, Laura. 2007. Trading on heterosexuality: College women's gender strategies and homophobia. *Gender & Society* 21:145–72.

Hanson, Karen V. 2005. *Not-so-nuclear families: Class, gender, and networks of care*. New Brunswick, NJ: Rutgers University Press.

Harding, Sandra. 1991. *Whose science? Whose knowledge? Thinking from women's lives*. Ithaca, NY: Cornell University Press.

Hartmann, Douglas. 2001. Notes on midnight basketball and the cultural politics of recreation, race, and at-risk urban youth. *Journal of Sport and Social Issues* 25:339–71.

Harvey, Jean, Maurice Levesque, and Peter Donnelly. 2007. Sport volunteerism and social capital. *Sociology of Sport Journal* 24:206–23.

Hays, Sharon. 1996. *The cultural contradictions of motherhood*. New Haven, CT: Yale University Press.

———. 2003. *Flat broke with children: Women in the age of welfare reform*. Oxford: Oxford University Press.

Henley, Nancy M. 1977. *Body politics: Power, sex, and nonverbal communication*. Englewood Cliffs, NJ: Prentice-Hall.

Hirschman, Linda R. 2005. Homeward bound. *American Prospect*, December.

———. 2006. *Get to work: A manifesto for women of the world*. New York: Viking.

Hochschild, Arlie Russell. 1983. *The managed heart: Commercialization of human feeling*. Berkeley: University of California Press.

———. 1989. *The second shift*. New York: Viking.

———. 2001. *The time bind: When work becomes home and home becomes work*. New York: Henry Holt.

Hondagneu-Sotelo, Pierrette, and Michael A. Messner. 1994. Gender displays and men's power: The "new man" and the Mexican immigrant man. In *Theorizing masculinities*, ed. Harry Brod and Michael Kaufman, 200–18. Thousand Oaks, CA: Sage Publications.

Hook, Jennifer L. 2004. Reconsidering the division of household labor: Incorporating volunteer work and informal support. *Journal of Marriage and Family* 66:101–18.

Jacobs, Jerry A., and Kathleen Gerson. 2001. Overworked individuals or overworked families? Explaining trends in work, leisure, and family time. *Work and Occupations* 28:40–63.

———. 2005. *The time divide: Work, family, and gender inequality.* Cambridge, MA: Harvard University Press.

Kane, Emily W. 2006. "No way my boys are going to be like that!" Parents' responses to gender nonconformity. *Gender & Society* 20:149–76.

Kane, Mary Jo. 1995. Resistance/transformation of the oppositional binary: Exposing sport as a continuum." *Journal of Sport and Social Issues* 19:191–218.

Kanter, Rosabeth Moss. 1977. *Men and women of the corporation.* New York: Basic Books.

Kimmel, Michael S. 1987. Men's responses to feminism at the turn of the century. *Gender & Society* 1:517–30.

———. 1990. Baseball and the reconstitution of American masculinity: 1880–1920. In *Sport, men, and the gender order: Critical feminist perspectives,* ed. Michael A. Messner and Donald F. Sabo, 55–66. Champaign, IL: Human Kinetics.

Kimmel, Michael S., and Abby Ferber, eds. 2003. *Privilege.* Boulder, CO: Westview Press.

Knoppers, Annelies. 1988. Men working: Coaching as a male dominated and sex segregated occupation. *Arena Review* 12:69–80.

———. 1994. Gender and the coaching profession. In *Women, sport, and culture,* ed. Susan Birrell and Cheryl L. Cole, 119–34. Champaign, IL: Human Kinetics Press.

Knoppers, Annelies, and Anton Anthonissen. 2005. Male athletic and managerial masculinities: Congruencies in discursive practices? *Journal of Gender Studies* 14:123–35.

Lamont, Michele, ed. 1999. *The cultural territories of race: Black and white boundaries.* Chicago: University of Chicago Press.

Lanctot, Neil. 2004. *Negro League baseball: The rise and ruin of a Black institution.* Philadelphia: University of Pennsylvania Press.

Lareau, Annette. 2003. *Unequal childhoods: Class, race, and family life.* Berkeley: University of California Press.

LaVoi, Nicole M., and Erin Becker. 2007. "Where have all the post–Title IX mothers gone? Exploring the scarcity of female coaches in youth sport. Working Paper, Tucker Center for Research on Girls and Women in Sport, University of Minnesota, Minneapolis.

Levin, Peter. 2001. "Gendering the market: Temporality, work, and gender on a national futures exchange. *Work and Occupations* 28:112–30.

Lichterman, Paul. 2005. Elusive togetherness: Church groups trying to bridge America's divisions. Princeton, NJ: Princeton University Press.

———. 2006. Social capital or group style? Rescuing Tocqueville's insights on civic engagement. *Theory and Society* 35:529–63.

Lorber, Judith. 1993. Believing is seeing: Biology as ideology, *Gender & Society* 7: 568–581.

Lytton, H., and D. M. Romney. 1991. Parents' differential socialization of boys and girls: A meta-analysis. *Psychological Bulletin* 109:267–96.

Martin, Patricia Yancy. 2001. "Mobilizing masculinities": Women's experiences of men at work." *Organization* 8:587–618.

———. 2003. "Said and done" versus "Saying and doing": Gendering practices, practicing gender at work." *Gender & Society* 17:342–66.

———. 2006. Practicing gender at work: Further thoughts on reflexivity. *Gender, Work and Organization* 13: 254–76.

Massey, Doreen. 1994. *Space, place, and gender.* Minneapolis: University of Minnesota Press.

McCaughey, Martha. 2008. *The caveman mystique: Pop-Darwinism and debates over sex, violence, and science.* New York: Routledge.

McDonagh, Eileen, and Laura Pappano. 2008. *Playing with the boys: Why separate is not equal in sports.* New York: Oxford University Press.

McKay, Jim. 1997. *Managing gender: Affirmative action and organizational power in Australian, Canadian, and New Zealand sport.* Albany: State University of New York Press.

McPherson, J. Miller, and Lynne Smith-Lovin. 1986. Sex segregation in voluntary associations. *American Sociological Review* 51:61–79.

Messerschmidt, James W. 2004. *Flesh and blood: Adolescent gender diversity and violence.* Lanham, MD: Rowman & Littlefield.

Messner, Michael A. 1988. Sports and male domination: The female athlete as contested ideological terrain. *Sociology of Sport Journal* 5:197–211.

———. 1990. Men studying masculinity: Some epistemological questions in sport sociology. *Sociology of Sport Journal* 7:136–53.

———. 1992. *Power at play: Sports and the problem of masculinity.* Boston: Beacon Press.

———. 2000. Barbie girls vs. sea monsters: Children constructing gender. *Gender & Society* 14:765–84.

———. 2002. *Taking the field: Women, men, and sports.* Minneapolis: University of Minnesota Press.

———. 2005. Still a man's world? Studying masculinities and sport. In *The handbook of studies on men and masculinities,* ed. Michael S. Kimmel, Jeff Hearn, and R. W. Connell, 313–25. Thousand Oaks, CA: Sage Publications.

Messner, Michael A., Margaret Carlisle Duncan, and Kerry Jensen. 1993. Separating the men from the girls: The gendered language of televised sports. *Gender & Society* 7:121–37.

Meyerson Milgraom, Eva M., and Trond Petersen. 2006. The glass ceiling in the United States and Sweden: Lessons from the family-friendly corner of the world, 1970–1990. In *The declining significance of gender?* ed. Francine D. Blau, Mary C. Brinton, and David B. Grusky, 156–211. New York: Russell Sage Foundation.

Miller, Kathleen, Merrill Melnick, Grace Barnes, Michael Farrell, and Don Sabo. 2005. Untangling the links among athletic involvement, gender, race, and adolescent academic outcomes. *Sociology of Sport Journal* 22:178–93.

Miller, Kathleen, Merrill Melnick, Michael Farrell, Grace Barnes, and Don Sabo. 2006. Jocks, gender, binge drinking, and adolescent violence. *Journal of Interpersonal Violence* 21:105–20.

Miller, Kathleen, Don Sabo, Michael Farrell, Grace Barnes, and Merrill Melnick. 1999. Sports, sexual activity, contraceptive use, and pregnancy among female and male high school students: Testing cultural resource theory." *Sociology of Sport Journal* 16:366–87.

Miller, Kathleen, Don Sabo, Merrill Melnick, Michael Farrell, and Grace Barnes. 2001. The Women's Sports Foundation report: Health risks and the teen athlete. East Meadow, NY: Women's Sports Foundation.

Montez de Oca, Jeffrey. 2005. As our muscles get softer, our missile race becomes harder: Cultural citizenship and the "muscle gap." *Journal of Historical Sociology* 18:145–71.

Morgan, Laurie A., and Karen A. Martin. 2006. Taking women professionals out of the office. *Gender & Society* 20:108–28.

Ollilainen, Marjukka, and Toni Calisanti. 2007. Metaphors at work: Maintaining the salience of gender in self-managing teams. *Gender & Society* 21:5–27.

Ortner, Sherry. 1974. Is female to male as nature is to culture? In *Woman, Culture, and Society,* ed. Michelle Zimbalist Rosaldo and Louise Lamphere, 67–87. Stanford, CA: Stanford University Press.

Petrzelka, Peggy, and Susan E. Mannon. 2006. Keepin' this little town going: Gender and volunteerism in rural America. *Gender & Society* 20:236–58.

Pierce, Jennifer. 1993. Rambo litigators: Emotional labor in a male-dominated occupation. In *Masculinities in Organizations,* ed. Cliff Cheng, 1–27. Thousand Oaks, CA: Sage Publications.

Pollack, William. 1999. *Real boys: Rescuing our sons from the myths of boyhood.* New York: Henry Holt.

Reskin, Barbara F. 1988. Bringing the men back in: Sex differentiation and the devaluation of women's work. *Gender & Society* 2:58–81.

Reskin, Barbara F., and Patricia A. Roos. 1990. *Job queues, gender queues: Explaining women's inroads into male occupations.* Philadelphia: Temple University Press.

Rhode, Deborah L., and Christopher J. Walker. 2008. Gender equity in college athletics: Women coaches as a case study. *Stanford Journal of Civil Rights and Civil Liberties* 4:1–50. Available at http://ssrn.com/abstract=922380.

Ridgeway, Cecilia. 2006. Gender as an organizing force in social relations: Implications for the future of inequality. In *The declining significance of gender?* ed. Francine D. Blau, Mary C. Brinton, and David B. Grusky, 265–87. New York: Russell Sage Foundation.

Ridgeway, Cecilia L., and Shelley J. Correll. 2004. Unpacking the gender system: A theoretical perspective on gender beliefs and relations. *Gender & Society* 18:510–31.

Ring, Jennifer. 2008. Waiting for Jackie: Why American girls don't play baseball. Paper presented at the annual meetings of the North American Society for the Sociology of Sport, Pittsburgh, PA, October 31–November 3.

Risman, Barbara J. 1998. *Gender vertigo: American families in transition.* New Haven, CT: Yale University Press.

Ryan, Joan. 1996. Little girls in pretty boxes: The making and breaking of elite gymnasts and figure skaters. New York: Warner Books.

Sabo, Don, and Ross Runfola, eds. 1980. *Jock: Sports and male identity.* Englewood Cliffs, NJ: Prentice- Hall.

Sabo, Don and Phil Veliz. 2008. *Go out and play: Youth sport and families.* East Meadow, NY: Women's Sports Foundation.

Sargent, Paul. 2001. *Real men or real teachers? Contradictions in the lives of men elementary school teachers.* Harriman, TN: Men's Studies Press.

Sharistanian, Janet, ed. 1987. *Beyond the public/domestic dichotomy: Contemporary perspectives on women's public lives.* Westport, CT: Greenwood Press.

Shields, David Light, Brenda Light Bredemeier, Nicole M. LaVoi, and F. Clark Power. 2005. The sport behavior of youth, parents, and coaches: The good, the bad, and the ugly. *Journal of Research in Character Education* 3:43–59.

Sprague, Joey. 2005. *Feminist methodologies for critical researchers: Bridging differences.* Lanham, MD: Altamira Press.

Stacey, Judith. 1997. *In the name of the family: Rethinking family values in the postmodern age.* Boston: Beacon Press.

Steiner, Leslie Morgan, ed. 2006. *Mommy wars.* New York: Random House.

Stevenson, Betsy. 2007. Title IX and the evolution of high school sports. *Contemporary Economic Policy* 25:486–505.

Stone, Pamela. 2007. *Opting out: Why women really quit careers and head home.* Berkeley: University of California Press.

Swidler, Anne. 1986. Culture in action: Symbols and strategies. *American Sociological Review* 51:273–86.

Talbot, Margaret. 2002. Playing with patriarchy: The gendered dynamics of sports organizations. In *Gender and sport: A reader,* ed. Sheila Scraton and Anne Flintoff, 277–91. London: Routledge.

Theberge, Nancy. 1988. Making a career in a man's world: The experiences and orientations of women in coaching. *Arena Review* 12:116–27.

———. 1989. Women athletes and the myth of female frailty. In *Women: A feminist perspective,* ed. Jo Freeman, 507–22. 4th ed. Mountain View, CA: Mayfield.

———. 1990. Gender, work, and power: The case of women in coaching. *Canadian Journal of Sociology* 15:59–75.

———. 1993. The construction of gender in sport: Women, coaching, and the naturalization of difference. *Social Problems* 40:301–13.

Thompson, Shona. 1999a. The game begins at home: Women's labor in the service of sport. In *Inside Sports,* ed. Jay Coakley and Peter Donnelly, 111–20. London: Routledge.

———. 1999b. *Mother's taxi: Sport and women's labor.* Albany: State University of New York Press.

Thorne, Barrie. 1993. *Gender play: Girls and boys in school.* New Brunswick, NJ: Rutgers University Press.

Thorne, Barrie, Cheris Kramarae, and Nancy Henley. 1983. *Language, gender, and society.* Rowley, MA: Newbury House.

Thorne, Barrie, and Marilyn Yalom, eds. 1992. (1982). *Rethinking the family: Some feminist questions.* Boston: Northeastern University Press.

Tucker Center for Research on Girls and Women in Sport. 2007. *The 2007 Tucker Center research report, Developing physically active girls: An evidence-based multidisciplinary approach.* Minneapolis: University of Minnesota.

Van Auken, Lance, and Robin Van Auken. 2001. *Play ball! The story of Little League Baseball.* University Park, PA: Pennsylvania State University Press.

Vavrus, Mary Douglas. 2007. Opting out moms in the news: Selling new traditionalism in the new millennium. *Feminist Media Studies* 7:47–63.

Wachs, Faye Linda. 2002. Leveling the playing field: Negotiating gendered rules in coed softball. *Journal of Sport and Social Issues* 26:300–316.

Wall, Glenda, and Stephanie Arnold. 2007. How involved is involved fathering? An exploration of the contemporary culture of fatherhood. *Gender & Society* 21:508–27.

Webber, Gretchen, and Christine Williams. 2008. Part-time work and the gender division of labor. *Qualitative Sociology* 31:15–36.

Weiss, Maureen R., Heather Barber, Vicki Ebbeck, and Becky L. Sisley. 1991. Developing competence and confidence in novice female coaches: II. Perceptions of ability and affective experiences following a season-long coaching internship. *Journal of Exercise Psychology* 13:336–63.

Weiss, Maureen R., and Susan D. Fretwell. 2005. The parent-coach/child-athlete relationship in youth sport: Cordial, contentious, or conundrum? *Research Quarterly for Exercise and Sport* 76:286–305.

Weiss, Maureen R., and Becky L. Sisley. 1986. Where have all the coaches gone? *Sociology of Sport Journal* 1:332–47.

West, Candace, and Don Zimmerman. 1987. Doing gender. *Gender & Society* 1:125–51.

Williams, Christine L. 1991. *Gender differences at work: Women and men in nontraditional occupations.* Berkeley: University of California Press.

Willis, Paul. 1983. Women in sport in ideology. In *Sport, culture, and ideology,* ed. Jennifer Hargreaves, 117–35. London: Routledge & Kegan Paul.

Wilson, John. 2000. Volunteering. *Annual Review of Sociology* 26:215–40.

Wilson, Robin. 2007. Where have all the women gone? *Chronicle of Higher Education,* May 4, A40–A44.

Yablonsky, Lewis, and Jonathan J. Brower. 1979. *The Little League game: How kids, coaches, and parents really play it.* New York: Times Books.

CHAPTER 4

HOW INEQUALITY WRECKS EVERYTHING WE CARE ABOUT

Consider the following questions as you read this chapter.

QUESTIONS TO CONSIDER

1 Name one specific example from the article of how inequality is damaging to our society.

2 How structures of inequality affect you depends on your social location. Think about your race, your gender, and your social class. How does this affect your opportunities in life? Do you face constraints or challenges someone in another social location might not?

3 What is the author's main point?

KEY TERMS

inequality
social solidarity
social mobility

HOW INEQUALITY WRECKS EVERYTHING WE CARE ABOUT

BY CHUCK COLLINS

> The reality is that U.S. society is polarizing and its social arteries are hardening. The sumptuousness and bleakness of the respective lifestyles of rich and poor represents a scale of difference in opportunity and wealth that is almost medieval—and a standing offense to the American expectation that everyone has the opportunity for life, liberty and happiness.
>
> —Will Hutton (b. 1951)

Inequality is wrecking the world. Not just poverty, which is destroying the lives of billions of people around the planet, but also inequality—the accelerating gap between the 99 percent and the 1 percent.

THE INEQUALITY DEATH SPIRAL

According to research in dozens of disciplines, the extreme disparities of wealth and power corrode our democratic system and public trust. They lead to a breakdown in civic cohesion and social solidarity, which in turn leads to worsened health outcomes.

Inequality undercuts social mobility and has disastrous effects on economic stability and growth. The notion of a "death spiral" may sound dramatic, but it captures the dynamic and reinforcing aspects of inequality.

And these inequalities were a major contributing factor to the 1929 and 2008 economic downturns. What follows is the case against inequality.

INEQUALITY WRECKS OUR DEMOCRACY AND CIVIC LIFE

Inequality is disenfranchising us, diminishing our vote at the ballot box and our voice in the public square. As dollars of the 1 percent displace the votes of the 99 percent as the currency of politics, the 1 percent wins. Not every time, but enough so that the tilt continues toward the agenda of the 1 percent.

The money of the 1 percent dominates our campaign finance system, even after efforts at reform. To run for U.S. Senate—or to win additional terms in the Senate after being elected—politicians must raise an estimated $15,000 a day in campaign contributions. To do this efficiently, politicians have to spend a lot of time courting people in the 1 percent, attending $1,000-a-plate fund-raising dinners and listening to their concerns and agenda. This means less time shaking hands in front of the Costco or Cracker Barrel. We all respond to the people we are surrounded by, and politicians are no different.

Elections do matter. Politicians care about votes on Election Day, and they campaign for those votes and work to get supporters to the polls. But candidates for the U.S. Congress know that every other day of the year they have to think about money.

The corporate 1 percent dominates the lobbying space around federal and state policies. In the last thirty years, the ranks of official lobbyists have exploded. In 1970, there were five registered lobbyists for every one of the 535 members of Congress. Today there are twenty-two lobbyists for every member.[1]

Who lobbies for the 99 percent? There are impressive organizations out there, such as Public Citizen and the Children's Defense Fund, that stand up, wave their arms, and say, "Hey, what about the 99 percent?" But they are severely underresourced, outgunned, and outmaneuvered by the organized 1 percent.

INEQUALITY MAKES US SICK

The medical researchers have said it. And now a growing body of public health research is arriving at the same conclusion: inequality is making us sick.

The more inequality grows between the 1 percent and the 99 percent, the less healthy we are. Unequal communities have greater rates of heart disease, asthma, mental illness, cancer, and other morbid illnesses.

Of course, poverty contributes to all kinds of bad health outcomes. But research shows that you are better off in a low-income community with greater equality than you are in a community with a higher income but more extreme inequalities.

Counties and countries with lower incomes but less inequality have better health outcomes. They have lower infant mortality rates, longer life expectancy, and lower incidences of all kinds of diseases. Counties with higher average incomes but greater disparities between rich and poor have the opposite indicators. They are less healthy places to live.[2]

Why is this so? According to British health researcher Richard Wilkinson, communities with less inequality have stronger "social cohesion," more cultural limits on unrestrained individualism, and more effective networks of mutual aid and caring. "The individualism and values of the market are restrained by a social morality," Wilkinson writes. The existence of more social capital "lubricates the workings of the whole society and economy. There are fewer signs of antisocial aggressiveness, and society appears more caring."[3]

INEQUALITY TEARS OUR COMMUNITIES APART

Extreme inequalities of wealth rip our communities apart with social divisions and distrust, leading to an erosion of social cohesion and solidarity. The 1 percent and the 99 percent today don't just live on opposite sides of the tracks—they occupy parallel universes.

New research shows that we're becoming more polarized by class and race in terms of where we live. A 2011 report based on U.S. Census data notes, "As overall income inequality grew in the last four decades, high- and low-income families have become increasingly less likely to live near one another. Mixed income neighborhoods have grown rarer, while affluent and poor neighborhoods have grown much more common."[4] As this distance widens, it is harder for people to feel like they are in the same boat.

High levels of inequality lead to the construction of physical walls. In many parts of the world, the members of the 1 percent reside in gated communities, surrounded by security systems and bodyguards. More than 9 million households in the United States live behind walls in gated communities, similar to the statistics in polarized societies such as Mexico and Brazil. Over a third of new housing starts in the southern United States are in gated communities.[5]

The relationship between the 1 percent and the 99 percent is characterized by fear, distance, misunderstanding, distrust, and class and racial antagonisms. As a result, there is less caring and a greater amount of individualistic behavior. Part of how people express care is support for public investments in health infrastructure and prevention that benefit everyone. As societies grow unequal, support for such investments declines.

Solidarity is characterized by people taking responsibility for one another and caring for neighbors. But for solidarity to happen, people must know one another and have institutions that transcend differences in class, culture, and race. In communities with great inequality, these institutions don't exist and solidarity is weakened.

INEQUALITY ERODES SOCIAL MOBILITY AND EQUAL OPPORTUNITY

Inequality undermines the cherished value of equality of opportunity and social mobility. Intergenerational mobility is the possibility of shifting up or down the income ladder relative to your parents' status. In a mobile society, your economic circumstances are not defined or limited by the economic origins of your family.

For many decades, economists argued that inequality in the United States was the price we paid for a dynamic economy with social mobility.[6] We didn't want to be like Canada or those northern European economies, economists would argue, with their rigid class systems and lack of mobility.

But here's the bad news: Canada and those European nations—with their social safety nets and progressive tax policies—are now more mobile than U.S. society. Research across the industrialized OECD countries has found that Canada, Australia, and the Nordic countries (Denmark, Norway, Sweden, and Finland) are among the most mobile. There is a strong correlation between social mobility and policies that redistribute income and wealth through taxation. The United States is now among the *least* mobile of industrialized countries in terms of earnings.[7]

INEQUALITY ERODES PUBLIC SERVICES

The 99 percent depends on the existence of a robust commonwealth of public and community institutions. As Bill Gates Sr., the father of the founder of Microsoft, wrote,

> The ladder of opportunity for America's middle class depends on strong and accessible public educational institutions, libraries, state parks and municipal pools. And for America's poor, the ladder of opportunity also includes access to affordable health care, quality public transportation, and childcare assistance.[8]

Historically, during times of great inequality, there is a disinvestment in the common-wealth.[9] There is less support provided for education, affordable housing, public health care, and other pillars of a level playing field. By contrast, in 1964, a time of relative equality, there was greater concern about poverty; in fact, we launched the War on Poverty to further reduce disadvantage.

Today, as the 1 percent delinks from our communities, it privatizes the services it needs. This leads to two bad outcomes. First, because the 1 percent does not depend on commonwealth services, it would rather not pay for them. They often prefer tax cuts and limited government, which leave them more of their money to spend on privatized services.

Second, the quality of life for the 99 percent suffers when the wealthy don't have a personal stake in maintaining quality public services. As we've seen, the 1 percent has tremendous clout. Its members have the ear of elected officials, command over charitable dollars, dominance of media ownership, and networking connections that are sometimes called "social capital." In a democratic society, good government and strong public institutions require civic engagement by everyone. But when those with the biggest amount of political power, largest number of connections, and greatest capacity don't have a stake, a cycle of disinvestment occurs.

The cycle of disinvestment begins when public services start to deteriorate after the withdrawal of tax dollars and the participation of the powerful. For example, if some-one doesn't use the neighborhood public swimming pool because he or she belongs to a private club or spends summers at a private beach house, that person doesn't have a stake in ensuring that the public swimming pool is open all summer, clean and well maintained, and staffed with qualified lifeguards. When services deteriorate and the powerful no longer participate, it leads to a decline in political support and resources, which in turn leads to a cycle of further disinvestment.

This lack of stake is even more visible in terms of public education, where the with-drawal of the 1 percent and even the top 30 percent of families has contributed to severe disinvestment in some school districts. This triggers a vicious circle of budget cuts, stakeholders pulling out, and declining public support for education.

The cycle of disinvestment accelerates when it becomes rational to abandon public and community services if one can afford to do so. Those who can get out do so, in a rush-to-the-exits moment. Families in the 99 percent work extra hard to privatize the services they need until there is a wholesale withdrawal from the public sphere.

If you can't depend on the bus to get to work, you buy a car. If you can't rely on the local public schools to educate your child, then you stretch to pay for private schools. If you can't depend on the lifeguards to show up at the public pool, then you join the private pool. If you can't depend on the police to protect your neighborhood, you hire a private security service or move to a gated community. The cycle of disinvestment continues and the costs of privatized services rise, trapping the remaining families in poor schools and neighborhoods lacking services.

INEQUALITY UNDERMINES ECONOMIC GROWTH

Remember the last time in history that the 1 percent had such a large share of the wealth pie? It was 1929, the eve of the Great Depression. Economic historians argue that this was not a coincidence. Too much inequality contributes to economic instability.

The corollary is that periods of shared prosperity have greater economic growth and stability. The period after World War II, 1947 to 1977, is often cited as a case study of a high-growth and high-equality period.

Making such comparisons is fraught with danger—we're not just comparing apples and oranges, we're comparing bicycles and dump trucks. The period after World War II was unprecedented in terms of the dominant and unrivaled role the United States played in the global economy. But international comparative data that look at inequality and economic performance reinforce this story. More-equal societies do better on most indicators.

The conventional wisdom, espoused in the 1960s by economists such as Arthur Okun of the Brookings Institution, was that there was a trade-off between growth and equity: policies that increased equality would slow economic growth, and aggressive pro-growth policies would worsen inequality. But this thinking is now being turned on its head.

Research by the International Monetary Fund (IMF) and the National Bureau of Economic Research point to the fact that more-equal societies have stronger rates of growth, experience longer economic expansions, and are quicker to recover from economic downturns. According to Jonathan Ostry, an economist at the IMF, trends toward unequal income in the United States mean that future economic expansions will be just one-third as long as they were in the 1960s, prior to the widening of the income divide. Less-equal societies are more vulnerable to both financial crises and political instability.[10]

In volatile markets, investors become gun-shy, even those in the 1 percent. When they perceive that financial markets are rigged in favor of insiders and the politically connected, they take their money somewhere else. "You're going to lose a generation of investors," observed Barry Ritholtz, an investor researcher with Fusion IQ. "And that's how you end up with a 25-year bear market. That's the risk if people start to think there is no economic justice."[11]

Many economists have drawn parallels between 1929 on the eve of the Great Depression and the 2008 economic meltdown. Raghuram Rajan, a former chief economist for the IMF, argues that both depressions were preceded by periods of extreme inequality. In his book *Fault Lines: How Hidden Fractures Still Threaten the World Economy*, Rajan observes that during the decade prior to both economic downturns, the 1 percent captured a gigantic percentage of income gains and wages were stagnant for the majority of Americans. Meanwhile, government policies and private corporate practices encouraged easy access to credit and borrowing among the poor and middle classes. Household debt nearly doubled during both periods.[12]

NOTES

1 According to the Center for Responsive Politics, there were 12,220 registered lobbyists in 2011. This is 22.84 lobbyists for every one of the 535 members of Congress. Center for Responsive Politics, "Lobbying Database," www.opensecrets.org/lobby/index.php?ql3 (accessed January 3, 2012).

2 For a good overview of health and inequality issues, see Sam Pizzigati, *Greed and Good: Understanding and Overcoming the Inequality That Limits Our Lives* (New York: Apex Press, 2004), 311–30. Also see Dr. Stephen Bezruchka's website, Population Health Forum (http://depts.washington.edu/eqhlth), for information on global and U.S. health and inequality information. Also see Stephen Bezruchka and M. A. Mercer, "The Lethal Divide: How Economic Inequality Affects Health," in M. Fort, M. A. Mercer, and O. Gish, eds., *Sickness and Wealth: The Corporate Assault on Global Health* (Boston: South End Press, 2004), 11–18.

3 See Richard Wilkinson, *Unhealthy Societies: The Afflictions of Inequality* (London: Routledge, 1996).

4 Sean F. Reardon and Kendra Bischoff, "Growth in the Residential Segregation of Families by Income, 1970–2009," Stanford University, US 2010 Project, Russell Sage Foundation, and American Communities Project at Brown University, November 2011, www.s4.brown.edu/us2010/Data/Report/report111111.pdf (accessed January 3, 2012).

5 Edward J. Blakely and Mary Gail Snyder, *Fortress America: Gated Communities in the United States* (Washington, DC: Brookings Institution Press, 1997); and Justice Policy Institute study, as reported in Jesse Katy, "A Nation of Too Many Prisoners?" *Los Angeles Times*, February 15, 2000.

6 Wojciech Kopczuk, Emmanuel Saez, and Jae Song, "Earnings Inequality and Mobility in the United States: Evidence from Social Security Data Since 1937," *Quarterly Journal of Economics* 125, 1 (February 2010): 91–128, http://ideas.repec.org/a/tpr/qjecon/v125y2010i1p91-128.html (accessed January 3, 2012).

7 OECD, "A Family Affair: Intergenerational Social Mobility Across OECD Countries," *Economic Policy Reforms: Going for Growth*, www.oecd.org/dataoecd/2/7/45002641.pdf (accessed January 3, 2012). Also see the Pew Charitable Trust's Economic Mobility Project (www.economicmobility.

org) and their study "Chasing the Same Dream, Climbing Different Ladders: Economic Mobility in the United States and Canada," January 2010, www.economicmobility.org/reports_and_research/other/other?id=0012(accessed January 3, 2012).

8 Bill Gates Sr. and Chuck Collins, *Wealth and Our Commonwealth: Why American Should Tax Accumulated Fortunes* (Boston: Beacon Press, 2003).

9 Ibid., 19–22.

10 David Lynch, "How Inequality Hurts the Economy," *Business Week Insider*, November 16, 2011, www.businessweek.com/magazine/how-inequality-hurts-the-economy-11162011.html?campaign_id=rss_topStories (accessed January 3, 2012).

11 Ibid.

12 Raghuram G. Rajan, *Fault Lines: How Hidden Fractures Still Threaten the World Economy* (Princeton, NJ: Princeton University Press, 2010).

CHAPTER 5

WHAT IS WHITE PRIVILEGE?

Consider the following questions as you read this chapter.

QUESTIONS TO CONSIDER

1. Give one specific example of white privilege discussed by Amico.

2. How does this situation of white privilege affect you personally? Is there anything you can do to ameliorate this?

3. What is the author's main point?

KEY TERMS

white privilege
racial domination

WHAT IS WHITE PRIVILEGE?

BY RICHARD P. AMICO

White privilege is a form of domination, hence it is a *relational* concept.[1] It positions one person or group over another person or group. It is a concept of racial domination that enables us to see this relationship from the perspective of those who benefit from such domination. Traditionally in the United States, racial domination has been portrayed as discrimination against people of color—that is, from the perspective of those who are disadvantaged by such domination. But you can't have one without the other—you can't have racial domination and disadvantage without racial dominators who are advantaged. This is the insight of Peggy McIntosh's seminal paper "White Privilege and Male Privilege: A Personal Account of Coming to See Correspondences through Work in Women's Studies": "As a white person, I realized I had been taught about racism as something which puts others at a disadvantage, but had been taught not to see one of its corollary aspects, white privilege, which puts me at an advantage."[2]

As a white male, I know what Peggy McIntosh is talking about. What we are taught to see and not see shapes our view of the world—of what is real. My education through high school, college, and graduate school never included any discussion of white privilege and only discussed racism as a historical phenomenon, something that happened to people of color centuries ago.

PERSONAL ANECDOTE

I remember watching television with my family in September 1957. I was ten years old and in the fifth grade. President Dwight D. Eisenhower had ordered the 101st Airborne Division of the US Army to Little Rock, Arkansas, to enforce the integration of Central High School and protect the nine black students enrolled that fall. My parents, like many whites at that time, thought that these black students were "troublemakers" who were trying to force themselves on people who didn't want to associate with them. They saw these black students as encroachers on "regular" people's freedom of association. I remember seeing the faces of all the angry white parents standing behind the line of troops and shouting racial epithets at these nine black children. I remember my parents making derogatory comments about African Americans that day and for many years after and telling me that people should "stick to their own kind." They made it clear to me that they did not approve of integration and wanted me to keep my distance from blacks. Three years after the *Brown v. Board of Education* decision, "separate but equal" was the prevailing norm in the world I inhabited. I believed my parents and parroted their views throughout my childhood—their view was my view. And white privilege was not even on the radar.

The natural question that arises from the introduction of the concept of white privilege is, What exactly are these advantages that white people enjoy at the expense and to the detriment of people of color? Since we whites have not been taught to see such advantages, we generally do not. Peggy McIntosh came to see some of her advantages as a white person through first understanding some of her disadvantages as a woman and observing men's inability or unwillingness to recognize their advantages as men: "I have often noticed men's unwillingness to grant that they are over-privileged in the curriculum, even though they may grant that women are disadvantaged. Denials, which amount to taboos, surround the subject of advantages, which men gain from women's disadvantages. These denials protect male privilege from being fully recognized, acknowledged, lessened, or ended."[3]

Again, as a male I know what Peggy McIntosh is talking about. For much of my life I believed that "it's a man's world" because we men deserve to be on top. We are simply better at certain things than women. The idea that we men are privileged was, in my view, "sour grapes" from women who couldn't make the grade. This unwillingness to acknowledge any male privilege is deeply connected to the American myth of meritocracy, which maintains that all advantage in society is based on merit. Some have more than others because they have earned it through hard work, perseverance, and right living. And conversely, those who have less have only themselves to blame. The idea that even some of my advantages are unearned and undeserved and are a function of my status as a male was in my mind, for many years, preposterous and unfounded. But the idea that we live in a meritocracy in the United States is a myth because it has proven to be inconsistent with sociological fact. Structured inequality would be impossible in a meritocracy. Those of every "race," ethnicity, and gender who worked hard, persevered, and lived right would excel in a meritocracy. Yet we have serious structured inequalities along racial, ethnic, and gender lines.[4]

White privilege and male privilege have the common feature that, in both cases, those who are advantaged cannot see their own advantage, although they can see that others are disadvantaged, and those who are privileged tend to fault those who are disadvantaged for their disadvantage. Conversely, those who are disadvantaged can see that they are disadvantaged and that some are advantaged, and they can see that both their disadvantage and the advantages of those who are privileged are unearned and undeserved. Ironically, then, those who enjoy privileges are epistemically disadvantaged, while those who are disadvantaged are epistemically advantaged! Hence, listening to someone who is epistemically advantaged due to her social disadvantage makes sense. The following anecdote illustrates my point.

PERSONAL ANECDOTE

Many years ago I was settling down with my partner to enjoy a TV movie at home. It was an action-adventure film, and I was excited to watch it. As we began to watch, my partner started to get agitated and said to me, "I am so sick and tired of watching television! Every time I turn it on, all I see is women being victimized, women being brutalized, women being assaulted sexually, women portrayed as stupid, helpless bimbos, as sexual objects! I can't watch another minute!" With that, she left the room. A lot of thoughts went through my mind all at once, and they were all dismissive and condescending: What's the matter with her? Is she having her period? Did she have a bad day? Something must have happened because this is a really good movie. I am embarrassed to reveal those thoughts even now. But although I discounted everything she said, I started to click the remote control (of course, I was always the one to hold the remote, to control the TV) to see what was on other channels. To my surprise I found quite a few programs showing women just the way my partner had described! At that point I could not have admitted this to her, but I did let it sink in. I wondered why I had never noticed it before. I am an educated, observant person; yet I was oblivious to what was obvious to her. That is how I understand epistemic disadvantage and advantage now.

Through comparative analysis with male privilege, Peggy McIntosh reached the following explanation of white privilege: "I have come to see white privilege as an invisible package of unearned assets, which I can count on cashing in each day, but about which I was 'meant' to remain oblivious. White privilege is like an invisible weightless backpack of special provisions, maps, passports, codebooks, visas, clothes, tools and blank checks."[5] After months of reflection McIntosh was able to list forty-six such advantages she enjoys as a white person. They include items like the following:

#13. Whether I use checks, credit cards, or cash, I can count on my skin color not to work against the appearance of financial reliability.

#15. I do not have to educate my children to be aware of systemic racism for their own daily physical protection.

#21. I am never asked to speak for all the people of my racial group.

#25. If a traffic cop pulls me over or if the IRS audits my tax return, I can be sure I haven't been singled out because of my race.[6]

For those of us who enjoy one form of privilege or another (e.g., race, gender, sexual orientation, socioeconomic class, ability, age, religion), why don't we feel privileged? As sociologist Allan Johnson explains, privilege attaches itself to social categories, not individuals.[7] So society values whiteness, not a particular person who is white; it values maleness, not a particular person who is male; it values heterosexuality, not any particular person who is heterosexual, and so forth. Hence, the perception that someone is white or male or heterosexual may be sufficient for that person to receive the privilege attached to that social category. And conversely, the perception that someone belongs to a social category that is disvalued in society may cause that person to receive the disadvantages attached to that category. So paradoxically, perception is more important than truth when it comes to who is advantaged and who is disadvantaged in society. How others perceive me may determine whether I am stopped by the police while driving my car, whether I am hired for a job, or whether I am followed in a department store by security. Because privilege does not attach itself to individuals for who they are, I may be privileged without feeling privileged. If I were a king, I would be privileged and feel privileged for who I was. But the kind of privilege we are talking about here is not like that. And the same holds true for disadvantage. Society disvalues certain social categories, and disadvantage attaches to them. Hence, it is possible to be disadvantaged without feeling disadvantaged.

PERCEPTION AND TRUTH

Earlier I said that perception is more important than truth, and that may have given the impression that there is a truth to the matter of whether the social category actually applies to a particular individual. Is the individual actually white? Well, the question itself presupposes that there is such a thing as actual whiteness, and there is not. We have learned from biology and history that "race" is a social construction; it is not a biologically real category. There is as much or more genetic variation between any two individuals of the same so-called race as there is between two individuals of two different so-called races.[8] In the late seventeenth century, wealthy, landowning, Christian men who invaded this land created the category of "race" based on superficial differences in skin tone and hair texture for the purpose of exploitation and permanent domination.[9] These men created social systems and institutions (e.g., laws, rules, practices, value systems) to reify "racial" difference and continually empower some and disempower others on the basis of this constructed "difference." Hence "race" is a social rather than a biological reality. Many of the social categories surrounding privilege and oppression—gender, sexual orientation, socioeconomic class, ability, and disability—are largely social constructions.

To be sure, there are real differences between people, but we define the social categories, and we assign meaning to those differences. For example, on the face of it, it would seem that nothing is more clear-cut than whether a person is male or female, whether a baby is born a boy or a girl. After all, that is the first question most ask when a baby is born: Is it a boy or a girl? But the experiences of many people born intersexed have led us to understand that whether someone is born a boy or a girl is a matter of definition. Some are born neither. Some are born both. Some simply defy such categorization and force us to realize that this scheme of categorization is a human invention. Some cultures recognize that a binary system of categorization is inadequate and have multiple categories within which to understand gender. Both sex and gender are more complicated than our binary categories allow.[10]

SYSTEMIC PRIVILEGE: WHAT DOES IT LOOK LIKE?

Understanding the relational nature of white privilege helps us see that white racism and white privilege are two sides of the same coin. Whereas some are undeservedly disadvantaged because they are perceived to be of color, others are undeservedly advantaged because they are perceived to be white. Here are a few examples to illustrate the ubiquity and systemic nature of white privilege.[11]

THE JOB MARKET

Tim Wise writes that a 2003 Milwaukee study

> had young black and white male job testers who were otherwise equally qualified apply for jobs in the metropolitan area. Some of the whites and some of the blacks claimed to have criminal records and to have served eighteen months in prison for possession of drugs with intent to distribute, while other whites and blacks presented themselves as having no prior criminal convictions. Whites without records received callbacks for interviews thirty-four percent of the time, compared to only fourteen percent for blacks, and whites with criminal records received callbacks seventeen percent of the time, compared to only five percent for blacks with records. So whites without records were 2.4 times more likely than comparable blacks to receive an interview, and whites with criminal records were 3.4 times more likely to receive a callback than similar blacks. So, at seventeen percent, whites with prior drug convictions were more likely than blacks without records (at fourteen percent) to be called back for an interview, even when all other credentials were equal.[12]

This study reveals the systemic nature of white privilege and white racism. Without the study a person looking for a job would only know that he either did or did not get a callback. From his experience alone, he would have no evidence that he was either privileged or disadvantaged because of his perceived race. The systemic nature of white privilege and white racism explains, in part, why those who receive such privilege are not aware of it and why those who are disadvantaged may not know it. From the outside it simply looks like one person got a callback and another did not. White privilege is embedded in the values, beliefs, and practices of those who are hiring. Even though it is illegal to discriminate in employment on the basis of perceived race, the practice is alive and well, but hidden. Only those explicitly looking for evidence of white privilege will find it.

HOUSING

In December 2011 Bank of America's Countrywide Financial agreed to pay $335 million to settle a lawsuit claiming it discriminated against black and Latino borrowers. The Justice Department alleged that Countrywide charged a higher interest rate on the mortgages of more than two hundred thousand minority borrowers, despite the fact that their creditworthiness was comparable to whites that received lower rates. The Justice Department called it the "largest residential fair lending settlement in history." According to the Center for Responsible Lending, borrowers of color are twice as likely to receive subprime loans than their white counterparts, and once the housing bubble burst, borrowers of color were more than twice as likely to lose their homes as white households.[13]

Subprime loans are five times more likely in black neighborhoods than in white neighborhoods. In predominantly black neighborhoods, high-cost subprime lending accounted for 51 percent of home loans in 1998—compared with only 9 percent in predominately white areas. Comparable 1993 figures were 8 percent in black neighborhoods and 1 percent in white neighborhoods. Homeowners in high-income black neighborhoods are twice as likely as homeowners in low-income white neighborhoods to have subprime loans. Only 6 percent of homeowners in upper-income white neighborhoods have subprime loans, while 39 percent of homeowners in upper-income black neighborhoods have subprime loans, more than twice the 18 percent rate for homeowners in low-income white neighborhoods.[14]

Again, without the studies, lawsuits, and statistics, we would be unable to see the systemic nature of white privilege and white racism. To the individual person pursuing a home mortgage loan, it either seems easy to obtain a prime lending rate or impossible. The white person who receives a prime mortgage loan will have no reason to think she or he is being privileged, and the person of color who receives the subprime rate may or may not understand that she or he is being discriminated against on the basis of perceived race.

ENVIRONMENT

A 1992 study by staff writers for the *National Law Journal* examined the Environmental Protection Agency's response to 1,177 toxic-waste cases and found that polluters of sites near the greatest white population received penalties 500 percent higher than polluters in minority areas—fines averaged $335,566 for white areas contrasted with $55,318 for minority areas. Income did not account for these differences. The penalties for violating all federal environmental laws regulating air, water, and waste pollution were 46 percent lower in minority communities than in white communities.[15]

Race has been found to be an independent factor, not reducible to class, in predicting exposure to a broad range of environmental hazards, including polluted air, contaminated fish, lead poisoning, municipal landfills, incinerators, and toxic-waste dumps.[16]

What white person would feel privileged not to live near toxic-waste dumps, breathe polluted air, or ingest chemicals that make people sick? Who would take the time and energy to investigate where toxic-waste dumps and incinerators are located if those facilities are not near one's neighborhood? As a white person, the first time I heard the term "environmental racism" I had no idea what it meant.

HEALTH

On average white Americans live 5.5 years longer than black Americans do. Blacks die from stroke 41 percent more often than whites, from heart disease 30 percent more often, and from cancer 25 percent more often. Asians, Pacific Islanders, and Hispanics all have lower heart disease rates than whites.

During the 1980s federal government researchers came up with a new way to measure "excess deaths" (i.e., deaths that would not have occurred if a minority population's mortality rate had been the same as the white population's). By that standard there were sixty-six thousand "excess deaths" of African Americans in 1940 and roughly one hundred thousand in 1999. That is the equivalent of one plane crash—with no survivors—occurring every day of the year.[17]

One can begin to see how multiple disadvantages compound the effects of each disadvantage and multiple privileges have a synergistic positive effect on those who receive them. It can begin to look like the "natural order" of things, but it is not. It is the result of interlocking systems of privilege and disadvantage in every aspect of life that maintain white supremacy and domination.

LAW ENFORCEMENT AND CRIME

In New York City, from 1997 to 1998, the Street Crimes Unit of the New York Police Department (NYPD) stopped and frisked 135,000 people, 85 percent of whom were people of color. Only 4,500 persons were ultimately arrested and prosecuted, meaning that over 95 percent of those harassed were innocent. Interestingly, whites who were stopped were significantly more likely to be found with drugs or other contraband, indicating not only that this policy of racial stops and searches was biased but that it failed the test as valid crime control on its own merits as well.[18]

A federal judge ruled on August 12, 2013, that the NYPD had violated the civil rights of New Yorkers with its broad "stop-and-frisk" policy. US District Court Judge Shira Scheindlin called for an independent monitor to oversee major changes to the policy. She did not end the policy, however, instead saying that an independent monitor would develop an initial set of reforms, as well as provide training, supervision, monitoring, and discipline. "The city's highest officials have turned a blind eye to the evidence that officers are conducting stops in a racially discriminatory manner," she wrote in a lengthy opinion. "In their zeal to defend a policy that they believe to be effective, they have willfully ignored overwhelming proof that the policy of targeting 'the right people' is racially discriminatory." Police brass had received warnings since at least 1999 that officers were violating rights, she said. "Despite this notice, they deliberately maintained and even escalated policies and practices that predictably resulted in even more widespread Fourth Amendment violations."[19]

Criminal Procedure Law § 140.50 (the stop-and-frisk law) became effective on September 1, 1971. That means that for more than forty years, it has been the law in New York City. According to the statistic cited above, in one year (1997–1998) NYPD officers stopped 135,000 people, 85 percent of whom were people of color—that is approximately 115,000 people of color stopped in one year. If we multiply that number by forty-three years (as of the time of this writing in 2014) we get just under 5 million people of color! I cannot verify the total number of people of color affected by this policy, but the New York Times reported in 2014, "At the height of the program, in the first quarter of 2012, the police stopped people—mostly black and Latino men—on more than 200,000 occasions. A vast majority of those stopped were found to have done nothing wrong."[20] That is at least two hundred thousand people stopped in three months! These policies and practices are known to be ineffective as law enforcement tools to fight crime. What white person living in New York City thinks that not being stopped and frisked on her or his way to work is a privilege? Yet it is.

GOVERNMENT POLICIES

Beginning in the 1930s the federal government began offering low-interest, taxpayer-guaranteed, underwritten loans through the Federal Housing Administration (FHA). Between the 1930s and the 1960s, more than $100 billion in home equity was loaned through these housing initiatives, boosting the overall rate of home ownership from 44 percent in 1934 to 66 percent in 1969. But loans went almost exclusively to white families. The Home Ownership Lending Corporation made it clear that these preferential loans were off-limits to people who lived in "declining" neighborhoods (every black neighborhood was rated as declining) and that loans were also to be denied to anyone whose receipt of the loan would result in a reduction in a neighborhood's racial homogeneity. The FHA underwriting manual stated to lenders, "If a neighborhood is to retain stability, it is necessary that properties shall continue to be occupied by the same social and racial classes." As a result of these policies, 27 million of the 28 million Americans who moved into suburban areas from 1950 until 1966 were white.[21]

The government, through the FHA, set up a national neighborhood appraisal system, explicitly tying mortgage eligibility to race. Integrated communities were deemed a financial risk ipso facto and made ineligible for home loans, a policy known today as "redlining." Between 1934 and 1962, the federal government backed $120 billion in home loans. More than 98 percent went to whites. Of the 350,000 new homes built with federal support in northern California between 1946 and 1960, fewer than 100 went to African Americans.[22]

These governmental policies and practices continue to affect the relative wealth of whites compared to African Americans and Latinos. The privileges of parents and grandparents get passed down to children, grandchildren, and great-grandchildren in the form of inherited wealth, giving each generation an ever-increasing advantage. How many whites today think of the FHA loans their grandparents received as an example of white privilege? Yet they are.

EDUCATION

The average black student attends a school with twice as many low-income students as the typical white youth, and schools that are mostly attended by black and Latino students are more than ten times as likely as mostly white schools to have concentrated levels of student poverty. Even black kids with family incomes higher than those of whites are more likely to attend schools with concentrated poverty levels.[23]

High-poverty schools (disproportionately serving a large number of students of color) have, on average, three times as many uncertified teachers or teachers who are teaching outside their field of study as teachers serving low-poverty and mostly white schools.[24]

Even when their prior performance would justify higher placement, students of color are still significantly less likely to be given honors or advanced-placement opportunities than whites, even when white students have lower grades or test scores. While this may be partly due to teacher bias, it is also the result of systematic inequity: schools serving mostly white students offer about three times as many advanced-level courses as schools serving mostly students of color. Thus, even in the total absence of racial bias on the part of school officials, the lack of certain course offerings deprives capable and hardworking students of color of opportunities available to their white counterparts.[25]

Because it is a policy and practice to fund public schools through property taxes, and because white students generally live in more affluent communities due in part to the practice of "redlining" cited above (which is responsible for much of the residential segregation in the United States), white students are again privileged from preschool and kindergarten all the way through their higher education. The educational, legal, housing, health-care, law enforcement, employment, and environmental policy systems all interlock to create a white hegemony in which we live and breathe, without noticing it so long as we are its beneficiaries—so long as we whites are breathing the clean air, drinking the clear water, attending the "good" schools, landing the best jobs, getting the prime loans, not being harassed by police, and living longer with fewer diseases—as long as we are on top! This is what white privilege looks like.

PERSONAL ANECDOTE

I graduated from the University of Massachusetts, Amherst, in 1970 with a bachelor's degree in philosophy. After graduation I traveled to Los Angeles, California, and took a job in a Danish restaurant as a sandwich preparer. I didn't yet know what I wanted to do as a career, so cooking was a useful way to make money while I figured that out. While I had experience working in restaurants, I'd never worked in a Danish restaurant, and I had a lot to learn about that. I worked alongside two Mexican guys who had been at the restaurant for a couple of years and knew the routine backward and forward. They were incredibly fast and skilled at their job and taught me how to prepare for and keep pace with a very busy luncheon service. I knew nothing about the lived experiences of Mexican people in Los Angeles. I was naive. After a month or two, I sensed that they resented me, and I didn't know why. Had I done something to offend them? There was a clear tension and hostility in our working environment, and I felt that hostility directed at me. The hostility finally came to a head with an argument between them and me. Management stepped in to quell the tempers. Why were they being so critical of my work? Why were they so belligerent? I had improved my speed since I started. Many of their verbal assaults were in Spanish, and I did not understand what they were saying. I only felt their anger. The manager, who was the daughter of the Danish couple who owned the restaurant, asked me if I had told my two coworkers how much I was being paid. I said yes; they had asked me one day, and I had told them. I still didn't get it. She told me not to discuss my salary with anyone. I wasn't being paid a lot, given the experience I had going into the restaurant, but my two Mexican coworkers, I found out, were being paid a lot less than I, even though they were more experienced and more skilled and had been on that job much longer than I had. I was surprised. My first thought was, Why would they work for so little? I wouldn't. And then I thought, Well, that's their problem, not mine! I've got my fair salary! That is white privilege.

SUMMARY

White privilege is a form of domination—it positions one group of people over an-other group. It is a relational concept that enables us to see clearly that some benefit and others suffer from racial oppression (racism). Both racial oppression and white privilege are two sides of the same coin; you cannot have one without the other. And both racial oppression and white privilege attach to social categories, not individuals. They describe how systems operate to benefit some and disadvantage others on the basis of perceived group membership (white or of color).

This chapter provides but a few examples of how our American social system manifests systemic white privilege and racial oppression of people of color. Once we begin to look at the extent of this system-wide domination, more and more features appear. As Joe Feagin explains, "Systemic racism encompasses a broad range of white-racist dimensions: racist ideology, attitudes, emotions, habits, actions, and institutions of whites in this society. Systemic racism is far more than a matter of racial prejudice and individual bigotry. It is a material, social and ideological reality that is well-imbedded in major U.S. institutions."[26] [...]

NOTES

1 Gary R. Howard, *We Can't Teach What We Don't Know: White Teachers, Multiracial Schools*, 2nd ed. (New York: Teachers College Press, 2006), 67.

2 Peggy McIntosh, "White Privilege and Male Privilege: A Personal Account of Coming to See Correspondences through Work in Women's Studies" (Working Paper 189, Wellesley College, 1988).

3 Ibid., 1.

4 See Adalberto Aguirre Jr. and David V. Baker, *Structured Inequality in the United States: Critical Discussions on the Continuing Significance of Race, Ethnicity, and Gender*, 2nd ed. (Upper Saddle River, NJ: Pearson Prentice Hall, 2008).

5 Peggy McIntosh, "White Privilege: Unpacking the Invisible Backpack," *Peace and Freedom* (July/August 1989).

6 McIntosh, "White Privilege and Male Privilege."

7 Allan G. Johnson, *Privilege, Power, and Difference*, 2nd ed. (New York: McGraw-Hill, 2006), 34–37.

8   See Christine Herbes-Sommers, dir., *Race: The Power of an Illusion*, Part 1 (San Francisco: California Newsreel, 2003), for an explanation of the work of evolutionary biologist Richard Lewontin, or see R. C. Lewontin, "The Apportionment of Human Diversity," *Evolutionary Biology* 6 (1972): 381–398.

9   See Ronald Takaki, *A Different Mirror: A History of Multicultural America*, rev. ed. (New York: Little, Brown and Co., 2008); Theodore W. Allen, *The Invention of the White Race*, Vol. 2: *The Origin of Racial Oppression in Anglo-America* (New York: Verso, 1997); Richard Delgado and Jean Stefancic, eds., *Critical White Studies* (Philadelphia: Temple University Press, 1997).

10 See Anne Fausto-Sterling, "The Five Sexes: Why Male and Female Are Not Enough," *Sciences* (March/April 1993): 20–24; Anne Fausto-Sterling, "The Five Sexes Revisited," in *Women's Voices, Feminist Visions*, ed. Susan Shaw and Janet Lee, 5th ed. (New York: McGraw-Hill, 2012), 121–125.

11 In fact I provide my students with a twenty-three-page, single-spaced, documented handout listing hundreds of such examples.

12 Tim Wise, *Affirmative Action: Racial Preference in Black and White* (New York: Routledge, 2005), 21, cited in Devah Pager, "The Mark of a Criminal Record," *American Journal of Sociology* 108, no. 5 (March 2003): 937–975.

13 Eyder Peralta, "BofA's Countrywide to Pay $335 Million, Settling Lending Discrimination Case," *The Two-Way*, December 21, 2011, www.npr.org/blogs/thetwo-way/2011/12/21/144083080/bofas-countrywide-will-pay-335-million-in-lending-discrimination-case.

14 US Department of Housing and Urban Development, "Unequal Burden: Income and Racial Disparities in Subprime Lending in America," HUD User, http://www.huduser.org/Publications/pdf/unequal_full.pdf.

15 George Lipsitz, *The Possessive Investment in Whiteness* (Philadelphia: Temple University Press, 1998), 8. Also see John R. Logan and Harvey Molotch, *Urban Fortunes: The Political Economy of Place* (Berkeley: University of California Press, 1987), 113.

16 Lipsitz, *The Possessive Investment*, 9. See also Robert D. Bullard, "Anatomy of Environmental Racism and the Environmental Justice Movement," in *Confronting Environmental Racism: Voices from the Grassroots*, ed. Robert D. Bullard (Boston: South End Press, 1993), 15–39.

17 David R. Williams and James Lardner, "Cold Truths about Class, Race and Health," in *Inequality Matters*, ed. James Lardner and David A. Smith (New York: The New Press, 2005), 105.

18 Tim Wise, "See No Evil," Tim Wise, August 2, 2001, http://www.timwise.org/2001/08/see-no-evil-perception-and-reality-in-black-and-white, originally published as a ZNet Commentary.

19 "Judge Rules NYPD's 'Stop-and-Frisk' Policy Violates Rights," Fox News, August 12, 2013, http://www.foxnews.com/politics/2013/08/12/judge-rules-nypd-stop-and-frisk-policy-violates-rights.

20 Benjamin Weiser and Joseph Goldstein, "Mayor Says New York City Will Settle Suits on Stop-and-Frisk Tactics," *New York Times*, January 30, 2014, http://www.nytimes.com/2014/01/31/nyregion/de-blasio-stop-and-frisk.html.

21 Wise, *Affirmative Action*, 31–32. For a detailed analysis of the FHA and Veterans Administration loan programs and how they discriminated racially, see Douglas Massey and Nancy Denton, *American Apartheid: Segregation and the Making of the Underclass* (Cambridge, MA: Harvard University Press, 1993); Melvin L. Oliver and Thomas Shapiro, *Black Wealth, White Wealth: A New Perspective on Racial Inequality* (New York: Routledge, 1997); Michael K. Brown et al., *Whitewashing Race: The Myth of a Color-Blind Society* (Berkeley: University of California Press, 2003); Leonard Steinhorn and Barbara Diggs-Brown, *By the Color of Our Skin: The Illusion of Integration and the Reality of Race* (New York: Dutton, 1999), 95–96.

22 Herbes-Sommers, *Race*.

23 Judith R. Blau, *Race in the Schools: Perpetuating White Dominance?* (Boulder, CO: Lynne Rienner, 2003), 48; Gary Orfield et al., "Deepening Segregation in American Public Schools: A Special Report from the Harvard Project on School Desegregation," *Equity and Excellence in Education* 30 (1997): 5–24; Gary Orfield and John T. Yun, "Resegregation in American Schools," eScholarship, June 6, 1999, http://escholarship.org/uc/item/6d01084d; Massey and Denton, *American Apartheid*, 153.

24 Deborah L. McKoy and Jeffrey M. Vincent, "Housing and Education: The Inextricable Link," in *Segregation: The Rising Costs for America*, ed. James H. Carr and Nandinee K. Kutty (New York: Routledge, 2008), 128.

25 Rebecca Gordon, *Education and Race* (Oakland, CA: Applied Research Center, 1998), 48–49; Claude S. Fischer et al., *Inequality by Design: Cracking the Bell Curve Myth* (Princeton, NJ: Princeton University Press, 1996), 164–165; Steinhorn and Diggs-Brown, *By the Color of Our Skin*, 47; Gary Orfield and Susan Eaton, *Dismantling Desegregation: The Quiet Reversal of Brown v. Board of Education* (New York: The New Press, 1996), 68.

26 Joe R. Feagin, *Systemic Racism: A Theory of Oppression* (New York: Routledge, 2006), 2.

SECTION III

SOCIAL INSTITUTIONS

Social institutions are parts of the social structure that serve some specific purpose. They *do* something. This section contains readings on health, the family, education, the economy, and religion. Of course there is overlap, as these are interconnected systems.

The first reading in this section, "Medicalizing the Aging Male Body: Andropause and Baldness" by Julie E. Szymczak and Peter Conrad, looks at gender and how it intersects with a medical system. The medical system of a society is an institution that exists to deal with sickness and injury. Sometimes, experiences and bodily events that are not technically sickness come to be treated as such. This process is referred to as "medicalization." This article looks at the process of medicalizing male aging.

"Social Support, Sex, and Food: Social Networks and Health" also looks at aspects of the medical system in its examination of how the linkages we have to other people—friends, family, acquaintances—help us to be healthy or might put our health at risk. We are social creatures, and the presence of others in our lives can affect our health and well-being in subtle ways. We also tend to behave similarly to those around us. So, if my friends have poor eating habits, I am likely to gain weight because I am likely to eat in a similar way.

"Concerted Cultivation and the Accomplishment of Natural Growth" by Annette Lareau looks at how one's parents intersect with one's social class. There are not only different levels of time and resources across social classes; there are also different value systems. This includes different goals or "outcomes" people are looking for in their children. This leads to different parenting styles and very different childhoods. Reading Nine, "Gender and Discrimination in Education" by Terence Fitzgerald, examines the intersection of gender and race in the education system. We find not only inequalities across racial lines but also differences in how males and females are treated within a minority group. This article highlights the voices of black males' experiences within the education system.

Our economic system is heavily intertwined with power structures in society. "A Late Capitalist World" by Steven M. Buechler gives some very good explanations of terms used in the analysis of political economy. The United States is a version of a capitalist economy, with power concentrated in a small portion of the population. This article lays out the roots of this, highlights some ways this structure is maintained, and gives some projections for where we might be headed.

Finally, in "Do Religious Children Care More and Provide More Care for Older Parents?" we have the examination of the intersection of religion and family life. As our society ages and birth rates decline, the question of who will provide care for our elders is a significant one.

Living in a society is complex. We have multiple layers of social structures that impinge upon our lives in many ways. So, while we might initially consider things such as religion and family life or race and education as separate things to be studied, in reality, these are interlinking, overlapping things. As you read this section, consider the ways different aspects of social structure affect your life. Some will be like the ones in the articles here. Some may include other parts of society not mentioned here. All in all, who you are is a function of being a person in a very complex, multilayered society.

CHAPTER 6

MEDICALIZING THE AGING MALE BODY

Consider the following questions as you read this chapter.

QUESTIONS TO CONSIDER

1. Is medicine strictly scientific, or is it linked to society?

2. How do ideas and expectations about masculinity affect men as they age? Are they able to fulfill social expectations?

3. If you are biologically male and also identify as male in terms of gender, think about what might happen as you age: how that might change how you view and experience yourself and how other people treat you. If you are not male, think about your male relatives (father, grandfather, etc.). How is aging affecting their masculinity?

4. What is the authors' main point?

KEY TERMS

medicalization
andropause

MEDICALIZING THE AGING MALE BODY

ANDROPAUSE AND BALDNESS

BY JULIE E. SZYMCZAK AND PETER CONRAD

INTRODUCTION

Aging men's lives and bodies are increasingly coming under medical jurisdiction. Images used to promote the latest erectile dysfunction medication, magazine articles about the best hair loss therapy, and television programs about successful aging consistently tell men to "see your doctor." The movement of aging from a natural life event to a medical problem in need of treatment (Estes and Binney 1989) is an example of medicalization. While earlier studies have pointed to the medicalization of women's bodies (Reissman 1983; Martin 1987; Riska 2003), we now see aging men's bodies becoming medicalized as well.

This chapter examines two clear cases of the medicalization of masculinity: one a commonly known bodily change, baldness, and the other an as yet lesser-known change, andropause. These cases raise interesting subtleties regarding the medicalization of masculinity. First, they point to a long-standing desire on the part of men and medical agents alike to achieve an old age that retains some of the essentially "masculine" and embodied qualities of youth and middle age—specifically, physical strength and energy, sexual vitality, and hirsutism. Thus the medicalization of male aging and baldness, while currently driven by the medical and pharmaceutical enterprises, is also fueled by men's own concerns with their masculine identities, capacities, embodiments, and presentations. Secondly, the medicalization of these "conditions" occurred only partially by design—while the pharmaceutical industry was actively seeking treatments for these conditions, current treatments emerged from research into other medical problems. Finally, these male "conditions" have only been partially medicalized. While medical and pharmaceutical enterprises have offered treatments for andropause and baldness, there is no consensus whether these constitute medical conditions, or if they do how their pathology is to be measured and assessed. These two conditions are provocative examples of the increasing medicalization of masculinity.

MEDICALIZATION

While medicalization describes a process by which "nonmedical problems become defined and treated as medical problems, usually in terms of illnesses or disorders" (Conrad 1992, 209), analysts of medicalization have primarily been concerned with overmedicalization, noting that the widening jurisdiction of medicine over everyday life has potentially troubling consequences (Zola 1972). Critics are concerned that medicalization transforms wider aspects of everyday life into pathology, narrowing the range of what is considered acceptable. Furthermore, by expanding medical jurisdiction, medicalization increases the amount of medical social control over human behavior (Zola 1972; Conrad 1992). Normal life events such as birth, sexuality, aging, and death were increasingly medicalized in the past several decades (see Conrad 1992, 2000).

Medicalization is not an all or nothing phenomenon, but rather is bidirectional and occurs along a continuum. By *bidirectional,* we mean that there can be both medicalization and demedicalization, but the trend in the past century has been overwhelmingly toward medicalization. For demedicalization to occur, problems must no longer be defined as medical and medical treatments not deemed appropriate. The two clearest examples of demedicalization are masturbation (Engelhardt 1974) and homosexuality (Conrad and Schneider 1992); although after demedicalization there is always the potential for remedicalization (Conrad and Angell 2004), this would be very rare. However, most cases of medicalization are not complete, so we conceptualize this as "degrees of medicalization." Some problems are nearly completely medicalized, such as childbirth, death, and severe mental illness; others are partially medicalized, such as opiate addiction and menopause; and still others are minimally medicalized, such as sexual addiction and spouse abuse. While we do not know all the factors that affect the degrees of medicalization, it is clear that medical categories can shift on the continuum toward or away from more complete medicalization.

Medicalization often occurs through the actions of advocates who support and promote a medical definition of a particular trouble. Advocates can be physicians, social movements, organized lay groups, medical technology industries (pharmaceutical companies and medical supply manufacturers), or patients. Early studies of medicalization focused largely on physicians, social movements, and moral entrepreneurs as important agents in medicalization. But more recently the advocacy is shifting to corporate interests, especially the pharmaceutical industry and consumers (Conrad and Leiter 2004).

The balance between physicians and the pharmaceutical industry as agents of medicalization is shifting. While physicians are still the gatekeepers for many drugs, the pharmaceutical companies have become a major player in medicalization. In the post-Prozac world, the pharmaceutical industry has been more aggressively promoting its wares to physicians and especially to the public. This includes promoting blockbuster drugs like various psychotropics for a range of human troubles (from depression to shyness to learning problems) and Viagra and its competitors for sexual dysfunction to more modest promotions for problems like baldness and andropause. But in all cases, the creation of new markets by the pharmaceutical industry engenders broader forms of medicalization.

It is important to remember that the pharmaceutical companies do not create the markets by themselves. Often there is an extant consumer demand that the pharmaceutical industry shapes and even exploits in its promotion. For example, male sexual dysfunction was clearly a problem for some men before Viagra, but Pfizer has expanded the definition of erectile dysfunction in order to enlarge its market (Carpiano 2001). In so doing, it has medicalized a wider range of sexual troubles, so that now virtually any man can be a candidate for Viagra or its competitors. Similarly with other problems often associated with male aging, such as baldness, vitality, and loss of muscle tone, we can begin to see more medical treatments for the aging male body. Definitions of masculinity may encourage some men to see bodily changes as threats to masculinity and lead them to pursue treatments that will maintain their youthful body image. These men become consumers of products that promise to retain youth or at least repair or postpone unwanted bodily changes. The pharmaceutical industry is more than happy to supply treatments and develop a market for its products.

GENDER AND MEDICALIZATION

Scholarly examinations of gender and medicalization have largely focused on the medicalization of women, ignoring the medicalization of men's lives. Some have argued that men are not as vulnerable to medicalization as are women (Reissman 1983): the substantial literature on the medicalization of childbirth, premenstrual syndrome, meno-pause, and anorexia in women (Wertz and Wertz 1989; Figert 1995; Bell 1990; Brumberg 2001) clearly shows that more of women's life experiences are medicalized than men's. Analysts have suggested several reasons for this. One of the reasons typically given for women's vulnerability to medicalization is the traditional definition of a healthy body. As Alan Petersen (1998a, 41) notes, "male bodies have been constructed through scientific and cultural practices as 'naturally' different from female bodies and [that] the bodies of white, European, middle-class, heterosexual men, have been constructed as the standard for measuring and evaluating other bodies." On the other hand, Catherine Reissman (1983) suggests that women are more vulnerable to medicalization than are men because their physiological processes are visible (menstruation, birth), their social roles expose them to medical scrutiny, and they are often in a subordinate position to men in the clinical domain. Reissman also argues that "routine experiences that are uniquely male remain largely unstudied by medical science and, consequently, are rarely treated by physicians as potentially pathological" (1983, 116).

However, while this may have been true when Reissman published her article in 1983, recent medical and scientific developments have engendered the medicalization of aging male bodies. Although it is not our intent to refute the claims that Reissman and others have made about women and medicalization, we would like to make a case for the increasing medicalization of men and to contribute to the understanding of medicalization as a truly gendered concept.[1] In this chapter, we examine two cases of the intersection of medical treatments, masculinity, and aging male bodies. We first examine the scientific identification of the male hormone testosterone and the "dis-covery" of andropause, purportedly caused by abnormal decrease of testosterone with age. Numerous medical testosterone based treatments were offered to alleviate this "disorder." Male hair loss, or baldness, is a common occurrence in aging men. Various elixirs and treatments have been introduced over the years, but in the past two decades new surgical and medical treatments have brought baldness further into the jurisdiction of medicine. Together these cases illustrate how medicine, expectations of masculinity, and the physiology of aging contribute to the medicalization of aging male bodies.

AGE, MASCULINITY, AND THE BODY

The medicalization of aging men's bodies is relevant to a range of disciplines besides sociology. Masculinity theorists, gender scholars, and anthropologists are concerned with the social processes and pressures that produce and constrain masculinity. The medicalization of men's aging bodies, through pressure to conform to certain standards of health, is one such source of constraint. A lack of discussion about the social factors that pressure men's lives, including medical factors, contributes to an incomplete picture of contemporary masculinity. Just as feminists consider the intersection of women's bodies and medicine to be an important issue, masculinity and gender studies can benefit from understanding the medicalization of men's bodies.

In addition to masculinity, such an analysis considers both age and the body as focal concerns and sheds light on a number of intersecting sociological themes. First, through the lens of medicalization, we can see a reflection of negative social beliefs about and fears of the aging process in men. We live in an ageist society where the aging process is resisted and often feared. Instead of accepting the natural progression of the life course, we medicalize old age in an attempt to control it (Marshall and Katz 2002; Katz and Marshall 2004; Gullette 1997). While researchers have paid attention to the aging process in women, particularly as it pertains to menopause (Friedan 1993b; Lock 1993), aging men have been overlooked, for several reasons. Edward Thompson (1994) suggests that older men are invisible, in part because of the stigma that is placed on men as they disengage from traditional social roles and become more dependent. The longer life expectancy of women and reduced percentage of men in older cohorts may also play a role in this invisibility. In addition, feminist writers (e.g., Sontag 1978) point to a double standard of aging, which suggests that men benefit from the aging process while women are stifled by it. As some have suggested, "sociocultural constructions of femininity place considerable value on physical attractiveness and youth, and aging therefore moves women away from these cultural ideals" (Halliwell and Dittmar 2003, 676). This chapter confronts the double standard of age and argues that a majority of men may not experience an increase in masculine traits as they age. Rather, the growing market for testosterone and hair loss treatments suggests that many men want to resist the aging process and may attempt to gain control of it by embracing its medicalization. If the desire for products to reverse the signs of age is any indication, men do not revere old age as a time in their lives when their masculine characteristics increase but instead are concerned about their decline. Thus, as we will discuss later, men often collude in the medicalization of their capacities, characteristics, and functions.

Medicalization can also provide insight into the sociocultural construction of the body—a burgeoning field (Gatens 1996; Turner 1992). There is a great deal of scholarship dedicated to understanding the body as a social and cultural artifact (Sauk 1994; Scheper-Hughes and Lock 1987). The body is the site where aging occurs, or as Christopher Faircloth (2003, 16) suggests, "the body visibly marks us as aging." Understanding how medicine acts upon the aging body through definition, control, and surveillance is a valuable step towards the creation of a fuller picture of the male experience of age. While aging can be understood on many levels, the body provides a salient frame of reference to comprehend the process. Age is characterized by bodily change and there is evidence that "the body [can] provide a key frame of reference for the male experience of health" (Watson 2000, 87). By looking at the different biotechnologies that "treat" the aging male body (here, testosterone and Propecia, Rogaine, and hair transplants) we can understand how it becomes socioculturally constructed. As Laura Mamo and Jennifer Fishman (2001, 14) suggest, "within the biomedicalization framework, medical technologies are part of programs and strategies of inscription that indicate the exercise of a rationalized, disciplining and regulating of bodies." The infiltration of biomedicine into everyday life through commonly used medical treatments redefines "healthy and "normal" with regard to bodily function. Men experience and understand their bodies differently when the aging process is constructed as pathological. Medical treatments for baldness and andropause arc part of a larger trend towards the discipline and regulation of male bodies.

ANDROPAUSE: RUNNING ON EMPTY

Testosterone is the most intriguing of the male hormones. Physiologically, it is claimed, testosterone increases sex drive, musculature, aggressive behavior, hair growth, and other traits traditionally considered masculine. Healthy men maintain a relatively high normal level of testosterone throughout early and middle age, but bodily production of testosterone may naturally decline with advancing age. For the last century, some physicians and other advocates have claimed that the age-related decline in testosterone levels results in a pathological condition known as andropause, which requires testosterone supplementation. Currently, older men are being prescribed testosterone replacement therapy for a set of vague symptoms, often referred to as andropause, male menopause, the male climacteric, or androgen deficiency in aging men (ADAM). A recent Institute of Medicine report estimates that "more than 1.75 million prescriptions were written in 2002, up from 648.000 in 1999" (Kolata 2003). Despite the widespread use of testosterone replacement therapy, there is a dearth of information and clinical studies about its risks and benefits. Amongst many in the scientific community, including the National Institute on Aging and the National Cancer Institute of the National Institute of Health, there is "growing concern about an increase in the use of testosterone by middle aged and older men who have borderline testosterone levels—or even normal testosterone levels—in the absence of adequate scientific information" (Institute of Medicine 2004, 1).

Uncertainty characterizes current medical knowledge of both the safety and efficacy of testosterone therapy and the existence of a male menopause. This uncertainty is not new, as scientists and physicians have debated the existence of andropause for over a century. A brief exploration of the history of testosterone therapy and andropause reveals that the pharmaceutical industry, endocrinologists, the media, and men in general have promoted a medicopathological definition of aging. With its perceived potential to return the aging male body to a state of socially rallied youthful vigor, testosterone has an almost magical attraction. Current media attention, the development of new pharmaceuticals, and the push to explore male aging and testosterone in medical terms are contributing to the further medicalization of the aging male body.

HISTORICAL CONTEXT FOR THE EMERGENCE OF TESTOSTERONE THERAPY

The discovery and isolation of testosterone undoubtedly contributed to the movement of male aging into the medical gaze. Although most of the scientific progress surrounding testosterone occurred during and after the nineteenth century, "both folklore and medicine had explored the sources of maleness, seeking ways to promote strength, vitality, and potency" before then (Rothman and Rothman 2003, 132). The medical definition of male aging had its origin in the work of the scientists who pioneered the field of endocrinology. One of the most important ways that scientists made connections between testosterone and masculinity was through observations of castrated men: men without functioning testicles do not exhibit typical "male" attributes. The recognition that the testicles had some powerful effect on the male body predated the discovery of testosterone. Rothman and Rothman (2003, 132) describe nineteenth-century common knowledge relating to the testicles and masculinity:

> After all, as every farmer knew, the testes affected energy and muscularity; to castrate a rooster produced a capon—fatter, softer, and less active. To castrate an aggressive farm animal (a horse, dog, or bull) rendered him more docile and manageable. Indeed, popular lore recognized that men castrated whether by accident or on purpose ... lost their manly characteristics.

Thus, according to this logic, an increase in the function of the testicles would amplify, enhance, or replace male traits from an undesirable level to a satisfactory one. Although they did not yet know that testosterone was produced in the testicles, many scientists, all of whom were male, applied this logic in exploring the testicles of a variety of animals.

It was not until 1889 that the endocrinologist Charles Edouard Brown Séquard made the connection between testosterone and aging. Brown Séquard completed a series of controversial experiments on himself. Motivated by a general feeling of malaise, weakness, and fatigue that had persisted for a few years, he injected himself ten times with "a solution composed of testicular blood, testicular extracts, and seminal fluids from dogs and guinea pigs" (Rothman and Rothman 2003, 134). The results were spectacular and dramatic: Brown Séquard reported that he was now able to work long hours in the laboratory, "his muscle strength, as measured on a dynamometer, increased dramatically, his urinary jet stream was 25 percent longer, and his chronic constipation had disappeared" (Rothman and Rothman 2003, 134). This sparked much interest in medical treatments for aging within both the scientific and lay communities. After a report of his presentation appeared in a French newspaper, "a geriatric horde descended on [his] laboratory at the College de France, demanding that he share his miracle potency restoring elixir with them" (Friedman 2001. 251). Some physicians in France and the United States were quick to adopt Brown Séquard's formula in the hope of rejuvenating their aging male patients. Although Brown Séquard's experiments could never be reproduced and he was eventually denounced as a quack, he was the first person to connect male aging to a biological process and to suggest a medical remedy for it.

Physiologists and early endocrinologists continued to be extremely interested in the science behind male physiology at the turn of the twentieth century. Not surprisingly, researchers were more interested in masculinity than fertility as "they defined the male not so much by his ability to reproduce, but by his manliness" (Rothman and Rothman 2003, 136). This concern with masculinity may have contributed to the medicalization of male aging and to the medicalized construction of andropause. In women, menopause is characterized by the cessation of fertility, a socially valued trait. This loss of fertility is considered the primary pathological event in the definition of menopause. Although men do not experience a decline in fertility when they age, they may notice a decrease in some of their allegedly masculine characteristics, such as libido, strength, and physical performance. Medicine, mirroring society, values these traits, and, as a result, provides a pathological definition for their diminution or disappearance.

Endocrinologists prescribed a variety of testicular extracts to male patients, which were identified as useless by the scientific community when the male hormone was isolated in 1935. The accurate isolation of testosterone and the ability of pharmaceutical companies to synthesize it were accompanied by increased optimism within the medical scientific community. As Rothman and Rothman assert, "the newfound ability to produce the male hormone in the laboratory ... sparked an even more zealous effort to establish its clinical uses" (2003, 151). Testosterone became a drug in search of a disease to treat. The excitement and increased optimism surrounding testosterone is particularly evident in medical journals following the 1935 discovery: published articles illustrated the dramatic effects that testosterone therapy could have on aging men. Many of these articles began by describing the pretreatment patient as desperate. In an early issue of the *Journal of the American Medical Association (JAMA)*, for example, Dr. August Werner wrote "in addition to markedly diminished sexual libido and inadequate penile erections, these patients, prior to treatment with testosterone propionate were disturbed, anxious and broken in spirit" (1939, 1442). Patients who had not yet received testosterone therapy are described as pathetic, broken men, with little ability to function in a society that demanded so much of them (Kearns 1939, 2257). By portraying the so-called male climacteric as a dire condition with potentially devastating consequences for male virility, physicians created a telling case for treatment.

Early pharmaceutical companies had a great deal at stake with testosterone. The optimism and excitement that surrounded the isolation of testosterone was easily translated into marketing strategies that targeted physicians. Companies such as Schering, Oreton, and Ciba promoted the use of testosterone to the medical community in a variety of ways. Schering produced a "clinical guide for physicians about male sex hormone therapy" (Rothman and Rothman 2003). Initially indicated for the treatment of sexual underdevelopment, hypogonadism, and testicular failure, Schering promoted testosterone therapy for the treatment of a broader scope of ailments, primarily the male climacteric. Pharmaceutical companies' promotion of testosterone for male menopause was profit driven, as "sexual underdevelopment was too rare to constitute a substantial market" (Rothman and Rothman 2003, 138), and they worked to develop a wider market for testosterone, with advertisements targeting physicians portraying testosterone as a magic pill that could work wonders for middle-aged male patients. A 1924 advertisement from the *Endocrine Herald* promoted the use of Orchotine, a testicular extract. The advertisement proclaimed that Orchotine was "The Modern Treatment of Mental and Physical Sub Efficiency For Men." The text of the advertisement suggests to physicians that the use of this wonder drug will, beyond a doubt, fix problems that afflict their aging male patients, such as fatigue, mental and physical subefficiency, and sexual apathy.

ANDROPAUSE: DISEASE OR MYTH?

Andropause is not a clear-cut, easily identifiable or definable condition. In a broad sense, andropause is defined as the age-related decline of testosterone levels in men that is accompanied by various symptoms, such as fatigue, lowered libido, and depression. The confusion surrounding the condition is "evident in the disputes over what to call it—andropause, veropause, male menopause, ADAM, and the male climacteric" (Mckinlay and Gemmel 2003). This conceptual confusion has existed for some time, as physicians and scientists have debated the use of each of these terms. A review of the current scientific literature on andropause reveals that describing the age-related decline of testosterone levels in men as "male menopause" and using terms like *andropause*, *male menopause*, and *the male climacteric* is misleading because, in Louis Gooren's (2003, 350) words, "terms like male menopause or andropause more or less suggest that, similarly to women, all men go through a profound decline of their androgen production from middle age on, but it should be stressed that the age related decline of androgens in men follows a totally different pattern in comparison to the menopause." In other words, *andropause* and *male menopause* are physiologically incorrect terms because, unlike women, men do not universally experience a cessation of gonadal function and reproductive capability. In fact, "aging in healthy men is normally not accompanied by abrupt or drastic alterations of gonadal function, and androgen production as well as fertility can be largely presented until very old age" (Nieschlag and Behre 1998, 437–438). Some in the medical community have suggested that the more accurate term *partial androgen deficiency in aging males* (PADAM) be used. This search for a scientific-sounding and accurate term is indicative of the process of medicalization, where a legitimate name for a condition promulgates its diagnosis.

While scientists agree that some men may experience a decrease in testosterone with age, the measure and meaning of testosterone levels remain contentious issues. Measuring testosterone levels is not straightforward: debates continue over whether it is the level of "free," bound, or total testosterone that is the most significant measure (Stas et al., 2003), and concerns that testosterone levels can vary from hour to hour and that "periodic declines can occur in some otherwise normal men" (American Association of Clinical Endocrinologists 2002, 442) fuel the debate as well. Thus, "there is currently no gold standard laboratory test" to determine testosterone levels (Tan and Culberson 2003, 16), and no agreement as to what measurement to use to arrive at a diagnosis of andropause. The American Association of Clinical Endocrinologists (AACE) suggests that "an important research goal is to establish a consistent method for determining free testosterone levels and to verify the results so that these levels can be more widely used and trusted" (2002, 442). In short, standardizing ways to measure testosterone levels and creating agreement on what levels are considered abnormal will facilitate a diagnosis of andropause and contribute to increased rates of treatment—a crucial step in the medicalization of masculinity.

Moreover, while there is a basic understanding of testosterone decline and aging, scientists and clinicians know very little about the mechanisms behind the decline and its connection to the physical manifestations of aging. It is clear that testosterone decreases with age, but whether or not this decline means that a man has a pathological condition such as andropause is not known. That professional societies such as the AACE are pushing for a resolution of diagnostic uncertainties, the acceptance of a standard laboratory analysis, and an accurate label to replace andropause is clear evidence that the medical and scientific communities are contributing to the medicalization of aging men's bodies. Indeed, despite the "humbling chasm of ignorance about testosterone therapy," as many as 1.5 million men are taking testosterone supplements (Vastag 2003, 971). The availability of testosterone as a supplement in a convenient form will increase the chance that healthy men will use it to help them "treat" the symptoms of aging.[2]

MODERN PHARMACEUTICAL COMPANIES AND THE MEDICALIZATION OF MALE AGING

Although testosterone therapy for the treatment of male menopause declined in popularity for most of the second half of the twentieth century, it never completely disappeared. Indeed, while the situation today is still somewhat ambiguous, the idea of a male menopause and the use of testosterone replacement therapy are reemerging, driven by technological advances made in the pharmaceutical realm and by the distribution of these drugs for an increasing range of male troubles, both of which facilitate medicalization.

First, the mode of delivery for testosterone has evolved over the past few decades. By providing a highly effective and convenient form of the drug, more men are likely to participate in treatment, and pharmaceutical companies continue to search for more convenient and attractive treatments. Oral preparations of testosterone, in the form of pills, are relatively easy to take but are problematic because they do not maintain a constant level of the hormone and may cause liver damage. Injections are uncomfortable for everyday use and "produce a sharp spike of the hormone, and then a fall, and these fluctuations are often accompanied by swings in mood, libido, and energy" (Groopman 2002, 1). Patches, worn on the abdomen, back, thighs, or upper arm, maintain a steady level of the hormone but may be uncomfortable or fall off. The most recent form of testosterone, a clear, odorless transdermal gel, can be rubbed into the shoulders once a day without any irritating effects. The main gel on the market today is AndroGel, a product of Unimed, an American division of the Belgian pharmaceutical company Solvay. The United States Food and Drug Administration (FDA) approved AndroGel in February of 2000. Shortly after the FDA approval Robert E. Dudley, president and CEO of Unimed, stated that "we believe that doctors and men who are waiting for a more convenient testosterone treatment will regard AndroGel as a very attractive alternative to existing testosterone replacement therapy" (Doctor's Guide Global Edition 2000).

Secondly, while AndroGel is currently only FDA approved for well-defined conditions associated with hypogonadism, such as Klinefelter's Syndrome,[3] "pharmaceutical companies often obtain FDA approval of a new product for a niche population with a relatively rare disease, hoping to expand later to a larger and more profitable market" (Groopman 2002, 3). This "off label" use of drugs is common medical practice and occurs when a physician prescribes a drug for conditions other than those for which the drug is approved. FDA regulations do not allow AndroGel to be advertised for any nonapproved uses, but pharmaceutical companies can use other avenues for promoting their product. For example, "they can run ads that 'raise awareness' of a condition without mentioning the proprietary therapy by name and they can align themselves with ... well known physicians whose views are thought to have influence among their peers' (Groopman 2002, 3), and Unimed/Solvay has used both of these tactics to promote the use of AndroGel in aging men. Perhaps the most interesting technique is a patient checklist titled "Could You Have Low Testosterone?" on AndroGel's Web site (www.androgel.com). The questionnaire is derived from a 1997 "Androgen Deficiency in Aging Men Questionnaire"; the questions are vague and mirror many life changes that occur as men age. Questions such as "Have you noticed a recent deterioration in your ability to play sports?" and "Are you falling asleep after dinner?" hardly seem like clear medical symptoms, yet the implicit promotion of AndroGel turns these common life events into symptoms of a medical problem and suggests that a physician review the checklist.

THE ALLURE OF TESTOSTERONE

Although pharmaceutical companies promoting andropause have been prominent advocates for the medicalization of male aging, they are not alone. The promise of testosterone therapy has an almost magical allure for many people, including clinicians, their patients, and even the lay public. Testosterone is often portrayed as a miraculous substance, with amazing power to restore or enhance masculinity. The metaphors for testosterone in the public media illustrate the magical light within which the male hormone is often viewed. Men become complicit in their own medicalization with the promise that such treatments can produce astonishing results.

An advertisement for AndroGel from the March 2003 issue of *Clinical Endocrinology* represents another way in which testosterone is framed to physicians and their male patients. The advertisement depicts a gas gauge with the arrow pointed to Empty.

The text states "Low Sex Drive? Fatigued? Depressed Mood? These could be indicators that your testosterone is running on empty." Here, testosterone is depicted as fuel for the male body that can be used up; the body does not naturally replace the material essential to sustaining its gender. Playing on the body-as-machine metaphor, the brightly colored dial illustrating two poles—Empty or Full—suggests that men and their physicians can simply "fill up" with testosterone supplementation to regain sex drive, energy, and optimism—essentially masculine qualities. Testosterone supplementation is promoted as something that many men will need as part of the regular maintenance of their body—not depicted as a rare condition, here andropause emerges as a mundane, typical, and predictable aspect of the daily life (and lived bodies) of men.

Testosterone therapy is also an attractive subject for the press. Different print sources publish stories that begin with headlines like "Testosterone: Shot in the arm for aging males" (Preidt 2002) or "Are You Man Enough? Testosterone can make a difference in bed and at the gym" (McLaughlin and Park 2000). These pieces almost always begin with the personal story of a man who was tired at work, uninterested in sex with his wife, failing on the football field/at the gym/on the squash court and whose life turned around after his physician prescribed testosterone. Using a metaphor redolent with images of man as a sleek, powerful, and fast machine, one journalist wrote, "if you happen to be a man, the very idea is bound to appeal to your inner hood ornament, to that image of yourself as all wind sheared edges and sunlit chrome" (McLaughlin and Park 2000, 58). This statement reflects a cultural preoccupation with reinvigorating the male body as a series of working parts that come together under the influence of "rocket fuel" (Friedman 2011). The millions of aging male baby boomers are an attractive market for both the media and pharmaceutical manufacturers (Friedan 1993b; Hepworth and Featherstone 1998). Coupled with the real and imagined aging male concerns with body failure, it seems likely that we will see testosterone replacement therapy as an important step in the medicalization of aging male bodies in the next decade.

BALDNESS: PLUGS AND DRUGS

Losing one's hair or going bald is a common bodily occurrence that can cause anxiety among aging men. While remedies ranging from tonics and elixirs to bear grease have a long history, and medicine has long been concerned with hair loss, baldness has only recently begun to become medicalized. Although the medical profession is reticent to call baldness a disease, the medicalization of baldness is gaining momentum in the light of new medical treatments for hair loss. Here, too, we see the invention and availability of medical therapies driving the process of medicalization.

A BRIEF LOOK AT HISTORICAL TREATMENTS FOR BALDNESS

Throughout history, men have been concerned with hair loss, as evidenced by an impressive range of remedies, potions, and concoctions used to treat baldness. One of the first known written medical records, the Ebers Papyrus, dates back to 1500 B.C. and contains eleven recipes for the treatment of baldness. One recipe "advised the sufferer to apply a mixture of burned prickles of a hedgehog immersed in oil, finger-nail scrapings, and a potpourri of honey, alabaster, and red ocher" (Segrave 1996, 3). Baldness treatments were understood in magical, mythical terms. For example, in the sixteenth century A.D., the alchemist Paracelsus prescribed an elixir that purportedly contained "blood from women in childbirth, the blood of a murdered new born baby, and 'vipers' wine'" (Cooper 1971, 153). The treatment of baldness was left to alchemists who created concoctions that were shrouded in mystery.

Until the late nineteenth century, there was little medical interest in the cause or potential treatments for baldness: medical science had limited legitimacy in an area where traditionally "the care of hair was left in the hands of charlatans, and treatments involved a mumbo jumbo of alchemy, magic, and superstition" (Cooper 1971, 157), and since most of the remedies for baldness were ineffective, medicine had little to offer for the treatment of hair loss. However, the late nineteenth century saw the emergence of several medical theories about baldness. Physicians and scientists conceived of a myriad of different causes of baldness, ranging from the logical to the bizarre. One of the most popular theories was that hats caused baldness because "they compressed the circulation system, thus reducing nourishment to the hair" (Segrave 1996, 14). Many physicians speculated on the hat theory, suggesting that the shape of the skull or the style of the hat were to blame. Accessing the new germ theory to present a pathological view of baldness, M. Sebouraud, a French physiologist, announced at the 1897 meeting of the Dermatological Society of Paris that a microbe caused baldness. Medical journals warned that "combs should he boiled regularly and frequently, and under no circumstances should members of precociously bald families use other combs or brushes than their own, or allow them to be used on them, in barber shops, unless they are assured of their sterilization beforehand" (JAMA 1903, 249). Late-nineteenth-ccntury dermatologists believed that irritating the scalp through blistering would cause hair regrowth. The procedure, known as vesication, "was believed to produce pooling of blood in the scalp, which provided more nourishment for the follicles there, causing hair regrowth" (Segrave 1996, 52). Other treatments included vacuum caps and electrical shock treatment. Men subjected themselves to painful treatments like vesication and electric shock in the hopes of medically producing hair growth. Interestingly, none of these alleged causes were specifically gendered.

CURRENT MEDICAL UNDERSTANDING OF BALDNESS

Despite or perhaps because of the quackery of the past, modern biomedicine has shown a keen interest in researching the causes of male pattern baldness (referred to in the scientific literature as "androgenetic alopecia"). Despite the fact that a MEDLINE search we conducted for articles from 1985 to 2003 on androgenetic alopecia produced 356 citations, and despite the fact that the term "androgenetic alopecia" evolved from the understanding that male baldness (alopecia) is dependent upon male hormones (androgens) and genetics, there is disagreement over whether androgenetic alopecia is actually a disease. One textbook states, "the human species is not the only primate species in which baldness is a natural phenomenon associated with sexual maturity" (Dawber and Van Neste 1995, 96). Other medical agents believe that "androgenetic alopecia becomes a medical problem only when the hair loss is subjectively seen as excessive, premature, and distressing" (Sinclair 1998, 865), with some distinguishing between androgenetic alopecia and hair changes that accompany "natural" aging, known as senescent baldness. The dermatologist David Whiting writes, "the clinical and histologic evidence for senescent alopecia is not clear cut and is still disputed" (1998, 564). However, the ambivalence scientific writings express over the identity (or lack thereof) of male baldness as a distinct pathology coexists with the medicalization of male pattern baldness as seen in the definition of androgenetic alopecia as a distinct entity from hair loss associated with "normal" aging.

Indeed, a science of hair loss has recently developed within this partially medicalized context: researchers have found that the male hormone dihydrotestosterone causes the hair follicle to produce the fine, unpigmented hair common in baldness. Growing evidence shows that male pattern baldness runs in families and has a genetic basis: a gene called "sonic hedgehog" has been implicated in baldness. A *Science News* article declares enthusiastically that "scientists suggest that a gene named after the combative [video game] character could prove a potent weapon in the battle against a fearsome foe: baldness" (*Science News* 1999, 283). A recent study published in *Nature Biotechnology* (April 2004) suggests that stem cells may be helpful in curing baldness. Such findings have been significant in providing a medical basis for baldness and its treatment.

According to a definition mentioned earlier (Sinclair 1998), androgenetic alopecia becomes a medical condition when hair loss is excessive. Determination of what constitutes excessive hair loss is subjective, yet medicine has created standards of hair loss through visual representations and quantitative means. Medical textbooks and journal articles contain diagrams that visually depict the progression of baldness, known as categorical classification systems. These diagrams represent categories of increasing severity from mild to severe hair loss. Surgeons and dermatologists commonly use them, and this system "has become the standard of classification for hair restoration physicians" (Stough and Haber 1996, 15).

Descriptions of baldness are awash in medical terminology. Consider the following description, which corresponds to a Norwood level V classification:

> *Type V.* The vertex region of alopecia remains separated from the frontotemporal region of alopecia. The separation is not as distinct as that in type IV because the band of hair across the crown is narrower and sparser. Both the vertex and frontotemporal areas of alopecia are larger than those in type IV. (Stough and Haber 1996, 16)

The language of this description is medically precise and docs not assign subjective value to the phenomenon. Other diagnostic criteria exist, including measurements such as hair density, hair length, hair diameter, and cosmetically significant hair, defined as "a hair with a defined thickness and length, usually >40/µm and at least 3cm long" (Van Neste 2002, 364). Medicine has attempted to quantify the exact length and diameter of a hair that would be considered attractive. Although the use of medical terms and measurements seems to remove the value judgments of baldness, the standards are still subjective and influenced by sociocultural expectations. Even M. D. Van Neste, a clinical dermatologist, admits to the capriciousness of this measurement when he writes, "fashion may ... limit the application of the method depending on what hair style is desirable for the patient (e.g., a close hair cut is the currently popular style compared with longer hair in 1970)" (2002, 364).

CURRENT TREATMENTS FOR BALDNESS

Modern medical, surgical, and pharmaceutical technology has yielded treatments for baldness that differ from the snake oils of the past in their efficacy and are currently the driving force in the medicalization of baldness; however, while effective, the drugs Rogaine and Propecia and hair transplant surgery are not miracle cures for baldness, but may be costly, painful, and useful for only some men. Despite such limitations, these treatments have been verified by the medical community, including the Food and Drug Administration, and are thus considered legitimate medical treatments. The cost of these treatments is significant, particularly for Rogaine and Propecia. Estimates from 1999 indicate that men spent nine hundred million dollars on medical treatments (Rogaine, Propecia, and hair transplant surgery) for baldness (Scow, Nolte and Shaughnessy 1999). Brand-name Rogaine costs three hundred dollars for a year's supply, and Propecia costs six hundred dollars (Scow, Nolte and Shaughnessy 1999). Because these two treatments must be continued indefinitely lest hair loss return, pharmaceutical companies are encouraged to develop and market these expensive and lucrative hair growth drugs. Moreover, hair transplants can cost anywhere from two thousand dollars to over ten thousand dollars depending on how many hairs are transplanted (Fischer 1997)—here too, many patients will require repeat surgeries to maintain the transplant, creating a lucrative market for hair restoration surgery.

SURGICAL TREATMENTS

There are three surgical treatments for male pattern baldness: transplants using a plug or graft technique, scalp reduction, and scalp flaps. As P. Bouhanna and J. C. Dardour assert, "the basic principle of the surgery of baldness consists in distributing the paucity of material as uniformly as possible" (2000, 29). Hair restoration techniques have limitations since baldness is a progressive condition: a transplant on a man in his thirties may look good at the time, but twenty years later his hair pattern could change significantly, rendering the cosmetic benefits of the transplant obsolete. Thus, although conceived of as a medical treatment for baldness, surgical procedures do not "cure" baldness but simply mask it. Textbooks and surgical atlases recognize this limitation. Marritt and Dzubow (1996, 30) contend that "hair restoration" is a misnomer, writing, "sadly, hair restoration has nothing at all to do with the restorative process. Hair cannot be restored or resuscitated, only rearranged."

Hair transplantation using plugs or grafts involves removing a section of the scalp from a part of the head that still has hair and sectioning this piece into "plugs" or "grafts" with a few follicles each. The plugs are then transplanted to the front of the scalp in an attempt to create a "natural" hairline. According to the surgical hair restoration literature, the creation of an "aesthetically pleasing" hairline is of utmost importance (Khan and Slough 1996), as is "naturalness." A goal of this surgery is to make it appear as if it were never done: one article even warns against "lowering the hairline to a position of youth ... If the hairline is restored in a middle aged person to the level of hair when they were 18 or so, it looks very unnatural" (Muiderman 2001, 142). This paradox characterizes the field of hair transplant surgery. Overall, the procedures available today are only moderately effective, with side effects including scarring, infection, and rejection of donor grafts. As a result, hair restoration surgery has had limited appeal as a medical treatment for baldness. The cutting edge of medical interventions for hair loss resides in pharmaceutical treatments.

ROGAINE

The pharmaceutical company UpJohn was not seeking a baldness cure when it happened upon minoxidil, the active chemical in Rogaine. In the mid-1960s, researchers found that minoxidil lowered heart rale. FDA approval followed for the drug, known as Loniten, in 1979 for the treatment of severe high blood pressure. Loniten was not expected to be a high-profit drug, since it had a relatively specific target group. However, during clinical trials for hypertension, researchers had noticed that one patient had grown new hair on the top of his head. This growth was significant because it was dark, thick terminal hair; the kind that is lost in baldness. When the media picked up research reports about this side effect of minoxidil, interested volunteers deluged dermatologists and physicians. As an associate of Dr. Howard Baden, a Harvard researcher involved with early trials of minoxidil, says, "it wasn't even necessary to advertise for volunteers. All you have to do is whisper in the corridors that you're doing a study of male baldness and you get all the volunteers you want" (Segrave 1996, 148). Clearly, the demand for an effective medical drug for male baldness was tremendous.

In the mid-1980s, even though the FDA had not approved the drug for treatment of baldness, many physicians were prescribing Loniten for their balding patients. This off-label use was so widespread that a 1986 survey estimated that "American dermatologists were prescribing topical minoxidil to over 100,000 patients per year" (Segrave 1996. 153). It was clear that this growth was not due to an expanding hypertension market. In December 1985, UpJohn presented their newly researched baldness treatment, Regaine topical solution, to the FDA for approval. After UpJohn modified its product information and changed the name of its minoxidil to Rogaine (which the FDA felt was less misleading than Regaine), the FDA granted approval on August 18, 1988.[4]

The availability of Rogaine changed dramatically on February 12, 1996, when the FDA approved both the over-the-counter sale of the drug and the production of generic formulations of minoxidil. Determined to stay a leader in the hair growth market, UpJohn released a 5-percent stronger formula of Rogaine in 1997 and launched an advertising campaign emphasizing the strength of the new formula and of the men who use it. A 1999 advertisement features the tennis player John McEnroe promoting the "return" of Rogaine. The advertisement tells consumers that McEnroe "attacked" his bald spot and "beat" it. It also poses the question, "Is John the first man to snatch victory from the follicles of defeat? Far from it." The message being communicated here is that using Rogaine can help men conquer their baldness by aggressively attacking it. Other Rogaine promotional materials utilize the slogan "stronger than heredity" and depict a bald father sitting next to his son with captions like "I love Dad. I'm just not in a rush to look like him." Rogaine is depicted as a drug that can give men power and control over a bodily change that was once perceived as inevitable. This is a seductive message, and one that reconfigures male aging as a vulnerable, though tenacious, foe.

PROPECIA

Rogaine's potential for profit was diminished when, on December 22, 1997, the FDA approved Merck's hair loss pill, Propecia. Researchers stumbled upon the hair growth properties of the drug finasteride while it was being tested for use in men with enlarged prostates. The effectiveness of finasteride for preventing hair loss has been evaluated in three studies comprising a total of 1,879 men (Scow, Nolte, and Shaughnessy 1999). Results are promising in that the drug is effective in preventing baldness in the early stages of androgenetic alopecia. Current scientific understanding supports the early use of Propecia because in most cases of androgenetic alopecia, "prevention and main-tenance are the most realistic therapeutic options" (Ramos e Silva 2000, 729). Propecia works well for men who have just begun to notice signs of baldness but will not regrow hair, and because it cannot reverse significant hair loss, it is not even technically a cure for baldness. To maintain the benefits of Propecia, men must take the medication for the rest of their lives, or they will revert to the normal progression of balding.

Propecia targets self-conscious men who are troubled by their hair loss, telling them that their impending baldness is preventable. Early Propecia advertisements depicted a man with a slight bald spot and a troubled, hopeless look on his face gazing into a bathroom mirror, seeing a reflection of himself as totally bald. The text of the advertisement reads, "If you think losing more hair is inevitable, think again." Another Propecia advertisement depicts a man with a bald spot staring at a dome. The text reads, "You don't need reminders about your hair loss. You need something to deal with it." Empowerment to attack hair loss and regain control is a central theme seen in both Rogaine and Propecia advertisements: even if a medical solution is not fully effective, the fact that one exists is enough to make men potentially empowered to do something about baldness. This is the attraction of drugs like Rogaine and Propecia, which contribute to medicalizing hair loss by providing men with medical treatments to conquer a troubling "disease."

PSYCHOSOCIAL CONSTRUCTION OF BALDNESS

Psychological effects of baldness serve as one of the main justifications for the treatment of hair loss as a disease. Medical textbooks and journal articles on the subject of treating baldness often have a separate section on psychosocial concerns or the effect of hair loss on quality of life. As Valerie Randall asserts early on in her chapter on androgenetic alopecia:

> In our youth oriented culture, the association of hair loss with increasing age has negative connotations and, since hair plays such an important role in human social and sexual communication, male pattern baldness often causes marked psychological distress and reduction in the quality of life, despite not being life threatening or physically painful. (2000, 125)

While such psychosocial connotations may or may not be accurate, making this connection allows Randall to justify treating hair loss as a disease, albeit a psychological one. Indeed, some physicians cite the negative psychological correlates of baldness as the justification for medical treatment of hair loss. Emanuel Marritt, a hair restoration surgeon, sees this as his medical responsibility: "that 'simple office procedure' has, in reality, just handed me a life sentence of follicular responsibility. The weight of this awareness is not only humbling, it can be at times, simply overwhelming" (1993, 4). While Marritt's views on treating hair loss are influenced by the fact that he specializes in a more invasive procedure than does a dermatologist prescribing Propecia, he expresses an increasingly common viewpoint: hair loss is a serious problem worthy of medical intervention.

Given the Western cultural view of hair loss, it is not surprising that men may hold negative views of baldness. A recent advertisement for Hershey's chocolate depicts the progression of baldness in a man with the text "change is bad." Although it has nothing to do with baldness therapy, the advertisement reinforces the view that bodily change due to age is not welcome and is stigmatized. Baldness often represents a loss of masculine traits and can affect male self-esteem. Psychological studies document the negative impact baldness can have on male mental health. Pamela Wells, Trevor Willmouth, and Robin Russell (1995) found that hair loss in men is associated with depression, low self-esteem, neuroticism, introversion, and feelings of unattractiveness. There are of course cultural counterexamples of bald men. Actors like Yul Brenner and sports stars like Andre Agassi or Michael Jordan are not considered unattractive because they are bald. These are examples of men who have embraced baldness and shaved their remaining hair. They have, in a sense, taken control of their hair loss. But these counterexamples stand in contrast to the generally negative views of baldness as an undesirable condition and one increasingly deemed appropriate for medical treatment.

CONCLUDING REMARKS

Andropause and baldness represent aspects of aging male bodies that have become partially medicalized in recent years. As new pharmaceuticals are developed and medical science understands more about the physiological basis of aging, it is likely that medicalization will continue. Men and masculinity have often been omitted from medicalization analyses, in part due to the belief that men are not as vulnerable to medical surveillance and control as women. But, as this chapter demonstrates, such a belief is no longer tenable.

Medicine has long been an avenue for women to resist aging bodies and reclaim fading youthful features. Now this avenue is available and becoming increasingly appealing to men. Youth and youthful manifestations of the body are paramount, as "contemporary expectations about health, fitness, and sexuality have pushed men to maintain youthful performance in all aspects of their lives" (Luciano 2001, 204). Medical treatments can help men achieve this youthful appearance, if not performance.

While both andropause and baldness are medicalized aspects of aging male bodies, they show some contrasting features. Male testosterone levels decline as men age, but it is unclear what this means. Unlike menopause in women, andropause has no distinct markers or "symptoms." Although claims have been made regarding the benefits of testosterone replacement therapy, there is precious little evidence of any efficacy or improvement from such treatments. Baldness, on the other hand, is a distinct physiological condition, similar in some ways to a disease or disorder; it appears to have a genetic basis and creates what could be called a "bodily dysfunction" but, until recently, was not considered a medical disorder, nor were medical treatments available for it. With the advent of surgical and pharmaceutical treatments, however, hair loss has been increasingly medicalized: while not yet conceptualized as a disease, baldness is an actual bodily change that can be treated through medical interventions, in a sense, andropause has a medical name but unclear symptoms and no efficacious treatment. In contrast, baldness has clear symptoms and a range of medical treatments, some of which have achieved success

In both cases, we see the infiltration of biomedicine into everyday life through definitions or treatments that redefine "healthy" and "normal" male bodily function. Men experience and understand their bodies differently if the aging process is constructed in pathological terms. The maintenance of masculinity is often connected to the functioning of the male body. As body function declines, self-conceptions of masculinity may be imperiled. This may invite men to seek medical solutions to repair or retain the body's abilities, especially in western culture where "all of us are encouraged to believe that our problem, aging, is natural, inevitable, awful, but controllable" (Gullette 1997, 231).

This male anxiety about aging and masculinity, while not ubiquitous, is sufficiently common in American society to create a strong market for medical solutions. Given the growing number of aging baby boomers in our generally youth-oriented culture, it is not surprising that male bodies are increasingly being seen as potential markets for medical solutions. The advent and promotion of products like AndroGel, Propecia and Rogaine, and Viagra, Levitra, and Cialis may just be the beginning of a new medicalization of aging male bodies. The potential market expands when one considers that certain types of body maintenance and prevention must begin long before the onset of "old age" (Katz and Marshall 2004). Pharmaceutical promotion of so-called "lifestyle drugs" that "treat conditions understood not as life threatening, but rather as life limiting" (Mamo and Fishman 2001, 16) is likely to be one of the forces pushing toward the medicalization of male bodies. The combination of corporate promotion and consumer demand together make medical definitions and treatments of human problems increasingly likely (Conrad and Leiter 2004).

Male concerns with aging bodies are propelling men to seek medical solutions for declining signs of masculinity. These threats to traditional characteristics of manliness are not universal, but seem to be increasing as pharmaceutical and medical entrepreneurs seek to establish markets, amplify male anxieties, and provide solutions to the problems of aging men. The medicalization of aging male bodies requires the joint action of men who seek solutions for perceived masculinity decline and the medical treatments that are offered to reinvigorate significant attributes of such masculinity. The huge success of Viagra and the partial medicalization of andropause and hair loss may be only the beginning. With the baby boomers coming into their sixties, one may expect an expansion of the medicalized categories and treatments for various ailments associated with aging men and masculinity.

NOTES

1 Indeed, this understanding is gaining recognition in the literature: Elianne Riska, writing two decades after Reissman, highlights the gendered nature of the medicalization thesis by examining type A behavioral patterns as risk factors for heart disease. She writes that "the original theory on Type A personality pointed indirectly to traditional masculinity as a risk factor" (2003, 75), suggesting that certain male-specific traits have come under medical jurisdiction.

2 The efficacy of testosterone replacement therapy is not well known, although a few small studies suggest some benefit for various age-related conditions. One study suggests that testosterone decreases LDL cholesterol in older men and may improve the quality of life in men with angina, or chronic chest pain (Morley and Perry 2003). One of the main health concerns among the aging

population is frailty, caused by sarcopenia, or a deterioration of lean muscle mass. Bodily frailty leaves the elderly population more prone to falls and broken bones. There is evidence that testosterone replacement therapy has the potential to increase lean muscle mass if accompanied by rehabilitation. As Morley and Perry (2003, 371) write, "well designed large clinical trials in sarcopenia and/or frail men are essential to determine whether this potential is a reality or merely a modern urban myth." While a small amount of clinical data suggests that testosterone therapy may have some benefit in terms of various bodily conditions later in life, it does not appear as if testosterone replacement therapy has the potential to completely reinvigorate aging male bodies. In short, testosterone replacement therapy has not yet demonstrated efficacy in reversing or correcting signs of the aging process (Wespes and Schulman 2002).

3 Klinefelter's syndrome is one of the more common developmental disorders of the reproductive tract in which a male has a chromosomal abnormality (XXY), undeveloped testes and gynecomastia, which is excessive development of the mammary glands in the male. Testosterone supplementation is often prescribed to individuals who have Klinefelter's syndrome.

4 As a topical solution, Rogaine is applied to the scalp twice a day. In clinical trials, Rogaine was moderately effective, although it could only be used in men with hair loss of a certain severity.

REFERENCES

BOOKS AND ARTICLES

American Association of Clinical Endocrinologists. 2002. "Medical Guidelines for Clinical Practice for the Evaluation and Treatment of Hypogonadism in Adult Male Patients." *Endocrine Practice* 8: 439–456.

Bell, Susan E. 1990. "Sociological Perspectives on the Medicalization of Menopause." *Annals of the New York Academy of Sciences* 592: 173–178.

Bouhanna, P., and J. C. Dardour. 2000. *Hair Replacement Surgery: Textbook and Atlas.* New York: Springer.

Brumberg, Joan Jacobs. 2001, "Anorexia Nervosa in Context." Pp. 94–108 in *The Sociology of Health and Illness: Critical Perspectives,* 6th ed., edited by P. Conrad. New York: Worth Publishers.

Carpiano, Richard M. 2001. "Passive Medicalization: The Case of Viagra and Erectile Dysfunction." *Sociological Spectrum* 21: 441–450.

Conrad, Peter. 1992. "Medicalization and Social Control." *Annual Review of Sociology* 18: 209–232.

Conrad, Peter. 2000. "Medicalization, Genetics, and Human Problems." Pp. 322–333 in *Handbook of Medical Sociology,* 5th ed., edited by C. Bird, P. Conrad, and A. M. Fremont. New York: Prentice Hall.

Conrad, Peter, and Allison Angell. 2004. "Homosexuality and Remedicalization." *Society* 41(5): 32–39.

Conrad, Peter, and Valeric Leiter. 2004. "Medicalization, Markets and Consumers, *Journal of Health and Social Behavior* 45(extra issue): 158–176.

Conrad, Peter, and Joseph W. Schneider. 1992. *Deviance and Medicalization: From Badness to Sickness.* Philadelphia: Temple University Press.

Cooper, Wendy. 1971, *Hair: Sex, Society, Symbolism.* New York: Stein and Day.

Dawber, Rodney, and Dominique Van Neste, eds. 1995. *Hair and Scalp Disorders: Common Presenting Signs, Differential Diagnosis and Treatment.* London: Martin Dunitz.

Doctor's Guide Global Edition. 2000. "FDA Approves Prescription Androgel for Low Testosterone." Buffalo Grove, IL: Doctor's Guide Publishing, http://www.pslgroup.com/dg/l780fa.htm (accessed June 14, 2004).

Engelhardt, H. Trisun. 1974. "The Disease of Masturbation: Values and the Concept of Disease." *Bulletin of the History of Medicine* 48: 234–248.

Estes, Caroll L., and Elizabeth A. Binney. 1989. "The Biomedicalisation of Aging: Dangers and Dilemmas." *The Gerontologist* 29: 587–596.

Faircloth, Christopher A. 2003. *Aging Bodies: Images and Everyday Experience.* Walnut Creek, CA: AltaMira Press.

Figert, Anne E. 1995. "The Three Faces of PMS: The Professional, Gendered, and Scientific Structuring of a Psychiatric Disorder." *Social Problems* 42: 56–73.

Fischer, David. 1997. "The Bald Truth: Americans Turn to Weaves. Rugs, Plugs, and Drugs to Alleviate Hair Loss." *U.S. News & World Report* (August 4), 44.

Friedan, Betty. 1993. "The New Menopause Brouhaha." Pp 472–499 in *The Fountain of Age.* New York: Simon and Schuster.

Friedman, David. 2001. *A Mind of Its Own: A Cultural History of the Penis.* New York: The Free Press.

Gatens, Moira. 1996. *Imaginary Bodies: Ethics, Power and Corporeality.* New York: Routledge.

Gooren, Louis. 2003. "Androgen Deficiency in the Aging Male: Benefits and Risks of Androgen Supplementation." *Journal of Steroid Biochemistry and Molecular Biology* 85: 349–355.

Groopman, Jerome. July 29, 2002. "Hormones for Men." *The New Yorker Magazine.*

Gullette, Margaret Morganroth. 1997. "All Together Now: The New Sexual Politics of Midlife Bodies." Pp. 221–247 in *The Male Body: Features, Destinies, Exposures,* edited by L. Goldstein. Ann Arbor, MI: University of Michigan Press.

Halliwell, Emma, and Helga Dittmar. 2003. "A Qualitative Investigation of Women's and Men's Body Image Concerns and their Attitudes Toward Aging." *Sex Roles* 49: 675–684.

Hepworth, Michael, and Mike Featherstone. 1998. "The Male Menopause: Lay Accounts and the Cultural Reconstruction of Midlife." Pp. 276–301 in *The Body in Everyday Life,* edited by S. Nettleton and J. Watson. London: Routledge.

Institute of Medicine. 2004. *Testosterone and Aging: Clinical Research Directions.* Washington, DC: The National Academies Press.

Journal of the American Medical Association. 1903. "Prophylaxis of Baldness." 40: 249.

Katz, Stephen, and Barbara Marshall 2004. "New Sex for Old: Lifestyle, Consumerism, and the Ethics of Aging Well." *Journal of Aging Studies* 17: 3–16.

Kearns, Waller. 1939. "The Clinical Application of Testosterone." *Journal of the American Medical Association* 112: 2257.

Khan, Sajjad and Dow B. Stough. 1996. "Determination of Hairline Placement." Pp. 425–429 in *Hair Replacement: Surgical and Medical,* edited by Dow B, Slough and Robert S. Haber. St. Louis, MO: Mosby.

Kolata, Gina. November 13, 2003. "Panel Recommends Studies on Testosterone Therapy." *New York Times.* Pg. A22.

Lock, Margaret. 1993. *Encounters with Aging: Mythologies of Menopause in Japan and North America.* Berkeley: University of California Press.

Luciano, Lynne. 2001. *Looking Good: Male Body Image in Modern America.* New York: Hill and Wang.

Mamo, Laura, and Jennifer R. Fishman. 2001. "Potency in All the Right Places: Viagra as a Gendered Technology of the Body,' *Body & Society* 7(4): 13–35.

Marritt, Emanuel. 1993. "The Overwhelming Responsibility." *Hair Transplant Forum International* Special Edition: 4.

Marritt, Emanuel, and Leonard M. Dzubow. 1990. "Reassessment of Male Pattern Baldness: A Reevaluation of the Treatment." Pp. 30–11 in *Hair Replacement: Surgical and Medical,* edited by D. W. Stough and R. S. Haber. St. Louis. MO: Mosby.

Marshall, Barbara L., and Stephen Katz, 2002. "Forever Functional: Sexual Fitness and the Ageing Male Body." *Body & Society* 8: 43–70.

Martin, Emily. 1987. *The Woman in the Body: A Cultural Analysis of Reproduction.* Boston: Beacon Press.

McKinlay, John B., and Allison Gemmel. 2003. "Hormone Replacement Therapy/Policy: There's Gold in Them Thar Pills." New England Research Institutes, Watertown, MA. Unpublished manuscript.

McLaughlin, Lisa, and Alice Park. 2000. "Are You Man Enough?" *Time* 155: 58–63.

Morley, John E„ and H. M. Perry III. 2003. "Androgen Treatment of Male Hypogonadism in Older Males," *Journal of Steroid Biochemistry & Molecular Biology* 85: 367–373.

Morris, Rebecca. Yaping Liu, Lee Marles. Zaixin Yang, Carol Trempus, Shulan Li, Jamie S. Lin, Janet A. Sawicki, and George Cotsarelis. 2004. "Capturing and Profiling Hair Follicle Stem Cells." *Nature Biotechnology* 22: 411–417.

Muiderman, Kevin. 2001. "Hair Restoration Surgery Through Micrografting Techniques." *Plastic Surgical Nursing* 21: 141–142.

Nieschlag, Eberhard, and Hermann M. Behre, eds. 1998. *Testosterone: Action, Deficiency and Substitution.* New York: Springer.

Petersen, Alan R. 1998a. *Unmasking the Masculine: 'Men' and 'Identity' in a Sceptical Age.* London: Sage Publications.

Preidt, Robert. July 26, 2002. "Testosterone: Shot in the Arm for Aging Males." *USA Today.*

Ramos e Silva, Marcia. 2000. "Male Pattern Hair Loss: Prevention Rather Than Regrowth." *International Journal of Dermatology* 39: 728–731.

Randall, Valerie A. 2000. "The Biology of Androgenetic Alopecia." Pp. 123–133 in *Hair and Its Disorders: Biology, Pathology and Management,* edited by F. Camacho. V. Randall and V. Price. London: Martin Dunilz.

Reissman, Catherine Kohler. 1983. "Women and Medicalization: A New Perspective." *Social Policy* 14(1): 46–63.

Riska, Elianne. 2003. "Gendering the Medicalization Thesis." Pp. 59–87 in *Gender Perspectives on Health and Medicine: Key Themes. Advances in Gender Research* 7(1–9), edited by M. S. Segal and V. Demos. Oxford, UK; Elsevier Press.

Rothman, Sheila M., and David J. Rothman. 2003. *The Pursuit of Perfection: The Promise and Perils of Medical Enhancement.* New York: Pantheon Books.

Sault, Nicole, ed. 1994. *Many Mirrors: Body Image and Social Relations.* New Brunswick, NJ: Rutgers University Press.

Scheper-Hughes, Nancy, and Margaret M. Lock. 1987. "The Mindful Body: A Prolegomenon to Future Work in Medical Anthropology." *Medical Anthropology Quarterly* 1: 6–41.

Science News. 1999. "Gene Therapy Tackles Hair Loss." October 30, 283.

Scow, Dean Thomas, Robert S. Nolte, and .Allen F. Shaughnessy. April 15, 1999. "Medical Treatments for Balding in Men." *American Family Physician.*

Segrave, Kerry. 1996. *Baldness: A Social History.* Jefferson. NC: McFarland.

Sinclair, Rodney. 1998. "Male Pattern Androgenetic Alopecia." *British Journal of Medicine* 317: 865–869.

Sontag, Susan. 1978. *Illness as Metaphor.* New York: Farrar, Straus and Giroux.

Stas, Sameer N., Aristotelis G. Anastasiadis, Harry Fisch, Mitchell C. Benson, and Ridwan Shabsigh. 2003. "Urologie Aspects of Andropause." *Urology* 61: 261–266.

Stough, Dow B., and Robert S. Haber, eds. 1996. *Hair Replacement: Surgical and Medical.* St. Louis, MO: Mosby.

Tan, Robert S., and John W. Culberson. 2003. "An Integrative Review on Current Evidence of Testosterone Replacement Therapy for the Andropause." *Maturitas* 45: 15–27.

Thompson. Edward H. 1994. "Older Men as Invisible Men in Contemporary Society." Pp. 1–21 in *Older Men's Lives,* edited by E. H. Thompson. Thousand Oaks, CA: Sage Publications.

Turner, Bryan S. 1992. *Regulating Bodies: Essays in Medical Sociology.* New York: Routledge.

Van Neste, M. D. 2002. "Assessment of Hair Loss: Clinical Relevance of Hair Growth Evaluation Methods." *Clinical Dermatology* 27: 362–369.

Vastag, Brian. 2003. "Many Questions, Few Answers for Testosterone Replacement Therapy." *Journal of the American Medical Association* 289: 971–972.

Watson, Jonathan. 2000. *Male Bodies: Health, Culture and Identity.* Buckingham: Open University Press.

Wells, Pamela A., Trevor Willmouth, and Robin Russell 1995. "Does Fortune Favor the Bald? Psychological Correlates of Hair Loss in Males." *British Journal of Psychology* 86: 337–344.

Werner, August A. 1939. "The Male Climacteric." *Journal of the American Medical Association* 112: 1441–1443.

Wertz, Richard, and Dorothy Wertz. 1989. *Lying In:* A *History of Childbirth in America,* expanded edition. New Haven. CT: Yale University Press.

Wespes. E., and C. C. Schulman. 2002. "Male Andropause: Myth, Reality, and Treatment." *International Journal of impotence Research* 14: S93–S98.

Whiting, David A. 1998. "Male Pattern Hair Loss: Current Understanding." *International Journal of Dermatology* 37: 561–566.

Zola, Irving K. 1972. "Medicine as an Institution of Social Control," *Sociological Review* 20: 487–504.

CHAPTER 7

SOCIAL SUPPORT, SEX, AND FOOD

As you read this section, consider the following questions.

QUESTIONS TO CONSIDER

1   What are social networks?

2   Why is the examination of our ties to other people important to understanding behavior that might increase health or increase health risks?

3   In your own life, do you think your health and well-being has been affected by your connections to others? Has your health and well-being been affected by a lack of connections to others at any time?

4   What is the authors' main point?

KEY TERMS

social networks
social support

SOCIAL SUPPORT, SEX, AND FOOD

SOCIAL NETWORKS AND HEALTH

BY GINA S. LOVASI, JIMI ADAMS, AND PETER BEARMAN

Patterns of social connection are essential to human health and well-being. Researchers are increasingly taking note of the importance of networks, exploring how social networks shape health and health behaviors, and examining how health contributes to the formation, dissolution, and maintenance of social relationships. While several resources are broadly devoted to describing social networks and health (Levy and Pescosolido 2002; Luke and Harris 2007; Smith and Christakis 2008), here we focus on a subset of the ways that networks affect health through their influence on social support, sex, and food consumption—topics both relevant to health and inherently social. In summarizing research in these areas, we highlight how three primary conceptualizations of networks shape what questions are addressed, how studies are designed, what researchers find, and the implications of those findings. (For a more systematic or historically oriented review of the literature on social networks and health, we recommend Hawe, Webster, and Shiell 2004; Luke and Harris 2007; Smith and Christakis 2008.)

FRAMING NETWORKS AND HEALTH RESEARCH

The key components of social networks are actors and the social ties between them (Hawe, Webster, and Shiell 2004). Although actors of interest are usually individual people, actors in a social network could also be organizations such as hospitals or community groups. Ties within social networks can include an array of potential relationships; here we follow Borgatti's classification strategy (2008). Some ties are based on direct interpersonal interactions. The social interactions that delineate social ties may include behaviors with direct health ramifications, such as sex, smoking, drinking, dining, and exercise. Another type of interpersonal interaction tie that has relevance for health is based on the transfer of material goods or information. The most commonly measured personal network tie is based on discussion of important matters (Bearman and Parigi 2004; Marsden 1987; McPherson, Smith-Lovin and Brashears 2006); discussion partners are an important source of social support and of health-relevant information. Other common ties are role based, including kin relationships, friendships, and cognitive relations based on whom an actor knows, likes/dislikes, and so on. Finally, ties may be purely association based, such as those that arise through shared memberships in organizations or shared participation in events. The diverse social ties that can exist between any two individuals are not mutually exclusive, and the overlaps between different tie types or different shared activities may themselves be of interest (Rothenberg, Woodhouse et al. 1995).

AN EPIDEMIC OF NETWORKS RESEARCH

Social networks were used as a metaphor in the social sciences, and even in literature, long before they became prominent in public health research (Luke and Harris 2007). Studies of social networks have increased markedly since the creation of International Network for Social Network Analysis in 1977, as evidenced by the growing number of journal articles on the subject. Informal searches of Medline and the Social Sciences Citation Index (SSCI) found parallel increases in the number of entries listing "social network" or "network analysis" (Figure 7.1). These sources listed 3,574 and 5,514 abstracts from 1977 to 2007, respectively, of which approximately two-thirds have been published in the last decade. Medline and SSCI are not mutually exclusive, so some manuscripts may appear in both databases. Of the social network abstracts identified in Medline, the most common subject categories were behavioral sciences, psychology, and sociology; the most common subject categories for social network abstracts

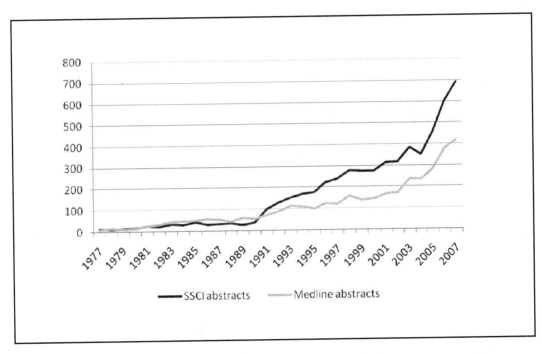

Figure 7.1. Temporal trend in the number of studies about social networks published annually

on SSCI were sociology, psychiatry, and public, environmental, and occupational health. Although fewer listings included the specific term "social network analysis" (99 and 313 in Medline and SSCI, respectively), these exhibited a similar increasing trend. In short, an enormous amount of research now considers network impacts on health.

PATHWAYS CONNECTING SOCIAL NETWORKS TO HEALTH

While individuals exert some control over their access to social support, sexual experiences, and diet, their choices are constrained and contingent on the behavior of others, on local norms, and in some cases on commercial distribution networks. Specific examples in the balance of this chapter highlight three ways that social networks are likely to affect health (see Figure 7.2).

First, an individual's health may be affected by connectivity to or isolation from others, and by the individual's position within a broader network (Figure 7.2a). Second, the qualities of the social network in which an individual is embedded may influence the individual's health-related behaviors (Figure 7.2b). And third, health-promoting or

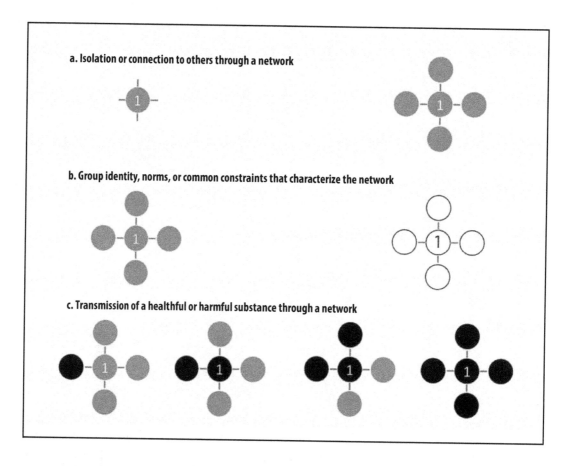

Figure 7.2. Three ways social networks can influence health

harmful substances may flow through networks in ways that protect health or increase risk (Figure 7.2c). Each potential pathway has important implications for the ways that research on social networks and health can be conducted.

These three ways that social networks affect health are shown schematically in Figure 7.2, using the convention that actors or nodes are connected by lines that represent social ties. Shading of the nodes can indicate actor characteristics, such as gender or disease status. Although in this simple representation relationships are either present or absent, more sophisticated characterizations of social ties may include information on their strength or direction. For example, if asked who individuals go to for advice, A may say she turns to B for advice, while B says she goes to C for advice. Such "directed ties" are usually displayed as an arrow rather than a line. In such directed networks, a double-headed arrow indicates a reciprocal relationship, such as where A turns to B for advice and B also turns to A. Similarly, lines could be assigned values to represent the strength of a relationship or the frequency of contact between two actors.

Suppose we want to characterize social networks in order to understand the health of a specific individual; such a focal individual is usually labeled "ego." Study participants may be asked about their social ties in order to generate "egocentric" social network data. Individuals with a social tie to ego are usually labeled ego's "alters." In some cases it may be sufficient to characterize only the immediate social environment of each study participant by asking that individual about alters of particular types, such as family, friends, sex partners, or other social ties. Those with no alters of a particular type would be classified as isolates without any further investigation. That they have zero such contacts would sufficiently characterize their position within the broader social network.

For certain health-related questions, the number of alters an ego has may be less important than who those alters are. The characteristics of alters may be collected by asking ego questions, but these characteristics may be reported with error or bias since ego may not know, or may not wish to report, the alters' characteristics or behavior patterns (Marsden 1990). Studies in which social environments are reported by a single focal individual provide an incomplete view of their social network but may be sufficient for some research questions, especially those in which ego's perceptions of alters' characteristics are seen to influence health-relevant behaviors.

Partial network designs not only collect information from index respondents about their alters but also subsequently recruit those alters into the study and ask about their relationships—a process that can be repeated as many times as desired. On the one hand, the value of such additional information must be weighed against the risks and costs involved in obtaining identifying information on alters (Klovdahl 2005). On the other hand, interviews with alters, or other corroboration of ego reports, may help address concerns about self-reported data. For example, an individual may falsely perceive their friends to have similar attitudes and beliefs (Baldassarri and Bearman 2007), while an interview with some or all of those friends would reveal new information about heterogeneity within the local network. Beyond confirming information between ego-alter pairs, partial network designs also provide some sense of the wider networks of interest. This extension of the network data collection can allow researchers to observe how individual characteristics, tie characteristics, and the patterning of those ties differ (or are similar) across the network as distance from the initially sampled respondents increases. In addition to the characteristics of an ego and its alters, we may also be interested in the arrangement of relationships among an interacting population of actors. Unfortunately, in the absence of population data, the position of an individual within their larger network must be estimated (Marsden 1990; Morris 2004).

A researcher may be interested in describing the overall network structure or in characterizing the social position of all individuals within a tangible social network.

Characterization of an entire network, while often desirable, is difficult and costly and may be impossible. The boundaries of such a sociocentric network may be clear-cut if the primary interest is in members of an organization or students within a school, but the relevant population boundaries are not always apparent. Sampling from a network may be an efficient strategy when measurement of the entire network is not feasible (Marsden 1990).

A range of structural characteristics may be relevant to the spread of pathogens, resources, or ideas through a population (Marsden 1990). Network structure can be characterized in terms of cohesion, distance, reachability, or density (Hawe, Webster, and Shiell 2004). Two actors within a network are said to have an indirect connection if there is a connected chain of actors leading from one to the other. Subgroups of a larger network may also be of interest, and are typically characterized as "components" (a group of actors connected to each other directly or indirectly) or "cliques" (a group of actors in which every pair of actors is directly connected). An individual's position within a network would commonly be characterized in terms of "centrality," which captures various estimates of network prominence or influence: for example, degree centrality is based simply on the number of direct ties, closeness centrality is based on the shortest distance to all directly and indirectly connected actors, and betweenness centrality is based on how many other actor pairs are indirectly connected through a given actor (Freeman 1979; Hawe, Webster, and Shiell 2004). The ability to measure the various types of network properties is constrained by the nature of network data collected and should be carefully considered in determining what approach to take in data collection (Marsden 1990; Morris 2004).

SOCIAL SUPPORT AND THE RISKS OF ISOLATION

Social isolation, the complete absence of social support, has been linked to psychological disturbances and increased mortality (Cacioppo et al. 2000; Cacioppo and Hawkley 2003; Hawkley and Cacioppo 2003; Seeman 1996). In fact, enforced social isolation in the form of exile or solitary confinement is occasionally used as a powerful punishment. Much of the health research on social support is based on samples of presumably independent individuals who report on the presence of relationships or the level of social support received. Other innovative approaches have considered ways that the health benefits of support might be deliberately cultivated or inadvertently undermined.

CONNECTIONS TO HEALTHFUL BEHAVIOR, STRESS BUFFERING, AND ILLNESS RECOVERY

Moderate amounts of social support, socially cohesive networks, and social contacts seem to be health enhancing across a range of health outcomes. In a large population of French employees, for example, an index of social integration was calculated based on several types of social ties (marital status/cohabitation, contacts with close friends and family, and affiliation with voluntary associations) and used to predict mortality (Berkman et al. 2004). A graded trend was seen across the four social integration groups, and for age-adjusted models, the mortality risk in the least integrated group was about three to four times higher than that of the most integrated group.

Some of the health benefits of social integration and social support may be mediated by healthful behavior patterns. Isolation, in contrast, has been linked to adolescent smoking (Ennett and Bauman 1994) and sedentary lifestyles (MacDougall et al. 1997). However, health behaviors do not fully explain the detrimental effects of social isolation (Cacioppo and Hawkley 2003; Hawkley and Cacioppo 2003).

Alternative explanations for the benefits of social support include a direct effect on the biological systems involved in repair and maintenance (S. Cohen 1988). Supportive social ties may also serve to reduce stress, or to counteract and buffer stressful or otherwise hazardous environments. The ways that individuals obtain support, resources, and ideas from the other people in their lives has been discussed as potentially buffering the harmful effects of stress (Wheaton 1985) or deprivation (Bobak et al. 1998). Such buffering may occur either because a harmful exposure is less harmful in the presence of social support, or because social support is mobilized in response to the harmful exposure (Wheaton 1985). These explanations are not mutually exclusive; social support may play a buffering role and also have a direct effect on health.

Social support may be particularly helpful to those who need to manage chronic health conditions (Gallant 2003) and is an important determinant of survival after a major health event such as a myocardial infarction (Mookadam and Arthur 2004). However, two careful attempts to improve social support for secondary prevention, the Enhancing Recovery in Coronary Heart Disease Patients (ENRICHD) trial and the Families in Recovery from Stroke Trial (FIRST), were unable to reduce mortality (Writing Committee 2003; Glass et al. 2004). Each of these trials randomized isolated or depressed individuals recovering from myocardial infarction or stroke to receive either standard care or additional psychosocial support. The intervention to address isolation developed for the ENRICHD trial employed cognitive behavior therapy techniques to address social skill deficits, cognitive factors contributing to low social support, and social outreach and network development (Writing Committee 2003). The FIRST intervention went a step further, by conducting the sessions at the participants' home and integrating participants' close alters, including family, friends, and caregivers, whenever possible (Glass et al. 2004). The psychosocial intervention did successfully decrease depression and isolation in the ENRICHD trial but did not significantly improve the primary health endpoints in either trial. These results raise the possibility that the beneficial effects of social support may accumulate across the life course such that new connections (or newly activated connections) late in life do not benefit otherwise isolated individuals. The trial findings also call into question the numerous observational studies of social support, which may have been biased by confounding or reverse causation.

RELATIONSHIP QUALITY AND SUPPORT SATISFACTION

The heterogeneity of relationships and interpersonal interactions may also help reconcile the observational and experimental literatures. One's interpretation of social support and evaluation of the supportive person may matter for determining behavior beyond the mere presence of social support. In a study by Tang and colleagues (2008), individuals with diabetes were asked about their experiences of positive and negative support, and these had different effects on diabetes self-care behaviors. Support perceived as negative was associated with poor medication adherence, while positive support predicted healthy physical activity and eating patterns. Future research may further elucidate the network characteristics, alter characteristics, behaviors, or communication patterns that contribute to the perception of support as positive or negative.

In a different setting, the potential benefits of so-called invisible support have been contrasted with the possible harms of receiving conspicuous help in a time of stress (Bolger, Zuckerman, and Kessler 2000). In a study of couples, Bolger and colleagues collected daily diary data on social support received and given during preparation for a difficult exam. Partners' reports of supportiveness were not necessarily associated with better health outcomes; only those who did not notice the support benefited from it. The authors suggest that acts of conspicuous support may increase distress by reminding stressed individuals about the source of stress, or a failure to adequately cope with the stress on their own. This contrary response to support may be evident even as the less salient acts of support reduce distress and depression. Notably, the advantages of invisible support could not be studied if only the support recipient were interviewed; obtaining information from an alter was necessary to reveal a nuanced effect of social support on short-term health and well-being.

SUPPORT FLOWS

Social support may provide benefits through specific and relatively intense interpersonal interactions, but the benefits may also accrue over time through a variety of more mundane experiences and exchanges. Supportive social networks can serve as a flexible infrastructure through which resources and services flow, though the benefits an individual receives may differ by relationship type or intensity, gender, and geographic proximity (Wellman and Wortley 1990).

Geographic variations in social connectedness, measured as social capital or social cohesion, may indicate differential potential for the exchange of goods and information, and these group-level measures have been correlated with geographic variations in health (Browning and Cagney 2002; Kawachi, Kennedy, and Wilkinson 1999; Sampson, Morenoff, and Gannon-Rowley 2002). In line with the literature on social support as a buffer against stress at the individual level, authors have suggested that the health effects of economic deprivation (D. Cohen, Farley, and Mason 2003) or inequalities (Wilkinson 1999) may be mediated or modified by the level of social cohesion within the local community.

Thus, social support may be thought of as the presence or abundance of interaction-based and role-based social connections, the quality of those connections, or the potential for such connections to serve as conduits for health-promoting resources and information. Although social isolation seems clearly linked to worse health, there is not a complete understanding of which types of social connections are most beneficial to health.

SEX: NUMBERS, NORMS, AND WEBS OF CONTACTS

Scholars of sexual health and behavior, along with public health practitioners, have played a central role in developing methods for gathering data on and analyzing interpersonal networks. Many network studies have focused on HIV/AIDS and other sexually transmitted infections (STIs) or on sexual and reproductive health in general. Given this research area's integral role in the history of social network analysis, investigations of sexual activity and networks are prime examples of the different conceptualizations of how networks can affect health.

PARTNER ACQUISITION

Researchers across the social and behavioral sciences have examined when people start engaging in sexual activity, as well as how often and with whom they continue to do so. This focus stems in part from the presumption that sexual activity itself is an important outcome for adolescent development (Laumann et al. 1994; Udry and Billy 1987), with researchers particularly interested in explaining differences in the timing of sexual debut across eras and societies (Cavanagh 2004; Mensch, Grant, and Blanc 2006; Zaba et al. 2004) or subcultures of societies (Browning, Leventhal, and Brooks-Gunn 2004, 2005). Sexual debut is also a predictor of individual life trajectories and behaviors, for example, delinquency (Armour and Haynie 2007); as well as of later sexual behavior, for example, condom use or "risky" sexual behaviors (Brückner and Bearman 2005; Uecker, Angotti, and Regnerus 2008). Individuals' involvement in a wide range of activities can substantially alter these trends, for example, research finds mixed effects of education attainment or religious participation on timing of sexual debut (DeRose, Dodoo, and Patil 2002; Rostosky, Regnerus, and Wright 2003).

The number of sexual partners individuals accumulate across their lifetime may also be important for health (Laumann et al. 1994), in part because it may be an important predictor of their risk of contracting an STI. For adult populations, the distribution of the number of partners individuals have can inform epidemic potential and inform intervention targets, for example, highlighting actors with numerous partners as targets for behavior change (Liljeros, Edling, and Nunes Amaral 2003; Liljeros, Edling, Stanley et al. 2003). Additionally, individuals who have multiple concurrent partnerships—overlapping in time—are epidemiologically important (Adimora et al. 2002; Adimora, Schoenbach, and Doherty 2007) especially for the spread of STIs (Morris and Kretzchmar 1997).

PATTERNING OF PARTNERSHIP SELECTION

Social networks play an important role in shaping the nature, timing, and extent of individuals' sexual behavior, along with the patterning of those relationships among potential partners. Peer groups frequently exhibit similarity or homophily across a range of sexual behavioral patterns, such that friends and other closely connected peers are alike in the timing of their sexual debuts (Cavanagh 2004; Kinsman et al. 1998), the number of lifetime sexual partners they accumulate (Santelli et al. 1998), and the types of behavior they engage in within those partnerships (Behrman, Kohler, and Watkins 2002; Morris et al. 1995).

In addition to controlling the extent and types of sexual behavior individuals engage in, social networks also encourage or discourage particular patterns of partner selection. Bearman and colleagues (2004) demonstrate that romantic relationships in a U.S. high school are relatively strictly patterned. Within studies of general relationship formation patterns, it is well known that local networks exhibit high probability of local closure—that is the notion of "a friend of a friend is a friend" (Holland and Leinhardt 1971). This finding applies across a wide range of tie types and is among the most common theoretical concepts and empirical findings cited in social network research. For sexual partnering the same pattern does not hold. Bearman and colleagues in fact demonstrate that local closure is virtually forbidden among romantic relationships. Specifically, they find that teens avoid partnering with their former partners' current partners' former partners (Bearman et al. 2004). This local relationship pattern has strong implications for overall network structure within the school, in this instance producing a partnership chain within the romantic network that directly or indirectly links 52 percent of those involved in a romantic relationship.

NETWORKS AS CONDUITS FOR THE SPREAD OF STIS

Studies of the spread and containment of infectious diseases have explicitly leaned on network insights and analytic strategies for decades, with STIs in particular receiving much of the attention. While questions about how often and with whom individuals have sex may scratch the surface of describing the potential spread of a pathogen within a population, fully mapping the structure of relevant contact networks provides an opportunity for more precise estimation. Sexual network structure both describes epidemic risk for entire populations (Helleringer and Kohler 2007; Morris 2007; Potterat et al. 1999, 2002; Woodhouse et al. 1994) and can improve estimations of the risk to individuals, based on their position within the network (Bell, Atkinson, and Carlson 1999; Rothenberg, Potterat et al. 1995).

Insights from network structure can usefully inform recommendations for preventing the spread of STIs. Individuals who have multiple sexual partners are a common prevention target, with the implication that reducing their numbers can substantially alter their personal risk of contracting or transmitting an STI. However, individual characteristics and simple social network summaries (e.g., number of partners) can misestimate a population's epidemic potential (Hamilton, Handcock, and Morris 2008; Handcock, Jones, and Morris 2003). Network structures with the same population distribution of partner numbers can plausibly generate a wide range of population-level epidemic outcomes (Handcock, Jones, and Morris 2003). Simulations show that reducing the number of high-risk actors in particular sets of conditions can actually *increase* population-level risk (Moody et al. 2007). In the best-case scenario, intervention efforts should make use of known network properties where available (Neaigus 1998; Ward 2007) or should target entire populations. One such example, for human papillomavirus (HPV) vaccination, is provided by Everett, Bearman, and Moody (2009).

FOOD CONSUMPTION AND BODY WEIGHT

Eating has a rich history as a social activity; in fact, the word "companion" is derived from the Latin words for "with bread." Meal sharing has been used to define social ties in some studies where other shared activities are of primary interest (Klovdahl et al. 1994). Shared meals mark moments of celebration and cement the social bonds within families, between romantic partners, and among friends. Lévi-Strauss (1969) discusses the roles of food and cuisine in delimiting culture and society, and modern groups and individuals also define and distinguish themselves by their culinary choices.

Nutritional epidemiologists and others interested in the health consequences of dietary intake face the difficulty of separating the role food plays in shaping social connections and identities from the more direct health effects of food. For example, although some research indicates that a vegetarian diet may be healthful (Appel 2003), vegetarians differ in other ways that may matter for their health. Back and Glasgow (1981) highlight the value vegetarians place on having other vegetarians in their social network, as well as the distinct socioeconomic correlates of a vegetarian lifestyle. They note also that discretionary food preferences like vegetarianism are more feasible for those with more resources: vegetarians tend to be middle class and from a metropolitan background. Thus a study reporting a health benefit of vegetarian diets or diet components may be confounded by class, geography, social context, or other aspects of the environment that influence both discretionary food choices and health.

While socially anchored, dietary patterns have long been linked to weight and health (Schwartz 1986). Excess calorie intake has become an increasingly prominent concern, and the production, distribution, and promotion of food have changed in ways that contribute to dietary excess and overweight (Nesse and Williams 1994; Nestle 2002; Pollan 2006). Socially enforced boundaries on when to eat have also been changing (Astrup et al. 2006). Against this backdrop of an obesigenic environment, social networks help explain some variations among individuals.

INTEGRATION VS. ISOLATION

Isolation from important peer networks can influence dietary patterns. Social isolation itself is associated with elevated hunger (Martin et al. 2004) and a higher risk of being overweight (Lemeshow et al. 2008). Isolation among the elderly, by contrast, is associated with insufficient food intake (Donini, Savina, and Cannella 2003). As with the evidence on individual isolation, the lack of collective efficacy within neighborhoods is also associated with obesity risk (D. Cohen et al. 2006). Social networks similarly affect other behavior patterns critical to energy balance and health, such as breastfeeding (Fonseca-Becker and Valente 2006; Wutich and McCarty 2008) and physical activity (McNeill, Kreuter, and Subramanian 2006).

RELATIONAL CONSTRAINTS ON FOOD CONSUMPTION

Predictable patterns of food selection within social networks provide avenues for understanding and changing patterns of excess caloric intake and dietary composition at a population level. In a partial network study by Feunekes and colleagues (1998), for example, fatty food intake was correlated within households but less so among friends. This study involved recruiting adolescents and their parents and then interviewing each of them plus their best friend, so that each mini-network included up to six individuals. These individuals were interviewed about their food consumption patterns, and correlation analyses were used to consider the similarities among pairs of individuals: matched friends, spouses, or parents and their children. For each pair type, the intake of some specific foods were correlated. In this study, friendship pairs, whether adult or adolescent, are likely to have similar intakes of snack foods and alcoholic beverages. Fat intake, however, was most correlated for child-parent pairs and between spouses. This suggests that adolescent friends share snacks and have influence on each other's overall calorie intake, while the consumption of fats is mainly determined by food-preparation decisions made at the household level. In this population, which was based in the Netherlands, a public health promotion effort aimed at reducing snacking among adolescents would likely be most successful if it includes friends and family, while an effort aimed at changing the types or amounts of fat consumed might do well to focus on the household food-preparation patterns. These conclusions suggest that the most relevant social leverage points for dietary interventions could depend on the type of dietary change sought.

Along with the social influence on intake of specific food items, there is evidence that body image responds to peer influence (Hutchinson and Rapee 2007). Such influence may contribute to both healthy and extreme weight-loss behavior. Paxton and colleagues (1999), for example, find that friendship cliques among adolescent girls are relatively homogenous with regard to body-image concern, eating behaviors, and the use of such extreme weight-loss strategies as fasting, crash dieting, or vomiting, and using laxatives, appetite suppressants, or diuretics. The role of social influence may deserve further consideration in the design of eating-disorder prevention programs, so that such interventions effectively discourage risky behaviors; previous evaluations suggest that effectiveness is limited when participants fail to identify with the information presented (Rosenvinge and Westjordet 2004), or identify with it so much that the risky behavior is inadvertently increased by the intervention (Mann et al. 1997).

As in much observational research, a study asserting that social influences cause dietary and weight changes may not be able to rule out the possibility that such an association is explained by reverse causation. Body weight may affect how future social interactions unfold (Janssen et al. 2004; Strauss and Pollack 2003), and the psychosocial effects of obesity among children are of particular concern (Wabitsch 2000). This does not exclude the possibility that social induction is also occurring and reinforcing the general tendency toward homophily within networks, but such a reciprocal relationship makes the effects difficult to disentangle. An individual who is both isolated and overweight may have gained weight in response to isolation, become isolated because of weight status, or had a combination of these two reinforcing processes. Likewise, friends who have similar weight status may have influenced each other to become more similar, chosen to be friends because of their similarity, or both.

CONTAGIOUS CONSUMPTION

Another recent study takes advantage of social network data collected incidentally within a long-term prospective cohort study and finds that weight changes are correlated within social networks over time (Christakis and Fowler 2007). At each study examination, participants identified their first-order relatives and at least one close friend, and many of these alters were themselves enrolled as study participants. During the study period, 1971 to 2003, U.S. obesity rates increased dramatically, and the study participants were also at risk for becoming obese (as defined by a body mass index of thirty or more). A direct social tie to an individual who became obese was associated with about a 45 percent increased risk of obesity. That is to say, if an alter recently became obese, then ego was likely to become obese in this same time period. If an alter's alter became obese, ego was about 20 percent more likely to become obese, and if an alter's alter's alter became obese, ego was about 10 percent more likely to become obese. Thus, the association remained significant up to three degrees of separation but decayed with social distance. The observed pattern also suggests that the type of social tie may determine the strength of the association, with spouse, same-sex sibling, and same-sex friend being especially influential. The authors consider three explanations for the observed associations: direct influence or "induction," shared behaviors, and bias due to confounding or selection. They interpret the observed pattern in which alter's sex mattered but geographic proximity did not to support the induction-based explanation of why obesity appears to flow through social networks. This suggests that changes in body size within one's social network may act through changing body-size norms and subsequent attention (or inattention) to dietary or physical activity choices.

Although we focus on networks of individuals, individuals' food choices are also constrained by the upstream networks within which food production and distribution take place (Sage 2003). A range of social policies and economic incentives influences the choices one faces at the market or in a restaurant (Nestle 2002; Pollan 2006). Further, the production networks may be important for their effect on the safety of the food supply. Cattle markets, for example, may be relevant to tracing the spread of illness among cattle (Ortiz-Pelaez et al. 2006; Robinson and Christley 2007) and its transmission to humans. Thus, consideration of social networks at multiple scales and across types of actors and ties may increase our understanding of the dietary choices individuals make.

USING NETWORKS TO PROMOTE HEALTH

In general, strategies to use what we know about social networks to improve health can be classified as efforts to change the network structure or as efforts to strategically use the network or leverage points within the network. A classic epidemiologic strategy might use contact tracing and quarantine to disrupt social contacts and halt the spread of illness through a network (Eichner 2003). Social network interventions can also be designed to enhance network activation and social integration (Israel 1985), although caution is warranted on the basis of the experience of social support intervention trials (e.g., Berkman et al. 2003; Glass et al. 2004). Another type of social network enhancement relevant to health could involve building coalitions of groups with a common interest in health promotion (Feinberg, Riggs, and Greenberg 2005; Schulz et al. 2005).

The strategic use of social networks to influence behavior change or the spread of information may involve targeting influential or otherwise strategically positioned individuals (Cross and Prusak 2002). Such social network strategies have been used in the implementation of interventions, for example, to encourage dietary change (Foley and Pollard 1998), smoking cessation (Valente et al. 2003), and STI prevention efforts (Amirkhanian et al. 2003). Social networks can also be used to find high-risk or difficult-to-recruit individuals for screening or targeted interventions (Salganik and Heckathorn 2004).

Another way that social network studies can support health promotion efforts is by explaining how population-level health changes occur. Changes to the structure of the social network, or the level of social support, could mediate some public health interventions, and understanding this may help justify strategic improvements or draw attention to other considerations. As an example, Fuemmeler and colleagues (2006) evaluated a church-based intervention to promote the consumption of fruits and vegetables and found that it works in part through increased social support and self-efficacy. Some researchers have also suggested that improvements to the physical environment could be mediated by social network changes (D. Cohen, Inagami, and Finch 2008), and these hypotheses warrant further testing. If social network changes mediate the effects of health promotion interventions, the health benefits may be contingent on a particular process of implementation that does not undermine the existing social networks (Fullilove 2004).

COMMON CHALLENGES AND CONVERGENT MECHANISMS

Our examination of how networks affect social support, sex, and food consumption and subsequent health raises a number of common research challenges. While each of these is important to an individual's health, the effects are difficult to isolate. Social ties form and dissolve in ways that respond to health or health behaviors, even as the ties themselves influence health. Endogeneity and complexity are commonplace in social network research, perhaps even more than in other observational research. Yet face validity makes the possibility of strong social induction difficult to dismiss: we all feel how people influence us, and that we can attempt to influence them in turn.

While social network data have sometimes been measured using individual questionnaires, any single person has a limited ability to report on the full social context that may be relevant to their health. In their work with social networks, Bolger, Zuckerman, and Kessler (2000) highlight a situation in which the discordance between reports of social support is itself informative, a finding that would have been overlooked in a study reliant upon the reports of only one member of the dyad. Likewise, studies of STIs have indicated that the number of sex ties one has is less important for an ego's contracting an STI than is the number of sex ties their alters have, or the temporal ordering or concurrency of such relationships (Morris 2007). Finally, in considering the social network influences on weight, Christakis and Fowler (2007) found that direct ties are the most influential, but that persons two and three degrees of separation away may also be important. Thus, there is reason to believe that a complete picture of the health-relevant social environment can best be attained in studies with multiple informants, despite the challenges inherent in doing so (Klovdahl 2005).

Studies of social networks are particularly valuable for the topics we have highlighted because individuals have limited ability to change the level of social support they receive, the amount and type of sex they have, and the foods they consume. Our choices are contingent on the choices of others around us, and on the broader cultural contexts and production networks that shape our options.

Social connections are cemented through shared conversations, sex acts, and meals, so while each come with risks, they also deliver a benefit to individuals who thus avoid isolation (Berkman and Syme 1979), and the meaning and importance of such activities may overshadow their health implications. Studies have documented a possible biological basis for the perceived benefits of these social behaviors and of avoiding isolation (Cacioppo and Hawkley 2003). The neuroendocrine consequences of social connections, sex, and food consumption are noteworthy, with oxytocin and dopamine apparently playing critical roles (Spanagel and Weiss 1999).

Even if beneficial effects overlap, the nature of the risks can vary greatly. Low levels of social support may leave a person vulnerable to chronic stress or sudden hardship. While the transmission of pathogens across networks has been particularly salient in the literature on sex ties and sexual networks, the gradual accumulation of harms has been the focus of the research on nutritional excess.

LINKING TO OTHER CONTEXTS FOR HEALTH BEHAVIOR

While most sampling and statistical analysis techniques are based on studying independent samples from a population, individuals are not autonomous or randomly affiliated. Social networks tend to be homophilous (McPherson, Smith-Lovin, and

Cook 2001). As a result, individuals sampled from a small population should not necessarily be assumed to be "independent" in the statistical sense—characteristics will be more highly correlated for socially connected individuals. But social networks overlap importantly with, and are complemented by, other types of context. Since further information on the surrounding social environment may be crucial for understanding an individual's access to resources and exposures to risk, we briefly consider these other contexts.

Institutional settings such as schools or workplaces define groups with potentially similar risks and exposures, and provide opportunities for health promotion interventions. These can also serve as settings for social network studies, as was the case for the Add Health study (Bearman, Jones, and Udry 1997). Characteristics of the physical environment or of geographically defined communities also determine exposure to risk and access to resources. The spatial proximity of individuals influences the probability of a social connection between them and may also affect opportunities for shared activities. A parallel between associations across spatial and social "distance" was explicitly drawn by Christakis and Fowler in their paper on obesity (2007). In fact, the social and physical environments of geographic areas may interact to determine the health of area residents. The degree to which physical environments predict obesity, for example, varies with social context (Lovasi et al. 2009). Several studies have explicitly considered how social networks overlap with physical or geographic settings to predict behavior and the spread of illness, but the data and analytic methods to capture these multiple layers of context simultaneously are not widely available (Schensul, Levy, and Disch 2003; Wylie, Cabral, and Jolly 2005; Wylie, Shah, and Jolly 2007).

Social network analysis is one of an interrelated set of tools that are useful for understanding the contexts in which individuals live. To capture spatial or other hierarchical patterns, geographic information systems, cluster analysis, generalized estimating equations, and multilevel modeling can be employed, as each of these is useful for accommodating the similarities among individuals with a shared group identity or physical space (Luke 2005).

Although social networks are only one of the contexts that shape health and health behavior, their effects are pervasive. The study of social networks is especially complex because of the need to protect human subjects and their confidentiality and the potential for bidirectional causation, that is, social networks affect health and health in turn affects social networks. The need to consider social networks at multiple scales—from interpersonal to organizational—further complicates the picture. Nonetheless, the potential for increased understanding and enhanced health promotion makes the incorporation of social networks into health research worthwhile.

REFERENCES

Adimora, Adaora A., Victor J. Schoenbach, Dana M. Bonas, Francis E. A. Martinson, Kathryn H. Donaldson, and Tonya R. Stancil. 2002. "Concurrent Sexual Partnerships among Women in the United States." *Epidemiology* 13(3): 320–327.

Adimora, Adaora A., Victor J. Schoenbach, and Irene A. Doherty. 2007. "Concurrent Sexual Partnerships among Men in the United States." *American Journal of Public Health* 97(12): 2230–237.

Amirkhanian, Yuri A., Jeffrey A. Kelly, Elena Kabakchieva, Timothy L. McAuliffe, and Sylvia Vassileva. 2003. "Evaluation of a Social Network HIV Prevention Intervention Program for Young Men Who Have Sex with Men in Russia and Bulgaria." *Aids Education and Prevention* 15(3): 205–20.

Appel, Lawrence J. 2003. "Lifestyle Modification as a Means to Prevent and Treat High Blood Pressure." *Journal of the American Society of Nephrology* 14, 7 Suppl. 2: S99–102.

Armour, Stacy, and Dana L. Haynie. 2007. "Adolescent Sexual Debut and Later Delinquency." *Journal of Youth and Adolescence* 36(2): 141–52.

Astrup, A., M. W. Bovy, K. Nackenhorst, and A. E. Popova. 2006. "Food for Thought or Thought for Food? A Stakeholder Dialogue around the Role of the Snacking Industry in Addressing the Obesity Epidemic." *Obesity Reviews* 7(3): 303–12.

Back, Kurt W., and Margaret Glasgow. 1981. "Social Networks and Psychological Conditions in Diet Preferences: Gourmets and Vegetarians." *Basic and Applied Social Psychology* 2(1): 1–9.

Baldassarri, Delia, and Peter Bearman. 2007. "Dynamics of Political Polarization." *American Sociological Review* 72(5): 784.

Bearman, Peter S., Jo Jones, and J. Richard Udry. 1997. "The National Longitudinal Study of Adolescent Health: Research Design." Chapel Hill: University of North Carolina at Chapel Hill, Carolina Population Center.

Bearman, Peter S., James Moody, and Katherine Stovel. 2004. "Chains of Affection: The Structure of Adolescent Romantic and Sexual Networks." *American Journal of Sociology* 110(1): 44–91.

Bearman, Peter S., and Paolo Parigi. 2004. "Cloning Headless Frogs and Other Important Matters: Conversation Topics and Network Structure." *Social Forces* 83(2): 535–57.

Behrman, Jere R., Hans-Peter Kohler, and Susan Cotts Watkins. 2002. "Social Networks and Changes in Contraceptive Use over Time: Evidence from a Longitudinal Study in Rural Kenya." *Demography* 39(4): 713–38.

Bell, David C., John S. Atkinson, and Jerry W. Carlson. 1999. "Centrality Measures for Disease Transmission Networks." *Social Networks* 21(1): 1–21.

Berkman, L. F., J. Blumenthal, M. Burg, R. M. Carney, D. Catellier, M. J. Cowan, S. M. Czajkowski, R. DeBusk, J. Hosking, A. Jaffe, P. G. Kaufmann, P. Mitchell, J. Norman, L. H. Powell, J. M. Raczynski, and N. Schneiderman. 2003. "Effects of Treating Depression and Low Perceived Social Support on Clinical Events after Myocardial Infarction: The Enhancing Recovery in Coronary Heart Disease Patients (ENRICHD) Randomized Trial." *Journal of the American Medical Association* 289:3106–16.

Berkman, Lisa F., Maria Melchior, Jean-François Chastang, Isabelle Niedhammer, Annette Leclerc, and Marcel Goldberg. 2004. "Social Integration and Mortality: A Prospective Study of French Employees of Electricity of France-Gas of France: The GAZEL Cohort." *American Journal of Epidemiology* 159(2): 167–74.

Berkman, Lisa F., and S. Leonard Syme. 1979. "Social Networks, Host Resistance, and Mortality: A Nine-Year Follow-Up Study of Alameda County Residents." *American Journal of Epidemiology* 109(2): 186–204.

Bobak, Martin, Hynek Pikhart, Clyde Hertzman, Richard Rose, and Michael Marmot. 1998. "Socioeconomic Factors, Perceived Control and Self-Reported Health in Russia. A Cross-Sectional Survey." *Social Science and Medicine* 47(2): 269–79.

Bolger, Niall, Adam Zuckerman, and Ronald C. Kessler. 2000. "Invisible Support and Adjustment to Stress." *Journal of Personality and Social Psychology* 79(6): 953–61.

Borgatti, Steve. 2008. "Network Reasoning: Keynote Address." Paper presented at Sunbelt XXVIII, annual meetings of the International Network for Social Network Analysis, St. Petersburg, Fla.

Browning, Christopher R., and Kathleen A. Cagney. 2002. "Neighborhood Structural Disadvantage, Collective Efficacy, and Self-Rated Physical Health in an Urban Setting." *Journal of Health and Social Behavior* 43(4): 383–99.

Browning, Christopher R., Tama Leventhal, and Jeanne Brooks-Gunn. 2004. "Neighborhood Context and Racial Differences in Early Adolescent Sexual Activity." *Demography* 41(4): 697–720.

———. 2005. "Sexual Initiation in Early Adolescence: The Nexus of Parental and Community Control." *American Sociological Review* 70(5): 758–78.

Brückner, Hannah, and Peter Bearman. 2005. "After the Promise: The STD Consequences of Adolescent Virginity Pledges." *Journal of Adolescent Health* 36(4): 271–78.

Cacioppo, John T., John M. Ernst, Mary H. Burleson, Martha K. McClintock, William B. Malarkey, Louise C. Hawkley, Ray B. Kowalewski, Alisa Paulsen, J. Allan Hobson, Kenneth Hugdahl, David Spiegel, and Gary G. Berntson. 2000. "Lonely Traits and Concomitant Physiological Processes: The MacArthur Social Neuroscience Studies." *International Journal of Psychophysiology* 35(2–3): 143–54.

Cacioppo, John T., and Louise C. Hawkley. 2003. "Social Isolation and Health, with an Emphasis on Underlying Mechanisms." *Perspectives in Biology and Medicine* 46, 3 Suppl.: S39–52.

Cavanagh, Shannon E. 2004. "The Sexual Debut of Girls in Early Adolescence: The Intersection of Race, Pubertal Timing, and Friendship Group Characteristics." *Journal of Research on Adolescence* 14(3): 285–312.

Christakis, Nicholas A., and James H. Fowler. 2007. "The Spread of Obesity in a Large Social Network over 32 Years." *New England Journal of Medicine* 357(4): 370–79.

Cohen, Deborah A., Thomas A. Farley, and Karen Mason. 2003. "Why Is Poverty Unhealthy? Social and Physical Mediators." *Social Science and Medicine* 57(9): 1631–41.

Cohen, Deborah A., Brian K. Finch, Aimee Bower, and Narayan Sastry. 2006. "Collective Efficacy and Obesity: The Potential Influence of Social Factors on Health." *Social Science and Medicine* 62(3): 769–78.

Cohen, Deborah A., Sanae Inagami, and Brian K. Finch. 2008. "The Built Environment and Collective Efficacy." *Health and Place* 14(2): 198–208.

Cohen, Sheldon. 1988. "Psychosocial Models of the Role of Social Support in the Etiology of Physical Disease." *Health Psychology* 7(3): 269–97.

Cross, Rob, and Laurence Prusak. 2002. "The People Who Make Organizations Go—Or Stop." *Harvard Business Review* 80(6): 104–12.

DeRose, Laurie F., F. Nii-Amoo Dodoo, and Vrushali Patil. 2002. "Schooling and Attitudes on Reproductive-Related Behavior in Ghana." *International Journal of Sociology of the Family* 30(1): 50–65.

Donini, Lorenzo M., Claudia Savina, and Carlo Cannella. 2003. "Eating Habits and Appetite Control in the Elderly: The Anorexia of Aging." *International Psychogeriatrics* 15(1): 73–87.

Eichner, Martin. 2003. "Case Isolation and Contact Tracing Can Prevent the Spread of Smallpox." *American Journal of Epidemiology* 158(2): 118.

Ennett, Susan T., and Karl E. Bauman. 1994. "The Contribution of Influence and Selection to Adolescent Peer Group Homogeneity: The Case of Adolescent Cigarette Smoking." *Journal of Personality and Social Psychology* 67(4): 653–63.

Everett, Katie, Peter Bearman, and James Moody. 2009. "Chain of Infection: A Sexual-Network-Based Model Evaluating the Impact of Human Papilloma Virus Vaccination on Infection Prevalence in an Adolescent Population." Unpublished paper.

Feinberg, Mark E., Nathaniel R. Riggs, and Mark T. Greenberg. 2005. "Social Networks and Community Prevention Coalitions." *Journal of Primary Prevention* 26(4): 279–98.

Feunekes, Gerda I. J., Cees de Graaf, Saskia Meyboom, and Wija A. van Staveren. 1998. "Food Choice and Fat Intake of Adolescents and Adults: Associations of Intakes within Social Networks." *Preventive Medicine* 27(5): 645–56.

Foley, Ruth M., and Christina M. Pollard. 1998. "Food Cent$: Implementing and Evaluating a Nutrition Education Project Focusing on Value for Money." *Australian and New Zealand Journal of Public Health* 22(4): 494–501.

Fonseca-Becker, Fannie, and Thomas W. Valente. 2006. "Promoting Breastfeeding in Bolivia: Do Social Networks Add to the Predictive Value of Traditional Socioeconomic Characteristics?" *Journal of Health, Population and Nutrition* 24(1): 71–80.

Freeman, Linton C. 1979. "Centrality in Social Networks: Conceptual Clarification." *Social Networks* 1(3): 215–39.

Fuemmeler, Bernard F., Louise C. Mâsse, Amy L. Yaroch, Ken Resnicow, Marci Kramish Campbell, Carol Carr, Terry Wang, and Alexis Williams. 2006. "Psychosocial Mediation of Fruit and Vegetable Consumption in the Body and Soul Effectiveness Trial." *Health Psychology* 25(4): 474–83.

Fullilove, Mindy T. 2004. *Root Shock: How Tearing Up City Neighborhoods Hurts America, and What We Can Do About It.* New York: Ballantine Books.

Gallant, Mary P. 2003. "The Influence of Social Support on Chronic Illness Self-Management: A Review and Directions for Research." *Health Education and Behavior* 30(2): 170–95.

Glass, Thomas A., Lisa F. Berkman, Elizabeth F. Hiltunen, Karen Furie, Maria M. Glymour, Marta E. Fay, and James Ware. 2004. "The Families in Recovery from Stroke Trial (FIRST): Primary Study Results." *Psychosomatic Medicine* 66(6): 889–97.

Hamilton, Deven T., Mark S. Handcock, and Martina Morris. 2008. "Degree Distributions in Sexual Networks: A Framework for Evaluating Evidence." *Sexually Transmitted Diseases* 35(1): 30–40.

Handcock, Mark S., James Holland Jones, and Martina Morris. 2003. "On 'Sexual Contacts and Epidemic Thresholds,' Models and Inference for Sexual Partnership Distributions." CSS Working Paper No. 31. Seattle: University of Washington, Center for Statistics and the Social Sciences.

Hawe, Penelope, Cynthia Webster, and Alan Shiell. 2004. "A Glossary of Terms for Navigating the Field of Social Network Analysis." *Journal of Epidemiology and Community Health* 58(12): 971–75.

Hawkley, Louise C., and John T. Cacioppo. 2003. "Loneliness and Pathways to Disease." *Brain Behavior and Immunity* 17, 1 Suppl.: S98–105.

Helleringer, Stephane, and Hans-Peter Kohler. 2007. "Sexual Network Structure and the Spread of HIV in Africa: Evidence from Likoma Island, Malawi." *AIDS* 21(17): 2323–32.

Holland, Paul W., and Samuel Leinhardt. 1971. "Transitivity in Structural Models of Small Groups." *Comparative Groups Studies* 2(2): 107–24.

Hutchinson, Delyse M., and Ronald M. Rapee. 2007. "Do Friends Share Similar Body Image and Eating Problems? The Role of Social Networks and Peer Influences in Early Adolescence." *Behavioral Research and Therapy* 45(7): 1557–77.

Israel, Barbara A. 1985. "Social Networks and Social Support: Implications for Natural Helper and Community Level Interventions." *Health Education and Behavior* 12(1): 65.

Janssen, Ian, Wendy M. Craig, William F. Boyce, and William Pickett. 2004. "Associations between Overweight and Obesity with Bullying Behaviors in School-Aged Children." *Pediatrics* 113(5): 1187–94.

Kawachi, Ichiro, Bruce P. Kennedy, and Richard G. Wilkinson. 1999. "Crime: Social Disorganization and Relative Deprivation." *Social Science and Medicine* 48(6): 719–31.

Kinsman, Sara B., Daniel Romer, Frank F. Furstenberg, and Donald F. Schwarz. 1998. "Early Sexual Initiation: The Role of Peer Norms." *Pediatrics* 102(5): 1185–92.

Klovdahl, Alden S. 2005. "Social Network Research and Human Subjects Protection: Towards More Effective Infectious Disease Control." *Social Networks* 27(2): 119–37.

Klovdahl, Alden S., John J. Potterat, Donald E. Woodhouse, John B. Muth, Stephen Q. Muth, and William W. Darrow. 1994. "Social Networks and Infectious Disease: The Colorado Springs Study." *Social Science and Medicine* 38(1): 79–88.

Laumann, Edward O., John H. Gagnon, Robert T. Michael, and Stuart Michaels. 1994. *The Social Organization of Sexuality: Sexual Practices in the United States.* Chicago: University of Chicago Press.

Lemeshow, Adina R., Laurie Fisher, Elizabeth Goodman, Ichiro Kawachi, Catherine S. Berkey, and Graham A. Colditz. 2008. "Subjective Social Status in the School and Change in Adiposity in Female Adolescents: Findings from a Prospective Cohort Study." *Archives of Pediatric and Adolescent Medicine* 162(1): 23–28.

Lévi-Strauss, Claude. 1969. *The Raw and the Cooked.* New York: Harper and Row.

Levy, Judith A., and Bernice A. Pescosolido, eds. 2002. *Social Networks and Health*. Vol. 8 of *Advances in Medical Sociology*. New York: Elsevier Science.

Liljeros, Fredrik, Christofer R. Edling, and Luis A. Nunes Amaral. 2003. "Sexual Networks: Implications for the Transmission of Sexually Transmitted Infections." *Microbes and Infection* 5(2): 189–96.

Liljeros, Fredrik, Christofer R. Edling, H. Eugene Stanley, Y. Åberg, and Luis A. Nunes Amaral. 2003. "Distributions of Number of Sexual Partnerships Have Power Law Decaying Tails and Finite Variance." arXiv:cond-mat/0305528v1.

Lovasi, Gina S., Kathryn M. Neckerman, James W. Quinn, Christopher C. Weiss, and Andrew Rundle. 2009. "Individual or Neighborhood Disadvantage Modifies the Association between Neighborhood Walkability and Body Mass Index." *American Journal of Public Health* 99(2): 279–84.

Luke, Douglas A. 2005. "Getting the Big Picture in Community Science: Methods That Capture Context." *American Journal of Community Psychology* 35(3–4): 185–200.

Luke, Douglas A., and Jenine K. Harris. 2007. "Network Analysis in Public Health: History, Methods and Applications." *Annual Review of Public Health* 28:69–93.

MacDougall, Colin, Richard Cooke, Neville Owen, Kristyn Willson, and Adrian Bauman. 1997. "Relating Physical Activity to Health Status, Social Connections and Community Facilities." *Australian and New Zealand Journal of Public Health* 21(6): 631–37.

Mann, Traci, Susuan Nolen-Hoeksema, Karen Huang, Debora Burgard, Alexi Wright, and Kaaren Hanson. 1997. "Are Two Interventions Worse Than None? Joint Primary and Secondary Prevention of Eating Disorders in College Females." *Health Psychology* 16(3): 215–25.

Marsden, Peter V. 1987. "Core Discussion Networks of Americans." *American Sociological Review* 52(1): 122–31.

———. 1990. "Network Data and Measurement." *Annual Review of Sociology* 16(1): 435–63.

Martin, Katie S., Beatrice L. Rogers, John T. Cook, and Hugh M. Joseph. 2004. "Social Capital Is Associated with Decreased Risk of Hunger." *Social Science and Medicine* 58(12): 2645.

McNeill, Lorna H., Matthew W. Kreuter, and S. V. Subramanian. 2006. "Social Environment and Physical Activity: A Review of Concepts and Evidence." *Social Science and Medicine* 63(4): 1011–22.

McPherson, Miller, Lynn Smith-Lovin, and James M. Cook. 2001. "Birds of a Feather: Homophily in Social Networks." *Annual Reviews in Sociology* 27(1): 415–44.

McPherson, Miller, Lynn Smith-Lovin, and Matthews E. Brashears. 2006. "Social Isolation in America: Changes in Core Discussion Networks over Two Decades." *American Sociological Review* 71(3): 353–75.

Mensch, Barbara S., Monica J. Grant, and Ann K. Blanc. 2006. "The Changing Context of Sexual Initiation in Sub-Saharan Africa." *Population and Development Review* 32(4): 699–727.

Moody, James, Martina Morris, jimi adams, and Mark Handcock. 2007. "Epidemic Potential in Low Degree Networks." Word document. Author files.

Mookadam, Farouk, and Heather M. Arthur. 2004. "Social Support and Its Relationship to Morbidity and Mortality after Acute Myocardial Infarction: Systematic Overview." *Archives of Internal Medicine* 164(14): 1514–18.

Morris, Martina. 2004. *Network Epidemiology: A Handbook for Survey Design and Data Collection*. London: Oxford University Press.

———. 2007. "Local Acts, Global Consequences: Networks and the Spread of HIV." Paper presented at NIH Director's Wednesday Afternooon Lecture Series. Washington, D.C. csde.washington.edu/news/spotlight/docs/wals042507.rm.

Morris, Martina, and Mirjam Kretzchmar. 1997. "Concurrent Partnerships and the Spread of HIV." *AIDS* 11(5): 641–48.

Morris, Martina, Anthony Pramualratana, Chai Podhisita, and Maria J. Wawer. 1995. "The Relational Determinants of Condom Use with Commercial Sex Partners in Thailand." *AIDS* 9(5): 507–15.

Neaigus, Alan. 1998. "The Network Approach and Interventions to Prevent HIV among Injection Drug Users." *Public Health Reports* 113, 1 Suppl.: 140–50.

Nesse, Randolph M., and George C. Williams. 1994. "Diseases of Civilization." In *Why We Get Sick: The New Science of Darwinian Medicine*, 143–57. New York: Random House.

Nestle, Marion. 2002. *Food Politics: How the Food Industry Influences Nutrition and Health*. Los Angeles: University of California Press.

Ortiz-Pelaez, A., D. U. Pfeiffer, R. J. Soares-Magalhaes, and F. J. Guitian. 2006. "Use of Social Network Analysis to Characterize the Pattern of Animal Movements in the Initial Phases of the 2001 Foot and Mouth Disease (FMD) Epidemic in the UK." *Preventive Veterinary Medicine* 76(1–2): 40–55.

Paxton, Susan J., Helena K. Schutz, Eleanor H. Wertheim, and Sharry L. Muir. 1999. "Friendship Clique and Peer Influences on Body Image Concerns, Dietary Restraint, Extreme Weight-Loss Behaviors, and Binge Eating in Adolescent Girls." *Journal of Abnormal Psychology* 108(2): 255–66.

Pollan, Michael. 2006. *The Omnivore's Dilemma: A Natural History of Four Meals*. New York: Penguin Press.

Potterat, John J., Helen Zimmerman-Rogers, Stephen Q. Muth, Richard B. Rothenberg, David L. Green, Jerry E. Taylor, Mandy S. Bonney, and Helen A. White. 1999. "Chlamydia Transmission: Concurrency, Reproduction Number and the Epidemic Trajectory." *American Journal of Epidemiology* 150:1331–39.

Potterat, John J., Richard B. Rothenberg, Helen Zimmerman-Rogers, David L. Green, Jerry E. Taylor, Mandy S. Bonney, and Helen A. White. 2002. "Sexual Network Structure as an Indicator of Epidemic Phase." *Sexually Transmitted Infections* 78: i152–58.

Robinson, S. E., and R. M. Christley. 2007. "Exploring the Role of Auction Markets in Cattle Movements within Great Britain." *Preventive Veterinary Medicine* 81(1–3): 21–37.

Rosenvinge, Jan H., and Marthe O. Westjordet. 2004. "Is Information about Eating Disorders Experienced as Harmful? A Consumer Perspective on Primary Prevention." *Eating Disorders* 12(1): 11–20.

Rostosky, Sharon S., Mark D. Regnerus, and Margaret L. C. Wright. 2003. "Coital Debut: The Role of Religiosity and Sex Attitudes in the Add Health Survey." *Journal of Sex Research* 40(4): 358–67.

Rothenberg, Richard B., John J. Potterat, Donald E. Woodhouse, William W. Darrow, Stephen Q. Muth, and Alden S. Klovdahl. 1995. "Choosing a Centrality Measure: Epidemiologic Correlates in the Colorado Springs Study of Social Networks." *Social Networks: Special Edition on Social Networks and Infectious Disease: HIV/AIDS* 17:273–97.

Rothenberg, Richard B., Donald E. Woodhouse, John J. Potterat, Stephen Q. Muth, William W. Darrow, and Alden S. Klovdahl. 1995. "Social Networks in Disease Transmission: The Colorado Springs Study." *NIDA Research Monographs* 151:3–19.

Sage, Colin. 2003. "Social Embeddedness and Relations of Regard: Alternative 'Good Food' Networks in South-West Ireland." *Journal of Rural Studies* 19(1): 47–60.

Salganik, Matthew J., and Douglas D. Heckathorn. 2004. "Sampling and Estimation in Hidden Populations using Respondent Driven Sampling." *Sociological Methodology* 34:193–240.

Sampson, Robert J., Jeffrey D. Morenoff, and Thomas Gannon-Rowley. 2002. "Assessing 'Neighborhood Effects': Social Processes and New Directions in Research." *Annual Review of Sociology* 28:443–78.

Santelli, John S., Nancy D. Brener, Richard Lowry, Amita Bhatt, and Laurie S. Zabin. 1998. "Multiple Sexual Partners among U.S. Adolescents and Young Adults." *Family Planning Perspectives* 30(6): 271–75.

Schensul, Jean J., Judith A. Levy, and William B. Disch. 2003. "Individual, Contextual, and Social Network Factors Affecting Exposure to HIV/AIDS Risk among Older Residents Living in Low-Income Senior Housing Complexes." *Journal of Acquired Immune Deficiency Syndrome* 33, 2 Suppl.: S138–52.

Schulz, Amy J., Srimathi Kannan, J. Timothy Dvonch, Barbara A. Israel, Alex Allen III, Sherman A. James, James S. House, and James Lepkowski. 2005. "Social and Physical Environments and Disparities in Risk for Cardiovascular Disease: The Healthy Environments Partnership Conceptual Model." *Environmental Health Perspectives* 113(12): 1817–25.

Schwartz, Hillel. 1986. *Never Satisfied: A Cultural History of Diets, Fantasies, and Fat*. New York: Doubleday.

Seeman, Teresa E. 1996. "Social Ties and Health: The Benefits of Social Integration." *Annals of Epidemiology* 6(5): 442–51.

Smith, Kirsten P., and Nicholas A. Christakis. 2008. "Social Networks and Health." *Annual Review of Sociology* 34(1): 405–29.

Spanagel, Rainer, and F. Weiss. 1999. "The Dopamine Hypothesis of Reward: Past and Current Status." *Trends in Neuroscience* 22(11): 521–27.

Strauss, Richard S., and Harold A. Pollack. 2003. "Social Marginalization of Overweight Children." *Archives of Pediatric and Adolescent Medicine* 157(8): 746–52.

Tang, Tricia S., Morton B. Brown, Martha M. Funnell, and Robert M. Anderson. 2008. "Social Support, Quality of Life, and Self-Care Behaviors among African Americans with Type 2 Diabetes." *Diabetes Educator* 34(2): 266–76.

Udry, J. Richard, and John O. G. Billy. 1987. "Initiation of Coitus in Early Adolescence." *American Sociological Review* 52(6): 841–55.

Uecker, Jeremy E., Nicole Angotti, and Mark D. Regnerus. 2008. "Going Most of the Way: 'Technical Virginity' among American Adolescents." *Social Science Research* 37:1200–1215.

Valente, Thomas W., Beth R. Hoffman, Annamara Ritt-Olson, Kara Lichtman, and C. Anderson Johnson. 2003. "Effects of a Social-Network Method for Group Assignment Strategies on Peer-Led Tobacco Prevention Programs in Schools." *American Journal of Public Health* 93(11): 1837–43.

Wabitsch, Martin. 2000. "Overweight and Obesity in European Children: Definition and Diagnostic Procedures, Risk Factors and Consequences for Later Health Outcome." *European Journal of Pediatrics* 159(1 Supplement): S8–13.

Ward, Helen. 2007. "Prevention Strategies for Sexually Transmitted Infections: Importance of Sexual Network Structure and Epidemic Phase." *Sexually Transmitted Infections* 83: i43–49.

Wellman, Barry, and Scot Wortley. 1990. "Different Strokes from Different Folks: Community Ties and Social Support." *American Journal of Sociology* 96(3): 558.

Wheaton, Blair. 1985. "Models for the Stress-Buffering Functions of Coping Resources." *Journal of Health and Social Behavior* 26(4): 352–64.

Wilkinson, Richard G. 1999. "Health, Hierarchy, and Social Anxiety." *Annals of the New York Academy of Science* 896:48–63.

Woodhouse, Donald E., Richard B. Rothenberg, John J. Potterat, William W. Darrow, Stephen Q. Muth, Alden S. Klovdahl, Helen P. Zimmerman, Helen L. Rogers, Tammy S. Maldonado, John B. Muth, and Judith U. Reynolds. 1994. "Mapping a Social Network of Heterosexuals at High Risk for HIV infection." *AIDS* 8(9): 1331–36.

Writing Committee for the ENRICHD Investigators. 2003. "Effects of Treating Depression and Low Perceived Social Support on Clinical Events after Myocardial Infarction: The Enhancing Recovery in Coronary Heart Disease Patients (ENRICHD) Randomized Trial." *Journal of the American Medical Association* 289(23): 3106–16.

Wutich, Amber, and Christopher McCarty. 2008. "Social Networks and Infant Feeding in Oaxaca, Mexico." *Maternal and Child Nutrition* 4(2): 15.

Wylie, John L., Teresa Cabral, and Ann M. Jolly. 2005. "Identification of Networks of Sexually Transmitted Infection: A Molecular, Geographic, and Social Network Analysis." *Journal of Infectious Diseases* 191(6): 899–906.

Wylie, John L., Lena Shah, and Ann Jolly. 2007. "Incorporating Geographic Settings into a Social Network Analysis of Injection Drug Use and Bloodborne Pathogen Prevalence." *Health and Place* 13(3): 617–28.

Zaba, Basia, Elizabeth Pisani, E. Slaymaker, and J. Ties Boerma. 2004. "Age at First Sex: Understanding Recent Trends in African Demographic Surveys." *Sexually Transmitted Infections* 80: ii28–35.

CHAPTER 8

CONCERTED CULTIVATION AND THE ACCOMPLISHMENT OF NATURAL GROWTH

As you read this selection, consider the following questions.

QUESTIONS TO CONSIDER

1 Note two ways the parenting styles of middle-class parents differ from each other in how they raise and interact with their children.

2 What research methods were used for this study? What were some of the costs and benefits of it?

3 Think about how you grew up. How did your parent (or parents) interact with you? Does your experience fit the model Lareau presents here?

4 What is the author's main point?

KEY TERMS

concerted cultivation
natural growth

CONCERTED CULTIVATION AND THE ACCOMPLISHMENT OF NATURAL GROWTH

BY ANNETTE LAREAU

Laughing and yelling, a white fourth-grader named Garrett Tallinger splashes around in the swimming pool in the backyard of his four-bedroom home in the suburbs on a late spring afternoon. As on most evenings, after a quick dinner his father drives him to soccer practice. This is only one of Garrett's many activities. His brother has a baseball game at a different location. There are evenings when the boys' parents relax, sipping a glass of wine. Tonight is not one of them. As they rush to change out of their work clothes and get the children ready for practice, Mr. and Mrs. Tallinger are harried.

Only ten minutes away, a Black fourth-grader, Alexander Williams, is riding home from a school open house.[1] His mother is driving their beige, leather-upholstered Lexus. It is 9:00 P.M. on a Wednesday evening. Ms. Williams is tired from work and has a long Thursday ahead of her. She will get up at 4:45 A.M. to go out of town on business and will not return before 9:00 P.M. On Saturday morning, she will chauffeur Alexander to a private piano lesson at 8:15 A.M., which will be followed by a choir rehearsal and then a soccer game. As they ride in the dark, Alexander's mother, in a quiet voice, talks with her son, asking him questions and eliciting his opinions.

Discussions between parents and children are a hallmark of middle-class child rearing. Like many middle-class parents, Ms. Williams and her husband see themselves as "developing" Alexander to cultivate his talents in a concerted fashion. Organized activities, established and controlled by mothers and fathers, dominate the lives of middle-class children such as Garrett and Alexander. By making certain their children have these and other experiences, middle-class parents engage in a process of *concerted cultivation*. From this, a robust sense of entitlement takes root in the children. This sense of entitlement plays an especially important role in institutional settings, where middle-class children learn to question adults and address them as relative equals.

Only twenty minutes away, in blue-collar neighborhoods, and slightly farther away, in public housing projects, childhood looks different. Mr. Yanelli, a white working-class father, picks up his son Little Billy, a fourth-grader, from an after-school program. They come home and Mr. Yanelli drinks a beer while Little Billy first watches television, then rides his bike and plays in the street. Other nights, he and his Dad sit on the sidewalk outside their house and play cards. At about 5:30 P.M. Billy's mother gets home from her job as a house cleaner. She fixes dinner and the entire family sits down to eat together. Extended family are a prominent part of their lives. Ms. Yanelli touches base with her "entire family every day" by phone. Many nights Little Billy's uncle stops by, sometimes bringing Little Billy's youngest cousin. In the spring, Little Billy plays baseball on a local team. Unlike for Garrett and Alexander, who have at least four activities a week, for Little Billy, baseball is his only organized activity outside of school during the entire year. Down the road, a white working-class girl, Wendy Driver, also spends the evening with her girl cousins, as they watch a video and eat popcorn, crowded together on the living room floor.

Farther away, a Black fourth-grade boy, Harold McAllister, plays outside on a summer evening in the public housing project in which he lives. His two male cousins are there that night, as they often are. After an afternoon spent unsuccessfully searching for a ball so they could play basketball, the boys had resorted to watching sports on television. Now they head outdoors for a twilight water balloon fight. Harold tries to get his neighbor, Miss Latifa, wet. People sit in white plastic lawn chairs outside the row of apartments. Music and television sounds waft through the open windows and doors.

The adults in the lives of Billy, Wendy, and Harold want the best for them. Formidable economic constraints make it a major life task for these parents to put food on the table, arrange for housing, negotiate unsafe neighborhoods, take children to the doctor (often waiting for city buses that do not come), clean children's clothes, and get children to bed and have them ready for school the next morning. But unlike middle-class parents, these adults do not consider the concerted development of children, particularly through organized leisure activities, an essential aspect of good parenting. Unlike the Tallingers and Williamses, these mothers and fathers do not focus on concerted cultivation. For them, the crucial responsibilities of parenthood do not lie in eliciting their children's feelings, opinions, and thoughts. Rather, they see a clear boundary between adults and children. Parents tend to use directives: they tell their children what to do rather than persuading them with reasoning. Unlike their middle-class counterparts, who have a steady diet of adult organized activities, the working-class and poor children have more control over the character of their leisure activities. Most children are free to go out and play with friends and relatives who typically live close by. Their parents and guardians facilitate the *accomplishment of natural growth*.[2] Yet these children and their parents interact with central institutions in the society, such as schools, which firmly and decisively promote strategies of concerted cultivation in child rearing. For working-class and poor families, the cultural logic of child rearing at home is out of synch with the standards of institutions. As a result, while children whose parents adopt strategies of concerted cultivation appear to gain a sense of entitlement, children such as Billy Yanelli, Wendy Driver, and Harold McAllister appear to gain an emerging sense of distance, distrust, and constraint in their institutional experiences.

America may be the land of opportunity, but it is also a land of inequality. This book identifies the largely invisible but powerful ways that parents' social class impacts children's life experiences. It shows, using in-depth observations and interviews with middle-class (including members of the upper-middle-class), working-class, and poor families, that inequality permeates the fabric of the culture. In the chapters that lie ahead, I report the results of intensive observational research for a total of twelve families when their children were nine and ten years old. I argue that key elements of family life cohere to form a cultural logic of child rearing.[3] In other words, the differences among families seem to cluster together in meaningful patterns. In this historical moment, middle-class parents tend to adopt a cultural logic of child rearing that stresses the concerted cultivation of children. Working-class and poor parents, by contrast, tend to undertake the accomplishment of natural growth. In the accomplishment of natural growth, children experience long stretches of leisure time, child-initiated play, clear boundaries between adults and children, and daily interactions with kin. Working-class and poor children, despite tremendous economic strain, often have more "childlike" lives, with autonomy from adults and control over their extended leisure time. Although middle-class children miss out on kin relationships and leisure time, they appear to (at least potentially) gain important institutional advantages. From the experience of concerted cultivation, they acquire skills that could be valuable in the future when they enter the world of work. Middle-class white and Black children in my study did exhibit some key differences; yet the biggest gaps were not within social classes but, as I show, across them. It is these class differences and how they are enacted in family life and child rearing that shape the ways children view themselves in relation to the rest of the world.

CULTURAL REPERTOIRES

Professionals who work with children, such as teachers, doctors, and counselors, generally agree about how children should be raised. Of course, from time to time they may disagree on the ways standards should be enacted for an individual child or family. For example, teachers may disagree about whether or not parents should stop and correct a child who mispronounces a word while reading. Counselors may disagree over whether a mother is being too protective of her child. Still, there is little dispute among professionals on the broad principles for promoting educational development in children through proper parenting.[4] These standards include the importance of talking with children, developing their educational interests, and playing an active role in their schooling. Similarly, parenting guidelines typically stress the importance of reasoning with children and teaching them to solve problems through negotiation rather than with physical force. Because these guidelines are so generally accepted, and because they focus on a set of practices concerning how parents should raise children, they form a *dominant set of cultural repertoires* about how children should be raised. This widespread agreement among professionals about the broad principles for child rearing permeates our society. A small number of experts thus potentially shape the behavior of a large number of parents.

Professionals' advice regarding the best way to raise children has changed regularly over the last two centuries. From strong opinions about the merits of bottle feeding, being stern with children, and utilizing physical punishment (with dire warnings of problematic outcomes should parents indulge children), there have been shifts to equally strongly worded recommendations about the benefits of breast feeding, displaying emotional warmth toward children, and using reasoning and negotiation as mechanisms of parental control. Middle-class parents appear to shift their behaviors in a variety of spheres more rapidly and more thoroughly than do working-class or poor parents.[5] As professionals have shifted their recommendations from bottle feeding to breast feeding, from stern approaches to warmth and empathy, and from spanking to time-outs, it is middle-class parents who have responded most promptly.[6] Moreover, in recent decades, middle-class children in the United States have had to face the prospect of "declining fortunes."[7] Worried about how their children will get ahead, middle-class parents are increasingly determined to make sure that their children are not excluded from any opportunity that might eventually contribute to their advancement.

Middle-class parents who comply with current professional standards and engage in a pattern of concerted cultivation deliberately try to stimulate their children's development and foster their cognitive and social skills. The commitment among working-class and poor families to provide comfort, food, shelter, and other basic support requires ongoing effort, given economic challenges and the formidable demands of child rearing. But it stops short of the deliberate cultivation of children and their leisure activities that occurs in middle-class families. For working-class and poor families, sustaining children's natural growth is viewed as an accomplishment.[8]

What is the outcome of these different philosophies and approaches to child rearing? Quite simply, they appear to lead to the *transmission of differential advantages* to children. In this study, there was quite a bit more talking in middle-class homes than in working-class and poor homes, leading to the development of greater verbal agility, larger vocabularies, more comfort with authority figures, and more familiarity with abstract concepts. Importantly, children also developed skill differences in interacting with authority figures in institutions and at home. Middle-class children such as Garrett Tallinger and Alexander Williams learn, as young boys, to shake the hands of adults and look them in the eye. In studies of job interviews, investigators have found that potential employees have less than one minute to make a good impression. Researchers stress the importance of eye contact, firm handshakes, and displaying comfort with bosses during the interview. In poor families like Harold McAllister's, however, family members usually do not look each other in the eye when conversing. In addition, as Elijah Anderson points out, they live in neighborhoods where it can be dangerous to look people in the eye too long.[9] The types of social competence transmitted in the McAllister family are valuable, but they are potentially less valuable (in employment interviews, for example) than those learned by Garrett Tallinger and Alexander Williams.

The white and Black middle-class children in this study also exhibited an emergent version of the *sense of entitlement* characteristic of the middle-class. They acted as though they had a right to pursue their own individual preferences and to actively manage interactions in institutional settings. They appeared comfortable in these settings; they were open to sharing information and asking for attention. Although some children were more outgoing than others, it was common practice among middle-class children to shift interactions to suit *their* preferences. Alexander Williams knew how to get the doctor to listen to his concerns (about the bumps under his arm from his new deodorant). His mother explicitly trained and encouraged him to speak up with the doctor. Similarly, a Black middle-class girl, Stacey Marshall, was taught by her mother to expect the gymnastics teacher to accommodate her individual learning style. Thus, middle-class children were trained in "the rules of the game" that govern interactions with institutional representatives. They were not conversant in other important social skills, however, such as organizing their time for hours on end during weekends and summers, spending long periods of time away from adults, or hanging out with adults in a nonobtrusive, subordinate fashion. Middle-class children also learned (by imitation and by direct training) how to make the rules work in their favor. Here, the enormous stress on reasoning and negotiation in the home also has a potential advantage for future institutional negotiations. Additionally, those in authority responded positively to such interactions. Even in fourth grade, middle-class children appeared to be acting on their own behalf to gain advantages. They made special requests of teachers and doctors to adjust procedures to accommodate their desires.

The working-class and poor children, by contrast, showed an emerging *sense of constraint* in their interactions in institutional settings. They were less likely to try to customize interactions to suit their own preferences. Like their parents, the children accepted the actions of persons in authority (although at times they also covertly resisted them). Working-class and poor parents sometimes were not as aware of their children's school situation (as when their children were not doing homework). Other times, they dismissed the school rules as unreasonable. For example, Wendy Driver's mother told her to "punch" a boy who was pestering her in class; Billy Yanelli's parents were proud of him when he "beat up" another boy on the playground, even though Billy was then suspended from school. Parents also had trouble getting "the school" to respond to their concerns. When Ms. Yanelli complained that she "hates" the school, she gave her son a lesson in powerlessness and frustration in the face of an important institution. Middle-class children such as Stacey Marshall learned to make demands on professionals, and when they succeeded in making the rules work in their favor they augmented their "cultural capital" (i.e., skills individuals inherit that can then be translated into different forms of value as they move through various institutions) for the future.[10] When working-class and poor children confronted institutions, however, they generally were unable to make the rules work in their favor nor did they obtain capital for adulthood. Because of these patterns of legitimization, children raised according to the logic of concerted cultivation can gain advantages, in the form of an emerging sense of entitlement, while children raised according to the logic of natural growth tend to develop an emerging sense of constraint.[11]

SOCIAL STRATIFICATION AND INDIVIDUALISM

Public discourse in America typically presents the life accomplishments of a person as the result of her or his individual qualities. Songs like "I Did It My Way," memoirs, television shows, and magazine articles, celebrate the individual. Typically, individual outcomes are connected to individual effort and talent, such as being a "type A" personality, being a hard worker, or showing leadership. These cultural beliefs provide a framework for Americans' views of inequality.

Indeed, Americans are much more comfortable recognizing the power of individual initiative than recognizing the power of social class. Studies show that Americans generally believe that responsibility for their accomplishments rests on their individual efforts. Less than one-fifth see "race, gender, religion, or class as very important for 'getting ahead in life.'"[12] Compared to Europeans, individuals in the United States are much more likely to believe they can improve their standard of living. Put differently, Americans believe in the American dream: "The American dream that we were all raised on is a simple but powerful one—if you work hard and play by the rules, you should be given a chance to go as far as your God-given ability will take you."[13] This American ideology that each individual is responsible for his or her life outcomes is the expressed belief of the vast majority of Americans, rich and poor.

Yet there is no question that society is stratified. As I show in the next chapter, highly valued resources such as the possession of wealth; having an interesting, well-paying, and complex job; having a good education; and owning a home, are not evenly distributed throughout the society. Moreover, these resources are transferred across generations: One of the best predictors of whether a child will one day graduate from college is whether his or her parents are college graduates. Of course, relations of this sort are not absolute: Perhaps two-thirds of the members of society ultimately reproduce their parents' level of educational attainment, while about one-third take a different path. Still, there is no question that we live in a society characterized by considerable gaps in resources or, put differently, by substantial *inequality*. As I explain in the next chapter, however, reasonable people have disagreed about how best to conceptualize such patterns. They also have disagreed about whether families in different economic positions "share distinct, life-defining experiences."[14] Many insist that there is not a clear, coherent, and sustained experiential pattern. In this book, I demonstrate the existence of a cultural logic of child rearing that tends to differ according to families' social class positions. I see these interweaving practices as coming together in a messy but still recognizable way. In contrast to many, I suggest that social class does have a powerful impact in shaping the daily rhythms of family life.

THE STUDY

It is a lot of work to get young children through the day, especially for their parents. When I embarked on this study, I was interested in understanding that labor process. In choosing to look at families, rather than just at children *or* parents, I hoped to capture some of the reciprocal effects of children and parents on each other. My approach also meant moving beyond the walls of the home to understand how parents and children negotiate with other adults in children's lives.

This book is based on intensive "naturalistic" observations of twelve families (six white, five Black, and one interracial) with children nine and ten years old. The twelve families are part of a larger study of eighty-eight children from the middle-class, working-class, and poor.[15] (For details of how the study was done, see Appendix A, Methodology.) I met most of these children when I visited their third-grade classrooms in an urban school, Lower Richmond, and a suburban school, Swan (both of which are described in the next chapter). With the help of white and Black research assistants, I carried out interviews first with the mothers and then with many of the fathers of these children. To better understand the expectations that professionals had of parents, I also interviewed the children's classroom teachers and other school personnel.

From this pool of children the research assistants and I selected twelve families for intensive observations.[16] We generally visited each family about twenty times in and around their home, usually in the space of one month. We followed children and parents as they went through their daily routines, as they took part in school activities, church services and events, organized play, kin visits, and medical appointments. Most visits lasted about three hours; sometimes, depending on the event (e.g., an out-of-town funeral, a special extended family event, or a long shopping trip), we stayed much longer. In most cases, we also arranged one overnight visit in each family's home. Often, especially after the families got used to us, we carried tape recorders.

When we introduced ourselves to each family, we said that, following a famous study, we wanted to be treated like "the family dog."[17] We wanted parents to step over and ignore us, but allow us to hang out with them. In reality, our presence had a more active character. Still, after some initial chatter, we often slipped into the background, letting the children and their parents set the pace. In the house, we sat on the floor with children and, as a rule, insisted on sitting in the backseat of cars when we rode along on family outings. Outside, we played ball with children or hung around while they played with their friends. Middle-class children, especially, spent quite a bit of time waiting for adults. We waited, too. As I explain in Appendix A, the rule of thumb was not to criticize and not to intervene unless a child was in imminent danger. We encouraged families not to worry about entertaining us, we told children to feel free to curse in front of us if they would do so normally, and we asked that other normal "guest" rules be dissolved.

Unquestionably, our presence changed the dynamics as we were sitting in living rooms watching television, riding along in the backseat of the car to a soccer game, watching children get into their pajamas, or sitting in church with them. Over time, however, we saw signs of adjustment (e.g., as families got used to us, yelling and cursing increased). Many families reported that, especially after the initial adjustment, their behavior changed only in modest ways, if at all.

The children found participating in the project enjoyable. They reported it made them feel "special." They were demonstrably happy to see the field-workers arrive and, at times, were reluctant to let them leave. Some parents also, at times, said they "had fun." Delight in the study was clearly stronger in the working-class and poor families, possibly because it was rare for these children to meet adults outside of their extended family, neighbors, and teachers. In middle-class families, children routinely interacted with nonfamilial adults outside of the home environment or school.

ENDURING DILEMMAS

In a seminar I attended recently, a Black anthropologist rebuffed another scholar's statement with the words, "Yes, but that is a white perspective." In this line of thought, membership in a particular racial or ethnic group crucially shapes a person's intellectual trajectory. Accordingly, there are those who believe that as a white woman, I should not have studied Black families. Conversely, they might object to having a Black research assistant visit a white middle-class family. They assert that it is more desirable, or even necessary, for gays to study gays or women to study women. Some worry that outsiders may get it wrong. Others assert that having white researchers in Black families is not a legitimate undertaking.

There are no easy answers to these contentious debates. In this study, the design grew out of the local context (see Appendix A for details). But more generally, I have a philosophical difference with the young woman in the seminar that evening. I question whether something called "a white perspective" exists.[18] To follow out the logic of her critique means that members of (dominant) racial and ethnic groups ought to refrain from studying social questions involving dominated groups. This does not strike me as the best approach for understanding complex social problems. (It also has the invidious effect of relegating every Black social scientist to studying Black Americans rather than whatever suits his or her fancy.) Moreover, the "groups" at hand are always diverse. What about members of the same ethnic group who are of a different gender: Are the walls blocking understanding equally high? In a series of ever-reflecting mirrors, does this tension mean that the only person you can truly "cross the divide" to study is yourself? This book takes the position that it is possible for outsiders of a group to study across boundaries. It reports findings from a study that used ethnographic methods to try to understand children in a wide variety of social locations: boys and girls, middle-class, working-class and poor families, and white and Black families.

In addition, the research teams were racially and ethnically diverse (as well as diverse by social class background), which, as I show in Appendix A, influenced what we learned in our visits.

Some reviewers worried that given the contested character of race relations in the United States, the behavior patterns described in this book might reinforce negative stereotypes of certain groups. The results could be taken out of context and exploited by others, particularly political conservatives. Some early readers encouraged me *not to report* results that might be used to reinforce negative images of, for example, poor Black families. The fact that the manuscript includes portraits of poor white families as well as Black families did not completely assuage these concerns. A key problem is that most readers will be middle class or, as college students, on the road to becoming middle class, even if they had working-class or poor origins. As readers, they will have their own childhoods and their own lives as parents or future parents as a base for what they consider appropriate. This cultural and historical frame can become the basis for interpreting the discussion. Indeed, some (middle-class) readers of earlier drafts felt that a child's life that consists of watching television all day would be "boring" or "bad" for the child. This interpretation, though, is rooted in a particular vision of childhood—one involving development and concerted cultivation. The historical and cultural character of readers' beliefs often are thrown into relief only through sharp cross-cultural or historical comparisons.[19]

In sum, the fear is that some readers will project their own cultural beliefs on the material. This pattern of projection makes it difficult to "see" alternative conceptions of child rearing as legitimate. As a result, although I make an assiduous effort to report the complexity of family life, at times I spend more time pointing out drawbacks of middle-class child rearing than I do drawbacks of working-class and poor families' approach. Still, it is in fact possible that the results of this study could be distorted or used to promote political positions that I find repugnant. But squelching results due to fears about how they could be interpreted (particularly worries that the examples could reinforce "deficit" theories of social life) seems wrong. Thus, although urged to do so, I have not omitted data on this criterion.

NOTES

1 Choosing words to describe social groups also becomes a source of worry, especially over the possibility of reinforcing negative stereotypes. I found the available terms to describe members of racial and ethnic groups to be problematic in one way or another. The families I visited uniformly described themselves as "Black." Recognizing that some readers have strong views that Black

---

should be capitalized, I have followed that convention, despite the lack of symmetry with the term white. In sum, this book alternates among the terms "Black," "Black American," "African American," and "white," with the understanding that "white" here refers to the subgroup of non-Hispanic whites.

2 Some readers have expressed concern that this phrase, "the accomplishment of natural growth," underemphasizes all the labor that mothers and fathers do to take care of children. They correctly note that working-class and poor parents themselves would be unlikely to use such a term to describe the process of caring for children. These concerns are important. As I stress in the text (especially in the chapter on Katie Brindle, Chapter 5) it does take an enormous amount of work for parents, especially mothers, of all classes to take care of children. But poor and working-class mothers have fewer resources with which to negotiate these demands. Those whose lives the research assistants and I studied approached the task somewhat differently than did middle-class parents. They did not seem to view children's leisure time as their responsibility; nor did they see themselves as responsible for assertively intervening in their children's school experiences. Rather, the working-class and poor parents carried out their chores, drew boundaries and restrictions around their children, and then, within these limits, allowed their children to carry out their lives. It is in this sense that I use the term "the accomplishment of natural growth."

3 I define a child-rearing context to include the routines of daily life, the dispositions of daily life, or the "habitus" of daily life. I focus on two contexts: concerted cultivation and the accomplishment of natural growth. In this book, I primarily use the concept of child rearing, but at times I also use the term *socialization*. Many sociologists have vigorously criticized this concept, noting that it suggests (inaccurately) that children are passive rather than active agents and that the relationship between parents and their children is unidirectional rather than reciprocal and dynamic. See, for example, William Corsaro, *Sociology of Childhood;* Barrie Thorne, *Gender Play;* and Glen Elder, "The Life Course as Development Theory." Nonetheless, existing terms can, ideally, be revitalized to offer more sophisticated understandings of social processes. Child rearing and socialization have the virtue of being relatively succinct and less jargon laden than other alternatives. As a result, I use them.

4 For discussions of the role of professionals, see Eliot Freidson, *Professional Powers;* Magali Sarfatti Larson, *The Rise of Professionalism;* and, although quite old, the still valuable collection by Amitai Etzioni, *The Semi-Professionals and Their Organizations.* Of course, professional standards are always contested and are subject to change over time. I do not mean to suggest there are not pockets of resistance and contestation. At the most general level, however, there is virtually uniform support for the idea that parents should talk to children at length, read to children, and take a proactive, assertive role in medical care.

5 Sharon Hays, in her 1996 book *The Cultural Contradictions of Motherhood,* studies the attitudes of middle-class and working-class mothers toward child rearing. She finds a shared commitment to "intensive mothering," although there are some differences among the women in her study in their views of punishment (with middle-class mothers leaning toward reasoning and working-class

women toward physical punishment). My study focused much more on behavior than attitudes. If I looked at attitudes, I saw fewer differences; for example, all exhibited the desire to be a good mother and to have their children grow and thrive. The differences I found, however, were significant in how parents *enacted* their visions of what it meant to be a good parent.

6 See Urie Bronfenbrenner's article, "Socialization and Social Class through Time and Space."

7 Katherine Newman, *Declining Fortunes,* as well as Donald Barlett and James B. Steele, *America: What Went Wrong?* See also Michael Hout and Claude Fischer, "A Century of Inequality."

8 Some readers expressed the concern that the contrast to natural would be "unnatural," but this is not the sense in which the term *natural growth* is used here. Rather, the contrast is with words such as cultivated, artificial, artifice, or manufactured. This contrast in the logic of child rearing is a heuristic device that should not be pushed too far since, as sociologists have shown, all social life is constructed in specific social contexts. Indeed, family life has varied dramatically over time. See Philippe Aries, *Centuries of Childhood,* Herbert Gutman, *The Black Family in Slavery and Freedom, 1750–1925,* and Nancy Scheper-Hughes, *Death without Weeping.*

9 Elijah Anderson, *Code of the Street;* see especially Chapter 2.

10 For a more extensive discussion of the work of Pierre Bourdieu see the theoretical appendix; see also David Swartz's excellent book *Culture and Power.*

11 I did not study the full range of families in American society, including elite families of tremendous wealth, nor, at the other end of the spectrum, homeless families. In addition, I have a purposively drawn sample. Thus, I cannot state whether there are other forms of child rearing corresponding to other cultural logics. Still, data from quantitative studies based on nationally representative data support the patterns I observed. For differences by parents' social class position and children's time use, see especially Sandra Hofferth and John Sandberg, "Changes in American Children's Time, 1981–1997." Patterns of language use with children are harder to capture in national surveys, but the work of Melvin Kohn and Carmi Schooler, especially *Work and Personality,* shows differences in parents' child-rearing values. Duane Alwin's studies of parents' desires are generally consistent with the results reported here. See Duane Alwin, "Trends in Parental Socialization Values." For differences in interventions in institutions, there is extensive work showing social class differences in parent involvement in education. See the U. S. Department of Education, *The Condition of Education, 2001,* p.175.

12 In this book, unless otherwise noted, the statistics reported are from 1993 to 1995, which was when the data were collected. Similarly, unless otherwise noted, all monetary amounts are given in (unadjusted) dollars from 1994 to 1995. The figure reported here is from Everett Ladd, *Thinking about America,* pp. 21–22.

13 This quote is from President Bill Clinton's 1993 speech to the Democratic Leadership Council. It is cited in Jennifer Hochschild, *Facing Up to the American Dream,* p. 18.

14 Paul Kingston, *The Classless Society,* p. 2.

15 As I explain in more detail in the methodological appendix, family structure is intertwined with class position in this sample. The Black and white middle-class children that we observed all resided with both of their biological parents. By contrast, although some of the poor children have regular contact with their fathers, none of the Black or white poor children in the intensive observations had their biological fathers at home. The working-class families were in between. This pattern raises questions such as whether, for example, the pattern of concerted cultivation depends on the presence of a two-parent marriage. The scope of the sample precludes a satisfactory answer.

16 As I explain in Appendix A, three of the twelve children came from sources outside of the schools.

17 Arlie Hochschild, *The Second Shift.*

18 My concern here is the vast diversity in views among white Americans as well as Black Americans. The phrase "a white perspective" seems inaccurate. This is not to say that whites don't experience considerable benefits from their race in our stratified society. They do. Whites benefit from racial discrimination in many ways, including their improved ability to secure housing loans and employment as well as relatively higher market values for their homes in racially segregated neighborhoods. There are also well-documented differences in street interaction, including the ability to secure a taxi on a busy street. Thus the question is not the amount of racial discrimination in our society. Instead the question is how much being a member of a dominant group, interested in studying racial differences in daily life, precludes one from "seeing" or "understanding" important dimensions of the phenomenon. See Douglas Massey and Nancy Denton, *American Apartheid;* Kathleen Neckerman and Joleen Kirschenmann, "Hiring Strategies, Racial Bias, and Inner-City Workers"; and Elijah Anderson, *Streetwise.* Finally, there is an extensive literature on "whiteness" and the benefits that whites gain from their position of privilege. See, among others, Phil Cohen, "Laboring under Whiteness."

19 See Julia Wrigley, "Do Young Children Need Intellectual Stimulation?" and Linda A. Pollock, *Forgotten Children.*

20 As I explain in more detail in Appendix A, some of the families in the study, including the Williamses, were upper–middle class. The project, however, was hampered by its small sample size and my desire to compare different racial and ethnic groups. As a result, the differences between middle-class and upper-middle-class families are not a major focus of the work. Within the scope of the sample of thirty-six middle-class families, however, clear differences did not emerge between the middle class and upper–middle class. As a result, in this book I use only the term *middle class* to encompass both.

BIBLIOGRAPHY

Adler, Patricia A., and Peter Adler. "Social Reproduction and the Corporate Other: The Institutionalization of Afterschool Activities." *The Sociological Quarterly* 35, 3 (1994): 309–28.

Adler, Patricia A., Peter Adler, and John M. Johnson. "Street Corner Society Revisited: New Questions about Old Issues." *Journal of Contemporary Ethnography* 21, 1 (1992): 3–10.

Alwin, Duane F. "Trends in Parental Socialization Values: Detroit, 1958–1983." *American Journal of Sociology* 90, 2 (1984): 359–82.

Anderson, Elijah. *Code of the Street: Decency, Violence, and the Moral Life of the Inner City.* New York: W. W. Norton and Company, 1999.

———. *Streetwise: Race, Class, and Change in an Urban Community.* Chicago: University of Chicago Press, 1990.

Anyon, Jean. *Ghetto Schooling: A Political Economy of Urban Educational Reform.* New York: Teachers College Press, 1997.

Archer-Banks, Diane A. M., and Linda S. Behar-Horenstein. "African American Parental Involvement in Their Children's Middle School Experiences." *Journal of Negro Education* 77, 2 (2008): 143–56.

Arendell, Teresa. "Soccer Moms and the New Care Work." Working paper. Center for Working Families, University of California, Berkeley, 2000. Published as: "The New Care Work of Middle Class Mothers: Managing Childrearing, Employment, and Time." Pp. 163–204 in *Minding the Time in Family Experience: Emerging Perspectives and Issues,* edited by Kerry J. Daly. Oxford: Elsevier Science, 2001.

Ariès, Philippe. *Centuries of Childhood: A Social History of the Family.* Translated by Robert Baldick. New York: Basic Books, 1962.

Attewell, Paul, and David E. Lavin. *Passing the Torch: Does Higher Education for the Disadvantaged Pay Off across the Generations?* New York: Russell Sage Foundation, 2007.

Averill, Patricia M., and Thomas G. Power. "Parental Attitudes and Children's Experiences in Soccer: Correlates of Effort and Enjoyment." *International Journal of Behavioral Development* 18, 2 (1995): 263–76.

Bagley, Carl. "Educational Ethnography as Performance Art: Towards a Sensuous Feeling and Knowing." *Qualitative Research* 8, 1 (2008): 53–72.

Barlett, Donald L., and James B. Steele. *America: What Went Wrong?* Kansas City: Andrews and McMeel Publishers, 1992.

Becker, Howard S. "How to Find Out How to Do Qualitative Research." *International Journal of Communication* 3 (2009): 545–53.

Bellah, Robert N., Richard Madsen, William M. Sullivan, Ann Swidler, and Steven M. Tipton. *Habits of the Heart: Individualism and Commitment in American Life.* 2nd ed. Berkeley: University of California Press, 1996.

Beller, Emily, and Michael Hout. "Intergenerational Social Mobility: The United States in Comparative Perspective." *The Future of Children* 16, 2 (2006): 19–36.

Belluck, Pam. "Parents Try to Reclaim Their Children's Time." In *New York Times* on the Web, 2000. www.nytimes.com/library/national/061300family-practices.html. Accessed February 24, 2011.

Bennett, Pamela R., Amy Lutz, and Lakshmi Jayaram. "Beyond the School Yard: The Contributions of Parenting Logics, Financial Resources, and Social Institutions to the Social Class Gap in Structured Activity Participation." *Sociology of Education,* forthcoming.

Berhau, Patricia. "Class and the Experiences of Consumers: A Study in the Practices of Acquisition." Ph.D. diss. Temple University, 2000.

Berhau, Patricia, Annette Lareau, and Julie E. Press. "Managing Children's Activities: Implications for the Gender Division of Household Labor." Pp. 43–60 in *At the Heart of Work and Family: Engaging the Ideas of Arlie Hochschild,* edited by Anita Ilta Garey and Karen V. Hansen. New Brunswick, N.J.: Rutgers University Press, 2011.

Berlage, Gai Ingham. "Are Children's Competitive Team Sports Teaching Corporate Values?" *ARENA Review* 6, 1 (1982): 15–21.

Bernstein, Basil B. *Class, Codes, and Control: Theoretical Studies towards a Sociology of Language*. New York: Routledge and Kegan Paul Ltd., 1971.

Best, Joel. *Threatened Children: Rhetoric and Concern about Child-Victims*. Chicago: University of Chicago Press, 1993.

Bettie, Julie. *Women without Class: Girls, Race, and Identity*. Berkeley: University of California Press, 2003.

Bianchi, Suzanne M. "Maternal Employment and Time with Children." *Demography* 37, 4 (2000): 401–14.

Bianchi, Suzanne M., and John P. Robinson. "What Did You Do Today? Children's Use of Time, Family Composition, and the Acquisition of Social Capital." *Journal of Marriage and the Family* 59, 2 (1997): 332–44.

Black, Timothy. *When a Heart Turns Rock Solid: The Lives of Three Puerto Rican Brothers on and off the Streets*. New York: Pantheon, 2009.

Blair-Loy, Mary. *Competing Devotions: Career and Family among Women Executives*. Cambridge, Mass.: Harvard University Press, 2003.

Bloom, Janice L. "(Mis)Reading Social Class in the Journey towards College: Youth Development in Urban America." *Teachers College Record* 109, 2 (2007): 343–68.

Bluestone, Cheryl, and Catherine S. Tamis-LeMonda. "Correlates of Parenting Styles in Predominantly Working- and Middle-Class African American Mothers." *Journal of Marriage and Family* 61, 4 (1999): 881–93.

Blum, Linda M. "Mother-Blame in the Prozac Nation: Raising Kids with Invisible Disabilities." *Gender and Society* 21, 2 (2007): 202–26.

Bodovski, Katerina. "Parental Practices and Educational Achievement: Social Class, Race, and Habitus." *British Journal of Sociology of Education* 31, 2 (2010): 139–56.

Bodovksi, Katerina, and George Farkas. "'Concerted Cultivation' and Unequal Achievement in Elementary School." *Social Science Research* 37, 3 (2008): 903–19.

Boelen, W. A. Marianne. "Street Corner Society: Cornerville Revisited." *Journal of Contemporary Ethnography* 21, 1 (1992): 11–51.

Bourdieu, Pierre. "Cultural Reproduction and Social Reproduction." Pp. 487–510 in *Power and Ideology in Education*, edited by Jerome Karabel and A. H. Halsey. New York: Oxford University Press, 1977.

———. *Distinction: A Social Critique of the Judgment of Taste*. Translated by Richard Nice. Cambridge, Mass.: Harvard University Press, 1984.

———. *The Logic of Practice*. Translated by Richard Nice. Stanford, Calif.: Stanford University Press, 1990; orig. pub. 1970.

———. "Marriage Strategies as Strategies of Social Reproduction." Translated by Elborg Forster and Patricia M. Ranum. Pp. 117–44 in *Family and Society: Selections from the Annales, Économies, Sociétés, Civilisations,* edited by Robert Forster and Orest A. Ranum. Baltimore: Johns Hopkins University Press, 1976.

———. *Outline of a Theory of Practice*. Translated by Richard Nice. Cambridge, Eng.: Cambridge University Press, 1977.

Bourdieu, Pierre, and Jean-Claude Passeron. *Reproduction in Education, Society, and Culture*. London: Sage Publications, 1990.

Bourdieu, Pierre, and Loïc J. D. Wacquant. *An Invitation to Reflexive Sociology*. Chicago: University of Chicago Press, 1992.

Bowen, William G., and Derek Bok. *The Shape of the River: Long-Term Consequences of Considering Race in College and University Admissions*. Princeton, N.J.: Princeton University Press, 1998.

Bowles, Samuel, and Herbert Gintis. *Schooling in Capitalist America*. New York: Basic Books, 1977.

Bronfenbrenner, Urie. "Socialization and Social Class through Time and Space." Pp. 362–77 in *Class, Status, and Power,* edited by Reinhard Bendix and Seymour Martin Lipset. New York: The Free Press, 1966.

Brooks, Scott N. *Black Men Can't Shoot*. Chicago: University of Chicago Press, 2009.

Brubaker, Rogers. "Rethinking Classical Theory: The Sociological Vision of Pierre Bourdieu." *Theory and Society* 14, 6 (1985): 745–75.

Buchmann, Marlis. *The Script of Life in Modern Society: Entry into Adulthood in a Changing World*. Chicago: University of Chicago Press, 1989.

Burawoy, Michael. *The Extended Case Method: Four Countries, Four Decades, Four Great Transformations, and One Theoretical Tradition.* Berkeley: University of California Press, 2009.

————. "Public Ethnography as Film: Michael Apted and the Up! Series." *Ethnography* 10, 3 (2009): 317–19.

————. "Revisits: An Outline of a Theory of Reflexive Ethnography." *American Sociological Review* 68, 5 (2003): 645–79.

Burton, Linda M. "Childhood Adultification in Economically Disadvantaged Families: A Conceptual Model." *Family Relations* 56 (2007): 329–45.

Burton, Linda M., Eduardo Bonilla-Silva, Victor Ray, Rose Buckelew, Elizabeth Hordge Freeman. "Critical Race Theories, Colorism, and the Decade's Research on Families of Color." *Journal of Marriage and Family* 72, 3 (2010): 440–59.

Burton, Linda M., Diane Purvin, and Raymond Garrett-Peters. "Longitudinal Ethnography: Uncovering Domestic Abuse in Low-Income Women's Lives." Pp. 70–92 in *The Craft of Life Course Research*, edited by Glen H. Elder Jr. and Janet Zollinger Giele. New York: Guilford Press, 2009.

Calhoun, Craig J., Edward LiPuma, and Moishe Postone, eds. *Bourdieu: Critical Perspectives.* Chicago: University of Chicago Press, 1993.

Caplow, Theodore, Howard M. Bahr, Bruce A. Chadwick, Reuben Hill, and Margaret Holmes Williamson. *Middletown Families: Fifty Years of Change and Continuity.* Minneapolis: University of Minnesota Press, 1982.

Carter, Prudence L. *Keepin' It Real: School Success beyond Black and White.* Oxford: Oxford University Press, 2005.

Cassell, Joan. "Risks and Benefits to Subjects of Fieldwork." *The American Sociologist* 13 (August 1978): 134–43.

Cheadle, Jacob E. "Educational Investment, Family Context, and Children's Math and Reading Growth from Kindergarten through the Third Grade." *Sociology of Education* 81, 1 (2008): 1–31.

————. "Parent Educational Investment and Children's General Knowledge Development." *Social Science Research* 38, 2 (2009): 477–91.

Cherlin, Andrew J. *The Marriage-Go-Round: The State of Marriage and the Family in America Today.* New York: Random House, 2009.

Chidekel, Dana. *Parents in Charge: Setting Healthy, Loving Boundaries for You and Your Child.* New York: Citadel Press Books, 2002.

Chin, Tiffani, and Meredith Phillips. "Social Reproduction and Child-Rearing Practices: Social Class, Children's Agency, and the Summer Activity Gap." *Sociology of Education* 77, 3 (2004): 185–210.

Chong, Kelly H. "Coping with Conflict, Confronting Resistance: Fieldwork Emotions and Identity Management in a South Korean Evangelical Community." *Qualitative Sociology* 31, 4 (2008): 369–90.

Choo, Hae Yeon, and Myra Marx Ferree. "Practicing Intersectionality in Sociological Research: A Critical Analysis of Inclusions, Interactions, and Institutions in the Study of Inequalities." *Sociological Theory* 28, 2 (2010): 129–49.

Chua, Amy. *Battle Hymn of the Tiger Mother.* New York: Penguin Press, 2011.

Cicourel, Aaron Victor, and John I. Kitsuse. *The Educational Decision-Makers: An Advanced Study in Sociology.* Indianapolis: Bobbs-Merrill, 1963.

Clough, Patricia. "The Case of Sociology: Governmentality and Methodology." *Critical Inquiry* 36 (2010): 627–41.

Cochran, Moncrieff, Mary Larner, David Riley, Lars Gunnarsson, and Charles R. Henderson Jr. *Extending Families: The Social Networks of Parents and Their Children.* Cambridge, Eng.: Cambridge University Press, 1990.

Cohen, Phil. "Laboring under Whiteness." Pp. 244–82 in *Displacing Whiteness: Essays in Social and Cultural Criticism*, edited by Ruth Frankenberg. Durham, N.C.: Duke University Press, 1997.

Coleman, James S. "Families and Schools." *Educational Researcher* 16, 6 (1987): 32–38.

————. "Social Capital in the Creation of Human Capital." *American Journal of Sociology* 94, Supplement (1988): S95–S120.

College Board. "The College Board Announces a New SAT." 2002. http://press.collegeboard.org/releas-es/2002/college-board-announces-new-sat supregsup. Accessed March 1, 2011.

Collins, Randall. *The Credential Society: An Historical Sociology of Education and Stratification*. New York: Academic Press, Inc., 1979.

———. *Max Weber: A Skeleton Key*. Beverly Hills: Sage Publications, 1986.

———. "Situational Stratification: A Micro-Macro Theory of Inequality." *Sociological Theory* 18, 1 (2000): 17–43.

Condron, Dennis J. "Social Class, School and Non-School Environments, and Black/White Inequalities in Children's Learning." *American Sociological Review* 74, 5 (2009): 683–708.

Conley, Dalton. *Being Black, Living in the Red: Race, Wealth, and Social Policy in America*. Berkeley: University of California Press, 1999.

———. *The Pecking Order: Which Siblings Succeed and Why*. New York: Pantheon Books, 2004.

Cookson, Peter W., Jr., and Caroline Hodges Persell. *Preparing for Power: America's Elite Boarding Schools*. New York: Perseus Books Group, 1985.

Cooper, Marianne. "Being the 'Go-To Guy': Fatherhood, Masculinity, and the Organization of Work in Silicon Valley." *Qualitative Sociology* 23, 4 (2000): 379–405.

———. *Doing Security in Insecure Times: Class and Family Life in the New Economy*. Berkeley: University of California Press, forthcoming.

Corsaro, William A. *The Sociology of Childhood*. Thousand Oaks, Calif.: Pine Forge, 1997.

Cose, Ellis. *The Rage of a Privileged Class*. New York: HarperCollins Publishers, 1993.

Covay, Elizabeth, and William Carbonaro. "After the Bell: Participation in Extracurricular Activities, Classroom Behavior, and Academic Achievement." *Sociology of Education* 83, 1 (2010): 20–45.

Crozier, Gill, and Jane Davies. "Hard to Reach Parents or Hard to Reach Schools? A Discussion of Home-School Relations, with Particular Reference to Bangladeshi and Pakistani Parents." *British Educational Research Journal* 33, 3 (2007): 295–313.

Daly, Kerry J., ed. *Minding the Time in Family Experience: Emerging Perspectives and Issues*. Vol. 3. of *Contemporary Perspectives in Family Research,* edited by Felix M. Berardo. New York: JAI Press, 2001.

Deater-Deckard, Kirby, Kenneth A. Dodge, John E. Bates, and Gregory S. Petit. "Physical Discipline among African American and European American Mothers: Links to Children's Externalizing Behaviors." *Developmental Psychology* 32, 6 (1996): 1065–72.

Demerath, Peter. *Producing Success: The Culture of Personal Advancement in an American High School*. Chicago: University of Chicago Press, 2009.

Denzin, Norman K., and Yvonna S. Lincoln. *The SAGE Handbook of Qualitative Research*. 3rd ed. Thousand Oaks, Calif.: Sage, 2005.

Deparle, Jason. *American Dream: Three Women, Ten Kids, and a Nation's Drive to End Welfare*. New York: Penguin Books, 2004.

DeVault, Marjorie L. *Feeding the Family: The Social Organization of Caring as Gendered Work*. Chicago: University of Chicago Press, 1991.

———. *People at Work: Life, Power, and Social Inclusion in the New Economy*. New York: New York University Press, 2008.

DeVault, Marjorie L., and Liza McCoy. "Institutional Ethnography: Using Interviews to Investigate Ruling Relations." Pp. 751–76 in *Handbook of Interview Research: Context and Method*, edited by Jaber F. Gubrium and James A. Holstein. Thousand Oaks, Calif.: Sage, 2002.

Devine, Fiona. *Class Practices: How Parents Help Their Children Get Good Jobs*. Cambridge, Eng.: Cambridge University Press, 2004.

Diamond, John. "Beyond Social Class: Cultural Resources and Educational Participation among Low-Income Black Parents." *Berkeley Journal of Sociology* 44 (2000): 15–54.

Diamond, John B., and Kimberly Williams Gomez. "African-American Parents' Educational Orientations: The Importance of Social Class and Parents' Perceptions of Schools." *Education and Urban Society* 36, 4 (2004): 383–427.

Dillon, Sam. "Study Finds High Rate of Imprisonment among Dropouts." *The New York Times*. October 8, 2009. www.nytimes.com/2009/10/09/education/09dropout.html. Accessed February 24, 2011.

DiPrete, Thomas A., Andrew Gelman, Tyler McCormick, Julian Teitler, and Tian Zheng. "Segregation in Social Networks Based on Acquaintanceship and Trust." *American Journal of Sociology,* in press.

Doherty, William J., and Barbara Carlson. *Putting Family First: Successful Strategies for Reclaiming Family Life in a Hurry-Up World.* New York: Henry Holt and Company, 2002.

Donzelot, Jacques. *The Policing of Families.* New York: Pantheon Press, 1979.

Downey, Douglas B., Paul T. von Hippel, and Beckett A. Broh. "Are Schools the Great Equalizer? School and Non-School Sources of Inequality in Cognitive Skills." *American Sociological Review* 69, 5 (2004): 613–35.

Dumais, Susan A. "Elementary School Students' Extracurricular Activities: The Effects of Participation on Achievement and Teachers' Evaluations." *Sociological Spectrum* 26, 2 (2006): 117–47.

Duncan, Greg J., and Jeanne Brooks-Gunn, eds. *Consequences of Growing Up Poor.* New York: Russell Sage Foundation, 1997.

Duneier, Mitchell. *Sidewalk.* New York: Farrar, Straus and Giroux, 1999.

———. "Transparency in Ethnography." *Sociological Methodology* 41 (forthcoming 2011).

Economic Policy Institute. *The State of Working America.* Washington, D.C.: Economic Policy Institute, 2011. www.stateofworkingamerica.org. Accessed March 1, 2011.

Edin, Kathryn, and Maria Kefalas. *Promises I Can Keep: Why Poor Women Put Motherhood Before Marriage.* Berkeley: University of California Press, 2005.

Edin, Kathryn, and Laura Lein. *Making Ends Meet: How Single Mothers Survive Welfare and Low-Wage Work.* New York: Russell Sage Foundation, 1997.

Elder, Glen H., Jr. "The Life Course as Developmental Theory." *Child Development* 69, 1 (1998): 1–12.

Elkind, David. *The Hurried Child: Growing Up Too Fast Too Soon.* 3rd ed. Cambridge, Mass.: Da Capo Press, 2001; orig. pub. 1981.

Ellis, Carolyn. "Emotional and Ethical Quagmires in Returning to the Field." *Journal of Contemporary Ethnography* 24, 1 (1995): 68–98.

Ellis, Carolyn S., and Arthur P. Bochner. "Analyzing Analytic Autoethnography: An Autopsy." *Journal of Contemporary Ethnography* 35, 4 (2006): 429–49.

Entwisle, Doris R., Karl L. Alexander, and Linda Steffel Olson. *Children, Schools, and Inequality.* Boulder, Colo.: Westview Press, 1997.

Epstein, Joyce L., and Mavis G. Sanders. "Connecting Home, School, and Community: New Directions for Social Research." Pp. 285–306 in *Handbook of the Sociology of Education,* edited by Maureen T. Hallinan. New York: Springer, 2000.

Erikson, Robert, and John H. Goldthorpe. *The Constant Flux: A Study of Class Mobility in Industrial Societies.* Oxford: Clarendon Press, 1992.

Etzioni, Amitai, ed. *The Semi-Professions and Their Organizations: Teachers, Nurses, Social Workers.* New York: The Free Press, 1969.

Feagin, Joe R., and Melvin P. Sikes. *Living with Racism: The Black Middle-Class Experience.* Boston: Beacon Press, 1994.

Fine, Gary Alan. "Towards a Peopled Ethnography: Developing Theory from Group Life." *Ethnography* 4, 1 (2003): 41–60.

———. *With the Boys: Little League Baseball and Preadolescent Culture.* Chicago: University of Chicago Press, 1987.

Fine, Michelle. *Framing Dropouts: Notes on the Politics of an Urban Public High School.* Albany: State University of New York Press, 1991.

Finkelhor, David, Richard Ormrod, Heather Turner, and Sherry L. Hamby. "The Victimization of Children and Youth: A Comprehensive, National Survey." *Child Maltreatment* 10, 1 (2005): 5–25.

Fischer, Claude S. *To Dwell among Friends: Personal Networks in Town and City.* Chicago: University of Chicago Press, 1982.

Fiske, Susan T. "Interpersonal Stratification: Status, Power, and Subordination." Pp. 941–82 in *Handbook of Social Psychology,* 5th ed., vol. 2, edited by Susan T. Fiske, Daniel T. Gilbert, and Gardner Lindzey. New York: McGraw-Hill, 2010.

Foreman, Gene. *The Ethical Journalist: Making Responsible Decisions in Pursuit of the News.* New York: Wiley-Blackwell, 2010.

Fredricks, Jennifer A., and Jacquelynne S. Eccles. "Participation in Extracurricular Activities in the Middle School Years: Are There Developmental Benefits for African American and European American Youth?" *Journal of Youth and Adolescence* 37, 9 (2008): 1029–43.

Freidson, Eliot. *Professional Powers: A Study of the Institutionalization of Formal Knowledge.* Chicago: University of Chicago Press, 1986.

Furstenberg, Frank F., Jr. "The Recent Transformation of the American Family: Witnessing and Exploring Social Change." In *Changing Families in an Unequal Society,* edited by Marcia J. Carlson and Paula England. Stanford, Calif.: Stanford University Press, 2011.

Furstenberg, Frank F., Jr., and Andrew J. Cherlin. *Divided Families: What Happens to Children When Parents Part.* Cambridge, Mass.: Harvard University Press, 1991.

Furstenberg, Frank F., Jr., Thomas D. Cook, Jacquelynne Eccles, Glen H. Elder, Jr., and Arnold Sameroff. *Managing to Make It: Urban Families and Adolescent Success.* Chicago: University of Chicago Press, 1999.

Future of Children. *America's High Schools* 19 (1). Princeton: Princeton-Brookings, 2009.

———. *Opportunity in America* 16 (2). Princeton: Princeton-Brookings, 2006.

Galinsky, Ellen. *Ask the Children: What America's Children Really Think about Working Parents.* New York: William Morrow and Company, Inc., 1999.

Gardner, Howard, and Thomas Hatch. "Multiple Intelligences Go to School: Educational Implications of the Theory of Multiple Intelligences." *Educational Researcher* 18, 8 (1989): 4–9.

Garey, Anita Ilta. *Weaving Work and Motherhood.* Philadelphia: Temple University Press, 1999.

Garey, Anita Ilta, and Terry Arendell. "Children, Work, and Family: Some Thoughts on 'Mother Blame.'" Pp. 293–303 In *Working Families: The Transformation of the American Home,* edited by Rosanna Hertz and Nancy L. Marshall. Berkeley: University of California Press, 2001.

Gaztambide-Fernández, Rubén A. *The Best of the Best: Becoming Elite at an American Boarding School.* Cambridge, Mass.: Harvard University Press, 2009.

Geertz, Clifford. *The Interpretation of Cultures: Selected Essays.* New York: Basic Books, 1973.

Gillies, Val. "Teaching and Learning Guide for *Childrearing, Class and the New Politics of Parenting.*" *Sociology Compass* 3, 2 (2009): 341–44.

Giordano, Peggy C. "Relationships in Adolescence." *Annual Review of Sociology* 29 (2003): 257–81.

Glasmeier, Amy K. *An Atlas of Poverty in America: One Nation, Pulling Apart, 1960–2003.* New York: Routledge, 2005.

Goffman, Alice. "On the Run: Wanted Men in a Philadelphia Ghetto." *American Sociological Review* 74, 3 (2009): 339–57.

Goldenberg, Claude N. "Low-Income Hispanic Parents' Contributions to Their First-Grade Children's Word-Recognition Skills." *Anthropology and Education Quarterly* 18, 3 (1987): 149–79.

Goldscheider, Frances K., and Linda J. Waite. *New Families, No Families?: The Transformation of the American Home.* Berkeley: University of California Press, 1991.

Gordon, Linda. *Heroes of Their Own Lives: The Politics and History of Family Violence.* New York: Penguin Books, 1989.

Granovetter, Mark S. "The Strength of Weak Ties: A Network Theory Revisited." *American Journal of Sociology* 78, 6 (1973): 1360–80.

Grasmuck, Sherri. *Protecting Home: Class, Race, and Masculinity in Boy's Baseball.* Piscataway, N.J.: Rutgers University Press, 2005.

Griffith, Alison I., and Dorothy E. Smith. *Mothering for Schooling.* London: RoutledgeFalmer, 2005.

Grusky, David, and Jesper Sørensen. "Can Class Analysis Be Salvaged?" *American Journal of Sociology* 103, 5 (1998): 1187–1234.

Grusky, David B., and Szonja Szelényi, eds. *The Inequality Reader: Contemporary and Foundational Readings in Race, Class, and Gender.* Boulder, Colo.: Westview Press, 2007.

Gutman, Herbert George. *The Black Family in Slavery and Freedom, 1750– 1925.* New York: Vintage Books, 1976.

Halbfinger, David M. "Our Towns; A Hockey Parent's Life: Time, Money, and Yes, Frustration." *New York Times,* January 12, 2002, p. 29.

Hale-Beson, Janice E. *Black Children: Their Roots, Culture, and Learning Styles.* Rev. ed. Baltimore: Johns Hopkins Press, 1982.

Hall, John R., ed. *Reworking Class.* Ithaca, N.Y.: Cornell University Press, 1997.

Halle, David. *America's Working Man: Work, Home, and Politics among Blue- Collar Property Owners.* Chicago: University of Chicago Press, 1984.

———. *Inside Culture: Art and Class in the American Home.* Chicago: University of Chicago Press, 1993.

Hammersley, Martyn, and Paul Atkinson. *Ethnography: Principles in Practice.* 3rd ed. London: Routledge, 2007.

Handel, Gerald. "Socialization and the Social Self." Pp. 3–10 in *Childhood Socialization,* edited by Gerald Handel. New York: Aldine de Gruyter, 1988. Revised 2nd ed., Piscataway, N.J.: Rutgers University Press, 2006.

Hanushek, Eric A., John F. Kain, and Steven G. Rivkin. "New Evidence about *Brown v. Board of Education*: The Complex Effects of School Racial Composition on Achievement." National Bureau of Economic Research, Working Paper 8741, 2002. www.nber.org/papers/w8741. Accessed February 24, 2011.

Harding, David J. *Living the Drama: Community, Conflict, and Culture among Inner-City Boys.* Chicago: University of Chicago Press, 2010.

Harding, David J., Michèle Lamont, and Mario Luis Small, eds. "Reconsidering Culture and Poverty." Special edition of *Annals of the American Academy of Political and Social Science* 629, 1 (2010): 6–27.

Harmon, Amy. "Target Cancer: New Drugs Stir Debates on Rules of Clinical Trials." *New York Times,* September 19, 2010, p. 1.

Harris, Judith Rich. *The Nurture Assumption: Why Children Turn Out the Way They Do.* New York: Free Press, 1998.

Hart, Betty, and Todd R. Risley. *Meaningful Differences in the Everyday Experiences of Young American Children.* Baltimore: Paul H. Brookes, 1995.

Haveman, Robert, and Timothy Smeeding. "The Role of Higher Education in Social Mobility." Special Issue, *Opportunity in America: The Future of Children* 16, 2 (2006): 125–50.

Hays, Sharon. *The Cultural Contradictions of Motherhood.* New Haven: Yale University Press, 1996.

Heath, Shirley Brice. *Ways with Words: Language, Life, and Work in Communities and Classrooms.* Cambridge, Eng.: Cambridge University Press, 1983.

Heimer, Carol Anne, and Lisa R. Staffen. *For the Sake of the Children: The Social Organization of Responsibility in the Hospital and the Home.* Chicago: University of Chicago Press, 1998.

Hertz, Rosanna, and Nancy L. Marshall, eds. 2001. *Working Families: The Transformation of the American Home.* Berkeley: University of California Press, 2001.

Hess, Robert D., and Gerald Handel. *Family Worlds: A Psychosocial Approach to Family Life.* Chicago: University of Chicago Press, 1974.

Heymann, Jody. *The Widening Gap: Why America's Working Families Are in Jeopardy and What Can Be Done About It.* New York: Basic Books, 2001.

Higginbotham, Elizabeth. *Too Much to Ask: Black Women in the Era of Integration.* Chapel Hill: University of North Carolina Press, 2001.

Hochschild, Arlie Russell. *The Time Bind: When Work Becomes Home and Home Becomes Work.* New York: Henry Holt, 1997.

Hochschild, Arlie, with Anne Machung. 1989. *The Second Shift: Working Parents and the Revolution at Home.* New York: Avon.

Hochschild, Jennifer L. *Facing Up to the American Dream: Race, Class, and the Soul of the Nation.* Princeton, N.J.: Princeton University Press, 1995.

Hofferth, Sandra L. "Family Reading to Young Children." Working paper, Ann Arbor, Michigan, 1999. Published as "Response Bias in a Popular Indicator of Reading to Children." *Sociological Methodology* 36, 1 (2006): 301–15.

Hofferth, Sandra L., and John Sandberg. "Changes in American Children's Time, 1981–1997." Pp. 26–47 in *Children at the Millennium: Where Have We Come From, Where Are We Going?*, edited by Sandra L. Hofferth and Timothy Joseph Owens. Vol. 6 of *Advances in Life Course Research.* Oxford: JAI, 2001.

———."How American Children Spend Their Time." *Journal of Marriage and the Family* 63, 2 (2001): 295–308.

Hoggart, Richard. *The Uses of Literacy.* Boston: Beacon Press, 1957.

Holloway, Susan D., Bruce Fuller, Marylee F. Rambaud, and Costanza Eggers-Piérola. *Through My Own Eyes: Single Mothers and the Cultures of Poverty.* Cambridge, Mass.: Harvard University Press, 1997.

Hoover-Dempsey, Kathleen V., and Howard M. Sandler. "Why Do Parents Become Involved in their Children's Education?" *Review of Education Research* 67, 1 (1997): 3–42.

Horvat, Erin McNamara, Elliot Weininger, and Annette Lareau. "From Social Ties to Social Capital: Class Differences in the Relations between Schools and Parent Networks." *American Educational Research Journal* 40, 2 (2003): 319–51.

Hout, Michael. "More Universalism, Less Structural Mobility: The American Occupational Structure in the 1980's." *American Journal of Sociology* 93, 6 (1988): 1358–1400.

Hout, Michael, and Claude S. Fischer. 2002. "A Century of Inequality: Family Income, Wealth, and Consumption, 1900–2000." Paper presented at the Conference on Education, Human Capital, and Social Inequality, of the Economy, Justice, and Society Program, University of California, Davis, May 3–4, 2002. Now expanded as: Claude S. Fischer and Michael Hout. *Century of Difference: How America Changed in the Last One Hundred Years.* New York: Russell Sage Foundation, 2006.

Howard, Adam, and Rubén A. Gaztambide-Fernández. *Educating Elites: Class Privilege and Educational Advantage.* Lanham, Md.: Rowman and Little-field, 2010.

Howard, Dennis R., and Robert Madrigal. "Who Makes the Decision, the Parent or the Child?: The Perceived Influence of Parents and Children on the Purchase of Recreation Services." *Journal of Leisure Research* 22, 3 (1990): 244–58.

Hubbard, Lea, Hugh Mehan, and Mary Kay Stein. *Reform as Learning: School Reform, Organizational Culture, and Community Politics in San Diego.* New York: Routledge, 2006.

Hulbert, Ann. *Raising America: Experts, Parents, and a Century of Advice about Children.* New York: Alfred A. Knopf, 2003.

Iceland, John. *Poverty in America: A Handbook.* 2nd ed. Berkeley: University of California Press, 2006.

"I Have a Dream" Foundation. www.ihad.org, 2002. Updated version (2008) accessed on February 24, 2011.

Imber, Jonathan B. "Doctor No Longer Knows Best." Pp. 298–317 in *America at Century's End,* edited by Alan Wolfe. Berkeley: University of California Press, 1991.

Irvin, George. *The Super Rich: The Rise of Inequality in Britain and the United States.* Cambridge, Eng.: Polity, 2008.

Irwin, Katherine. "Into the Dark Heart of Ethnography: The Lived Ethics and Inequality of Intimate Field Relationships." *Qualitative Sociology* 29, 2 (2006): 155–75.

Jackson, Kenneth T. *Crabgrass Frontier: The Suburbanization of the United States.* New York: Oxford University Press, 1985.

Jackson, Mathew O. *Social and Economic Networks.* Princeton, N.J.: Princeton University Press, 2008.

Jacobs, Jerry A., and Kathleen Gerson. *The Time Divide: Work, Family, and Gender Inequality.* Cambridge, Mass.: Harvard University Press, 2004.

———. "Who Are the Overworked Americans?" *Review of Social Economy* 56, 4 (1998): 442–59.

Jacobson, Jennifer. "Help Not Wanted: Parents Are More Involved Than Ever in the Admissions Process, But They Can Do More Harm Than Good." *The Chronicle of Higher Education* 49, 45 (2003): A27.

Jencks, Christopher, Susan Bartlett, Mary Corcoran, James Cruse, David Eagles-field, Gregory Jackson, Kent McClelland, Peter Mueser, Michael Olneck, Joseph Schwartz, Sherry Ward, and Jill Williams. *Who Gets Ahead? The Determinants of Economic Success in America.* New York: Basic Books, 1979.

Jencks, Christopher, and Meredith Phillips, eds. *The Black-White Test Score Gap.* Washington, D.C.: Brookings Institution Press, 1998.

Jencks, Christopher, Marshall Smith, Henry Acland, Mary Jo Bane, David Cohen, Herbert Gintis, Barbara Heyns, and Stephan Michelson. *Inequality: A Reassessment of the Effect of Family and Schooling in America*. New York: Basic Books, 1972.

Jepperson, Ronald L. 1991. "Institutions, Institutional Effects, and Institutionalism." Pp. 143–63 in *The New Institutionalism in Organizational Analysis*, edited by Walter W. Powell and Paul J. DiMaggio. Chicago: University of Chicago Press, 1991.

Kalleberg, Arne L., Barbara F. Reskin, and Ken Hudson. "Bad Jobs in America: Standard and Nonstandard Employment Relations and Job Quality in the United States." *American Sociological Review* 65, 2 (2000): 256–78.

Karabel, Jerome. *The Chosen: The Hidden History of Admission and Exclusion at Harvard, Yale, and Princeton*. New York: Houghton Mifflin, 2005.

Karen, David, and Robert E. Washington, eds. *The Sport and Society Reader*. New York: Routledge, 2009.

Katz, Jack. "On the Rhetoric and Politics of Ethnographic Method." *ANNALS of the American Academy of Political and Social Science* 595, 1 (2004): 280–308.

Katz, Michael B. *Class, Bureaucracy, and Schools: The Illusion of Educational Change in America*. New York: Praeger, 1975.

———. *The Price of Citizenship: Redefining the American Welfare State*. New York: Henry Holt, 2001.

———. *The Undeserving Poor: From the War on Poverty to the War on Welfare*. New York: Pantheon Books, 1989.

Kefalas, Maria. *Working Class Heroes*. Berkeley: University of California Press, 2003.

Keller, Bill, and the *New York Times*. *Class Matters*. New York: Times Books, 2005.

KidsHealth.org. "Is Your Child Too Busy?" The Nemours Foundation/Kids Health, 2010. Available at http://kidshealth.org/parent/growth/growing/child_too_busy.html. Accessed February 24, 2011.

Kindlon, Daniel J. *Too Much of a Good Thing: Raising Children of Character in an Indulgent Age*. New York: Hyperion, 2001.

Kingston, Paul W. *The Classless Society*. Stanford, Calif.: Stanford University Press, 2000.

Kohn, Melvin L. *Class and Conformity: A Study in Values*. 2nd ed. Chicago: University of Chicago Press, 1977.

Kohn, Melvin L., and Carmi Schooler, eds. *Work and Personality: An Inquiry Into the Impact of Social Stratification*. Norwood, N.J.: Ablex, 1983.

Kohn, Melvin L., and Kazimierz M. Slomczynski. *Social Structure and Self-Direction: A Comparative Analysis of the United States and Poland*. Cambridge, Eng.: Basil Blackwell, 1990.

Kombo, Eddah Mutua. "Their Words, Actions, and Meaning: A Researcher's Reflection on Rwandan Women's Experience of Genocide." *Qualitative Inquiry* 15, 2 (2009): 308–23.

Kornblum, William. *Sociology: The Central Questions*. Belmont, Calif.: International Thomson Publishing, 1998.

Kozol, Jonathan. *Savage Inequalities: Children in America's Schools*. New York: HarperCollins, 1992.

Kremer-Sadlik, Tamar, Carolina Izquierdo, and Marilena Fatigante. "Making Meaning of Everyday Practices: Parents' Attitudes toward Children's Extracurricular Activities in the United States and in Italy." *Anthropology and Education Quarterly* 41, 1 (2010): 35–54.

Kropp, Paul. *I'll Be the Parent, You Be the Child: Encourage Excellence, Set Limits, and Lighten Up*. New York: Fisher Books, 2001.

Kurz, Demie. "I Trust Them, but I Don't Trust Them: Issues and Dilemmas in Monitoring Teenagers." Pp. 260–70 in *Who's Watching?: Daily Practices of Surveillance among Contemporary Families*, edited by Margaret K. Nelson and Anita Ilta Garey. Nashville: Vanderbilt University Press, 2009.

Lacy, Karyn R. *Blue-Chip Black: Race, Class, and Status in the New Black Middle Class*. Berkeley: University of California Press, 2007.

Ladd, Everett. "Thinking about America." *The Public Perspective* 4, 5 (1993): 19–34.

Lamborn, Susie D., Nina S. Mounts, Laurence Steinberg, and Sanford M. Dornbusch. "Patterns of Competence and Adjustment among Adolescents from Authoritative, Authoritarian, Indulgent, and Neglectful Families." *Child Development* 62, 5 (1991): 1049–65.

Lamont, Michèle. *The Dignity of Working Men: Morality and the Boundaries of Race, Class, and Immigration.* Cambridge, Mass.: Harvard University Press, 2000.

————. *Money, Morals, and Manners.* Chicago: University of Chicago Press, 1992.

Lamont, Michèle, and Marcel Fournier, eds. *Cultivating Differences: Symbolic Boundaries and the Making of Inequality.* Chicago: University of Chicago Press, 1992.

Lamont, Michèle, and Annette Lareau. "Cultural Capital." *Sociological Theory* 6 (1988): 153–68.

Lamont, Michèle, and Virag Molnar. "The Study of Boundaries across the Social Sciences." *Annual Review of Sociology* 28 (2002): 167–95.

Lamont, Michèle, and Patricia White. *Workshop on Interdisciplinary Standards for Systematic Qualitative Research.* Washington: National Science Foundation, 2009. Available at www.nsf.gov/sbe/ses/soc/ISSQR_workshop_rpt.pdf. Accessed February 24, 2011.

Lareau, Annette. *Doing Ethnography in the Real World: A Companion Guide.* Unpublished manuscript. Department of Sociology, University of Pennsylvania, 2010.

————. *Home Advantage.* 2nd ed. Lanham, Md.: Rowman and Littlefield, 2000.

————. "My Wife Can Tell Me Who I Know: Methodological and Conceptual Problems in Studying Fathers." *Qualitative Sociology* 23, 4 (2000): 407–33.

————. "Studying Families: A Realistic Account." Unpublished manuscript. Temple University, 2002.

————. "Taking Stock of Class." Pp. 3–25 in *Social Class: How Does it Work?,* edited by Annette Lareau and Dalton Conley. New York: Russell Sage Foundation, 2008.

Lareau, Annette, and Dalton Conley, eds. *Social Class: How Does It Work?* New York: Russell Sage Foundation, 2008.

Lareau, Annette, and Amanda Cox. "Class and the Transition to Adulthood: Differences in Parents' Interactions with Institutions." Pp. 134–64 in *Changing Families in an Unequal Society,* edited by Marcia J. Carlson and Paula England. Stanford, Calif.: Stanford University Press, 2011.

Lareau, Annette, and Erin McNamara Horvat. "Moments of Social Inclusion and Exclusion: Race, Class, and Cultural Capital in Family-School Relationships." *Sociology of Education* 72, 1 (1999): 37–53.

Lareau, Annette, and Jeffrey Shultz, eds. *Journeys through Ethnography: Realistic Accounts of Fieldwork.* Boulder, Colo.: Westview Press, 1996.

Lareau, Annette, and Elliot Weininger. "Concerted Cultivation Continues: Class, Culture, and Child Rearing." Pp. 118–51 in *Social Class: How Does It Work?,* edited by Annette Lareau and Dalton Conley. New York: Russell Sage Foundation, 2008.

————. "The Context of School Readiness: Social Class Differences in Time Use in Family Life." Pp. 155–88 in *Early Disparities in School Readiness,* edited by Alan Booth and Anne Crouter. Mahwah, N.J.: Lawrence Erlbaum, 2007.

————. "Time, Work, and Family Life: Reconceptualizing Gendered Time Patterns through the Case of Children's Organized Activities." *Sociological Forum* 3, 23 (2008): 419–54.

————. "Translating Bourdieu into the American Context: The Question of Social Class and Family-School Relationships." *Poetics* 31 (October/December 2003): 375–402.

Larson, Magali Sarfatti. *The Rise of Professionalism: A Sociological Analysis.* Berkeley: University of California Press, 1977.

Larson, Reed W., and Suman Verma. "How Children and Adolescents Spend Time across the World: Work, Play, and Developmental Opportunities." *Psychological Bulletin* 125, 6 (1999): 701–36.

Lassiter, Luke Eric. *The Chicago Guide to Collaborative Ethnography.* Chicago: University of Chicago Press, 2005.

Lee, Jennifer, and Frank D. Bean. "America's Changing Color Lines: Immigration, Race/Ethnicity, and Multiracial Identification." *Annual Review of Sociology* 30 (August 2004): 221–42.

Lever, Janet. "Sex Differences in the Complexity of Children's Games." Pp. 325–44 in *Childhood Socialization,* edited by Gerald Handel. New York: Aldine de Gruyter, 1988.

Levey, Hilary. *Playing to Win: Raising Children in a Competitive Culture.* Berkeley: University of California Press, forthcoming.

Levine, Madeline. *The Price of Privilege: How Parental Pressure and Material Advantage Are Creating a Generation of Disconnected and Unhappy Kids.* New York: HarperCollins, 2006.

Lewis, Amanda E., and Tyrone A. Forman "Contestation or Collaboration? A Comparative Study of Home-School Relations." *Anthropology and Education Quarterly* 33, 1 (2002): 60–89.

Louv, Richard. *Childhood's Future*. New York: Houghton Mifflin, 1990.

Lubrano, Alfred. *Limbo: Blue-Collar Roots, White-Collar Dreams*. New York: John Wiley, 2004.

Lucas, Samuel Roundfield. *Tracking Inequality: Stratification and Mobility in American High Schools*. New York: Teachers College Press, 1999.

Luthar, Suniya S. "The Culture of Affluence: Psychological Costs of Material Wealth." *Child Development* 74, 6 (2003): 1581–93.

Lynd, Robert S., and Helen Merrell Lynd. *Middletown*. New York: Harcourt Brace Jovanovich, 1929.

————. *Middletown in Transition: A Study in Cultural Conflicts*. New York: Harcourt Brace Jovanovich, 1965.

Maccoby, Eleanor E. *The Two Sexes: Growing Up Apart, Coming Together*. Cambridge, Mass.: Harvard University Press, 1998.

MacLeod, Jay. *Ain't No Makin' It: Aspirations and Attainment in a Low-Income Neighborhood*. 3rd ed. Boulder, Colo.: Westview Press, 2008; orig. pub. 1995.

Maier, Kimberly S., Timothy G. Ford, and Barbara Schneider. "Are Middle-Class Families Advantaging Their Children?" Pp. 134–48 in *The Way Class Works: Readings on School, Family, and the Economy*, edited by Lois Weis. New York: Routledge, 2008.

Maier, Shana L., and Brian A. Monahan. "How Close Is Too Close? Balancing Closeness and Detachment in Qualitative Research." *Deviant Behavior* 31, 1 (2010): 1–32.

Marquand, John Phillips. *Point of No Return*. Boston: Little Brown, 1949.

Massey, Douglas S. *Categorically Unequal: The American Stratification System*. New York: Russell Sage Foundation, 2007.

Massey, Douglas, and Nancy Denton. *American Apartheid*. Cambridge, Mass.: Harvard University Press, 1993.

Matthews, Stephen A., Linda M. Burton, and James Detwiler. "Geo-ethnography: Coupling Geographic Information Analysis Techniques with Ethnographic Methods in Urban Research." *Cartographica* 40, 4 (2005): 75–90.

Mayer, Susan E. *What Money Can't Buy: Family Income and Children's Life Chances*. Chicago: University of Chicago Press, 1997.

McCall, Michal M., and Howard S. Becker. "Performance Science." *Social Problems* 37, 1 (1990): 117–32.

McLaughlin, Milbrey W., Merita A. Irby, and Juliet Langman. *Urban Sanctuaries: Neighborhood Organizations in the Lives and Futures of Inner-City Youth*. San Francisco: Jossey-Bass Publishers, 1994.

Medrich, Elliot, Judith A. Roizen, Victor Rubin, and Stuart Buckley. *The Serious Business of Growing Up*. Berkeley: University of California Press, 1982.

Mehan, Hugh, Lea Hubbard, Irene Villanueva, and Angela Lintz. *Constructing School Success: The Consequences of Untracking Low-achieving Students*. Cambridge and New York: Cambridge University Press, 1996.

Menaghan, Elizabeth G. "Work Experiences and Family Interaction Processes: The Long Reach of the Job?" *Annual Review of Sociology* 17 (1991): 419–44.

Meyers, David G., and Ed Diener. "Who Is Happy?" *Psychological Science* 6, 1 (1995): 10–19.

Mezzacappa, Dale. "Ten Years of Learning, Living, Loving: The Say Yes to Education Program Celebrates Success Stories on Its Anniversary." *Philadelphia Inquirer*, July 28, 1997, pp. A1, A28.

Mills, C. Wright. *The Sociological Imagination*. Oxford: Oxford University Press, 1959.

Mintz, Steven. *Huck's Raft: A History of American Childhood*. Cambridge, Mass.: Belknap Press, 2004.

Mishel, Lawrence, Jared Bernstein, and John Schmitt. *The State of Working America 1998–99*. Ithaca, N.Y.: Cornell University Press, 1999.

Morgan, William R., Duane F. Alwin, and Larry J. Griffin. "Social Origins, Parental Values, and the Transmission of Inequality." *American Journal of Sociology* 85, 1 (1979): 156–66.

National Collegiate Athletic Association. "Estimated Probability of Competing in Athletics beyond the High School Interscholastic Level." 2010. www.ncaa.org/wps/portal/ncaahome?WCM_GLOBAL_

CONTEXT=/ncaa/ncaa/academics+and+athletes/education+and+research/probability+of+com-peting/methodology+-+prob+of+competing. Accessed February 24, 2011.

Neckerman, Kathryn M., ed. *Social Inequality*. New York: The Russell Sage Foundation, 2004.

Neckerman, Kathryn M., and Joleen Kirschenmann. "Hiring Strategies, Racial Bias, and Inner-City Workers." *Social Problems* 38 (November 1991): 433–47.

Nelson, Margaret K. *Parenting Out of Control: Anxious Parents in Uncertain Times*. New York: New York University Press, 2010.

Nelson, Margaret K., and Anita Ilta Garey, eds. *Who's Watching?: Daily Practices of Surveillance among Contemporary Families*. Nashville: Vanderbilt University Press, 2009.

Nelson, Margaret K., and Rebecca Schutz. "Day Care Differences and the Reproduction of Social Class." *Journal of Contemporary Ethnography* 36, 3 (2007): 281–317.

Newman, Katherine S. *Declining Fortunes: The Withering of the American Dream*. New York: Basic Books, 1993.

Newman, Maria. "Timeout! (for Overextended Families): A Town Takes a Rare Break from the Frenzy of Hyperscheduling." *New York Times*, March 27, 2002, p. B1. Available online as "A Town Calls a Timeout for Overextended Families"; www.hyper-parenting.com/nytimes5.htm; accessed March 22, 2011.

Ochs, Elinor, Anthony P. Graesch, Angela Mittmann, Thomas Bradbury, and Rena Repetti. "Video Ethnography and Ethnoarchaeological Tracking." Pp. 387–409 in *The Work-Family Handbook: Multi-Disciplinary Perspectives and Approaches to Research*, edited by Marcie Pitt-Catsouphes, Ellen Ernst Kossek, and Stephen A. Sweet. Mahwah, N.J.: Lawrence Erlbaum Associates, 2006.

Ochs, Elinor, Merav Shohet, Belinda Campos, and Margaret Beck. "Coming Together for Dinner: A Study of Working Families." Pp. 57–70 in *Workplace Flexibility: Realigning 20th-Century Jobs for a 21st-Century Workforce*, edited by Kathleen Christensen and Barbara Schneider. Ithaca, N.Y.: Cornell University Press, 2010.

Oliver, Melvin L., and Thomas M. Shapiro. *Black Wealth/White Wealth: A New Perspective on Racial Inequality*. New York: Routledge, 1997.

Orlandella, Angelo Ralph. "Boelen May Know Holland, Boelen May Know Barzini, But Boelen 'Doesn't Know Diddle about the North End!'" *Journal of Contemporary Ethnography* 21, 1 (1992): 69–79.

Pager, Devah. *Marked: Race, Crime, and Finding Work in an Era of Mass Incarceration*. Chicago: University of Chicago Press, 2007.

Pakulski, Jan, and Malcolm Waters. *The Death of Class*. London: Sage Publications, 1996.

Pallas, Aaron M., and Jennifer L. Jennings. "Cumulative Knowledge about Cumulative Advantage." *Swiss Journal of Sociology* 35, 2 (2009): 211–29.

Patillo-McCoy, Mary. *Black Picket Fences: Privilege and Peril among the Black Middle Class*. Chicago and London: University of Chicago Press, 2000.

Pollock, Linda A. *Forgotten Children: Parent-Child Relations from 1500 to 1900*. Cambridge, Eng.: Cambridge University Press, 1983.

Pollock, Mica. *Colormute*. Princeton, N.J.: Princeton University Press, 2004.

Portes, Alejandro. "Social Capital: Its Origins and Applications in Modern Sociology." *Annual Review of Sociology* 24 (1998): 1–24.

Portes, Alejandro, and Dag MacLeod. "Educational Progress of Children of Immigrants: The Roles of Class, Ethnicity, and School Context." *Sociology of Education* 69, 4 (1996): 255–75.

Putnam, Robert D. *Bowling Alone: The Collapse and Revival of American Community*. New York: Simon and Schuster, 2000.

Rabinow, Paul. *Reflections on Fieldwork in Morocco*. 2nd ed. Berkeley: University of California Press, 2007.

Ragin, Charles, Joane Nagel, and Patricia White. *Workshop on Scientific Foundations of Qualitative Research*. Washington, D.C.: National Science Foundation, 2004. Available at www.nsf.gov/pubs/2004/nsf04219/nsf04219.pdf. Accessed February 24, 2011.

Rainwater, Lee, and Timothy M. Smeeding. 1995. "Doing Poorly: The Real Income of American Children in a Comparative Perspective." 1995. Available at www.lisproject.org/publications/liswps/127.pdf. Accessed March 2, 2011.

————. *Poor Kids in a Rich Country: America's Children in Comparative Perspective*. New York: Russell Sage Foundation, 2003.

Ramazanoğlu, Caroline, and Janet Holland. *Feminist Methodology: Challenges and Choices*. Thousand Oaks, Calif.: Sage, 2002.

Reay, Diane. *Class Work: Mothers' Involvement in Their Children's Primary Schooling*. London: University College London Press, 1998.

————. "Doing the Dirty Work of Social Class? Mothers' Work in Support of Their Children's Schooling." *The Sociological Review* 53 (2005): 104–16.

Reay, Diane, Gill Crozier, and David James. *White Middle Class Identities and Urban Schooling*. Hampshire, U.K.: Palgrave Macmillan, in press.

Redford, Jeremy, Jennifer A. Johnson, and Julie Honnold. "Parenting Practices, Cultural Capital, and Educational Outcomes: The Effects of Concerted Cultivation on Academic Achievement." *Race, Gender and Class* 16, 1–2 (2009): 25–44.

Reich, Jennifer A. *Fixing Families: Parents, Power, and the Child Welfare System*. New York: Routledge, 2005.

Reinharz, Shulamit, and Lynn Davidman. *Feminist Methods in Social Research*. New York: Oxford University Press, 1992.

Risman, Barbara J. *Families as They Really Are*. New York: W. W. Norton, 2009.

Ritzer, George. *The McDonaldization of Society*. Thousand Oaks, Calif.: Pine Forge Press, 2000.

Rivera, Lauren. "Ivies, Extracurriculars, and Exclusion: Credentialism in Elite Labor Markets." *Research in Social Stratification and Mobility*, in press.

Robinson, John P., and Geoffrey Godbey. *Time for Life*. University Park: Pennsylvania State University Press, 1997.

Rosenbaum, James E. *Beyond College for All: Career Paths for the Forgotten Half*. New York: Russell Sage Foundation, 2001.

Rosenbaum, James E., Regina Deil-Amen, and Ann E. Person. *After Admission: From College to College Success*. New York: Russell Sage Foundation, 2006.

Rosenfeld, Alvin, and Nicole Wise. *The Over-Scheduled Child*. New York: St. Martin's Griffin, 2000.

Roy, Kevin. "Three-Block Fathers: Spatial Perceptions and Kin-Work in Low-Income Neighborhoods." *Social Problems* 51, 4 (2004): 528–48.

Roy, Kevin, and Linda Burton. "Mothering through Recruitment: Kinscription of Nonresidential Fathers and Father Figures in Low-Income Families." *Family Relations* 56, 1 (2007): 24–39.

Royster, Deirdre Alexia. *Race and the Invisible Hand: How White Networks Exclude Black Men from Blue-Collar Jobs*. Berkeley: University of California Press, 2003.

Rubin, Lillian B. *Worlds of Pain: Life in the Working-Class Family*. New York: Basic Books, 1976.

Rubinowitz, Leonard S., and James E. Rosenbaum. *Crossing the Class and Color Lines: From Public Housing to White Suburbia*. Chicago: University of Chicago Press, 2000.

Sandberg, John F., and Sandra L. Hofferth. "Changes in Children's Time with Parents, U.S. 1981–1997." *Demography* 38, 3 (2001): 423–36.

Scheper-Hughes, Nancy. *Death without Weeping: The Violence of Everyday Life in Brazil*. Berkeley: University of California Press, 1992.

————. "Ire in Ireland." *Ethnography* 1, 1 (2000): 117–40.

————. *Saints, Scholars, and Schizophrenics: Mental Illness in Rural Ireland*. 2nd ed. Berkeley: University of California Press, 2001.

Sennett, Richard, and Jonathan Cobb. *The Hidden Injuries of Class*. New York: Norton, 1972.

Settersten, Richard A., Jr., Frank F. Furstenberg Jr., and Rubén G. Rumbaut. *On the Frontier of Adulthood: Theory, Research, and Public Policy*. Chicago: University of Chicago Press, 2005.

Sewell, William H., and Robert M. Hauser. "The Wisconsin Longitudinal Study of Social and Psychological Factors in Aspirations and Achievements." *Research in Sociology of Education and Socialization* 1 (1980): 59–99.

Shehan, Constance L., ed. *Through the Eyes of the Child: Re-Visioning Children as Active Agents of Family Life.* Vol. 1 of *Contemporary Perspectives on Family Life*, edited by Felix M. Berardo. Stamford, Conn.: JAI Press, 1999.

Shorter, Edward. *The Making of the Modern Family.* New York: Basic Books, 1977.

Shulman, James L., and William G. Bowen. *The Game of Life: College Sports and Educational Values.* Princeton, N.J.: Princeton University Press, 2001.

Sibley, David. "Families and Domestic Routines: Constructing the Boundaries of Childhood." Pp. 123–37 in *Mapping the Subject: Geographies of Cultural Transformation,* edited by Steve Pile and Nigel Thrift. New York: Routledge, 1995.

Simons, Ronald L., Les B. Whitbeck, Rand D. Conger, and Wu Chyi-In. "Intergenerational Transmission of Harsh Parenting." *Developmental Psychology* 27, 1 (1991): 159–71.

Skolnick, Arlene. *Embattled Paradise: The American Family in an Age of Uncertainty.* New York: Basic Books, 1991.

Small, Mario Luis. "How Many Cases Do I Need?: On Science and the Logic of Case Selection in Field-Based Research." *Ethnography* 10, 1 (2009): 5–38.

———. *Unanticipated Gains: Origins of Network Inequality in Everyday Life.* New York: Oxford University Press, 2009.

Smalls, Ciara. "African American Adolescent Engagement in the Classroom and Beyond: The Roles of Mothers' Racial Socialization and Democratic-Involved Parenting." *Journal of Youth and Adolescence* 38, 2 (2009): 204–13.

Smetana, Judith, and Susan Chuang. "Middle-Class African American Parents' Conceptions of Parenting in Early Adolescence." *Journal of Research on Adolescence* 11, 2 (2001): 177–98.

Smith, Dorothy E. *The Everyday World as Problematic: A Feminist Sociology.* Boston: Northeastern University Press, 1987.

———. *Institutional Ethnography: A Sociology for People.* Oxford: AltaMira Press, 2005.

Smith, Sandra. "'Don't Put My Name on It': Social Capital Activation and Job-Finding Assistance among the Black Urban Poor." *American Journal of Sociology* 111, 1 (2005): 1–57.

Stein, Arlene. "Sex, Truths, and Audiotape: Anonymity and the Ethics of Exposure in Public Ethnography." *Journal of Contemporary Ethnography* 39 (2010): 554–68.

Steinberg, Jacques. "One Show's Unexpected Lessons in Reality." *New York Times,* March 16, 2005, p. E1.

Steinberg, Laurence, Susie D. Lamborn, Sanford M. Dornbusch, and Nancy Darling. "Impact of Parenting Practices on Adolescent Achievement." *Child Development* 63, 5 (1992): 1266–81.

Stempel, Carl. "Adult Participation Sports as Cultural Capital: A Test of Bourdieu's Theory of the Field of Sports." *International Review for the Sociology of Sport* 40, 4 (2005): 411–32.

Stevens, Mitchell L. *Creating a Class: College Admissions and the Education of Elites.* Cambridge, Mass.: Harvard University Press, 2007.

Stone, Pamela. *Opting Out?: Why Women Really Quit Careers and Head Home.* Berkeley: University of California Press, 2007.

Stuber, Jenny M. "Class, Culture, and Participation in the Collegiate Extra-Curriculum." *Sociological Forum* 24, 4 (2009): 877–900.

Subedi, Binaya, and Jeongeun Rhee. "Negotiating Collaboration across Differences." *Qualitative Inquiry* 14, 6 (2008): 1070–92.

Swartz, David. *Culture and Power: The Sociology of Pierre Bourdieu.* Chicago: University of Chicago Press, 1997.

Tatum, Beverly Daniel. *Why Are All the Black Kids Sitting Together in the Cafeteria? And Other Conversations about Race.* New York: Basic Books, 1997.

Tavory, Iddo, and Stefan Timmermans. "Two Cases of Ethnography: Grounded Theory and the Extended Case Method." *Ethnography* 10, 3 (2009): 243–63.

ten Have, Paul. *Understanding Qualitative Research and Ethnomethodology.* Thousand Oaks, Calif.: Sage, 2004.

Thacker, Lloyd, ed. *College Unranked: Ending the College Admissions Frenzy.* Cambridge, Mass.: Harvard University Press, 2004.

Thompson, Shona M. *Mother's Taxi*. Albany: State University of New York Press, 1999.

Thorne, Barrie. "'The Chinese Girls' and the 'Pokémon Kids': Children Negotiating Differences in Urban California." Pp. 73–97 in *Figuring the Future: Globalization and the Temporalities of Children and Youth*, edited by Jennifer Cole and Deborah Durham. Santa Fe, N.M.: School for Advanced Research Press, 2008.

———. *Gender Play: Girls and Boys in School*. New Brunswick, N.J.: Rutgers University Press, 1993.

———. "Growing Up in Oakland." Paper presented at ASA Annual Meeting. Anaheim, Calif., August 2001. Revised and published as: "The Crisis of Care." Pp. 165–78 in *Work-Family Challenges for Low-Income Parents and Their Children*, edited by Nan Crouter and Alan Booth. Hillsdale, N.J.: Lawrence Erlbaum Publishers, 2003.

Tierney, Joseph P., Jean Baldwin Grossman, with Nancy L. Resch. *Making a Difference: An Impact Study of Big Brothers/Big Sisters*. Philadelphia: Public/Private Ventures, 1995. Available at www.ppv.org. Accessed February 24, 2011.

Tulgan, Bruce. *Not Everyone Gets a Trophy: How to Manage Generation Y*. San Francisco: Jossey-Bass, 2009.

Tyack, David B. *The One Best System: A History of American Urban Education*. Cambridge, Mass.: Harvard University Press, 1974.

Tyler, John H. "The Economic Benefits of the GED: Lessons from Recent Research." *Review of Educational Research* 73, 3 (2003): 369–403.

Tyler, John H., and Magnus Lofstrom. "Finishing High School: Alternative Pathways and Dropout Recovery." *The Future of Children* 19, 1 (2009): 77–103.

Tyson, Karolyn. *Integration Interrupted: Tracking, Black Students, and Acting White after Brown*. New York: Oxford University Press, 2011.

U.S. Census Bureau. "Educational Attainment—People 25 Years Old and Over, by Total Money Earnings in 2009, Work Experience in 2009, Age, Race, Hispanic Origin, and Sex." Current Population Survey. Annual Social and Economic Supplement. 2010. www.census.gov/hhes/www/cpstables/032010/perinc/new03_000.htm. Accessed March 2, 2011.

U.S. Department of Education. "Academic Preparation for College in the High School Senior Class of 2003–04." NCES 2010-169. Washington, D.C.: National Center for Education Statistics, 2010.

———. "Access to Post-Secondary Education for 1992 High School Graduates." NCES 98–105, 1997. http://nces.ed.gov/pubs98/98105.pdf. Accessed March 3, 2011.

———. *The Condition of Education, 1995*. Washington, D.C.: National Center for Educational Statistics, 1995.

———. *The Condition of Education, 2001*. Washington, D.C.: National Center for Education Statistics, 2001.

———. "Educational Aspirations." Youth Indicators, 2005. Washington, D.C.: National Center for Education Statistics, 2005. Available at http://nces.ed.gov/programs/youthindicators/Indicators.asp?PubPageNumber=18=18&ShowTablePage=TablesHTML/18.asp. Accessed March 1, 2011.

———. "Event Dropout Rates of 15-through-24-year-olds Who Dropped Out of Grades 10–12, by Family Income: October 1972 through October 2006." Washington, D.C.: National Center for Education Statistics, 2008. Available at http://nces.ed.gov/pubs2008/dropout06/figures/figure_01.asp. Accessed March 1, 2011.

———. "First-Generation College Students." Washington, D.C.: National Center for Education Statistics, 2005. Available at http://nces.ed.gov/pubs2005/2005171.pdf. Accessed February 24, 2011.

———. "Students Whose Parents Did Not Go to College: Postsecondary Access, Persistence, and Attainment." NCES 2001–126. Washington, D.C.: National Center for Education Statistics, 2001. http://nces.ed.gov/pubs2001/2001126.pdf. Accessed February 24, 2011.

Useem, Elizabeth L. "Student Selection into Course Sequences in Mathematics: The Impact of Parental Involvement and School Policies." *Journal of Research on Adolescence* 1, 3 (1991): 231–50.

Valdes, Guadalupe. *Con Respecto: Bridging the Distances between Culturally Diverse Families and Schools*. New York: Teachers College Press, 1996.

Van Ausdale, Debra, and Joe Feagin. "Using Racial and Ethnic Concepts: The Critical Case of Very Young Children." *American Sociological Review* 61, 5 (1996): 779–93.

Van Maanen, John. *Tales of the Field: On Writing Ethnography.* Chicago: University of Chicago Press, 1988.

Vanneman, Reeve, and Lynn Weber Cannon. *The American Perception of Class.* Philadelphia: Temple University Press, 1987.

Vidich, Arthur J., and Joseph Bensman. *Small Town in Mass Society: Class, Power, and Religion in a Rural Community,* rev. ed. Champaign: University of Illinois Press, 2000.

Wacquant, Loïc J. D. "Negative Social Capital: State Breakdown and Social Destitution in America's Urban Core." *Netherlands Journal of Housing and the Built Environment* 13, 1 (1998): 25–40.

Waksler, Frances. *Studying the Social Worlds of Children.* London: Routledge-Falmer Press, 1991.

Walker, Karen. "'Always There For Me': Friendship Patterns and Expectations among Middle- and Working-Class Men and Women." *Sociological Forum* 10, 2 (1995): 273–96.

Waller, Maureen R., and Raymond Swisher. "Fathers' Risk Factors in Fragile Families: Implications for 'Healthy' Relationships and Father Involvement." *Social Problems* 53, 3 (2006): 392–420.

Warner, William Lloyd, J. O. Low, Paul S. Lunt, and Leo Srole. *Yankee City.* New Haven: Yale University Press, 1963.

Warr, Mark, and Christopher G. Ellison. "Rethinking Social Reactions to Crime." *American Journal of Sociology* 106, 3 (2000): 551–78.

Warren, Mark. "A Collaborative Approach to Ethnographic Case Study Research: The Community Organizing and School Reform Project at Harvard University." Paper presented at a colloquium, Department of Sociology, University of Pennsylvania, October 8, 2010.

Waters, Mary C. *Black Identities.* New York: Russell Sage Foundation, 1999.

Weininger, Elliot B. "Class and Causation in Bourdieu." Pp. 49–114 in *Current Perspectives in Social Theory,* vol. 21, edited by Jennifer M. Lehmann. Oxford, Eng.: Elsevier, 2002.

———. "Foundations of Bourdieu's Class Analysis." Pp. 82–118 in *Approaches to Class Analysis,* edited by Erik O. Wright. Cambridge: Cambridge University Press, 2005.

Weininger, Elliot, and Annette Lareau. 2002. "Children's Participation in Organized Activities and the Gender Dynamics of the 'Time Bind.'" Paper presented at American Sociological Association Annual Meetings. Chicago, 2002. Published as: Lareau and Weininger. "Time, Work, and Family Life: Reconceptualizing Gendered Time Patterns through the Case of Children's Organized Activities." *Sociological Forum* 3, 23 (2008): 419–54.

———. "Cultivating the Religious Child." Paper presented at American Sociological Association, Las Vegas, Nev., 2011.

———. "Paradoxical Pathways: An Ethnographic Extension of Kohn's Findings on Class and Childrearing." *Journal of Marriage and Family* 71, 3 (2009): 680–95.

Weininger, Elliot, Annette Lareau, Dalton Conley, and Melissa Velez. "Concerted Cultivation and Natural Growth among American Children." Unpublished manuscript. Department of Sociology, University of Pennsylvania, 2011.

Weis, Lois. *Class Reunion: The Remaking of the American White Working Class.* New York: Routledge, 2004.

———, ed. *The Way Class Works: Readings on School, Family, and the Economy.* New York: Routledge, 2008.

Wells, Amy Stuart, and Robert L. Crain. *Stepping over the Color Line: African American Students in White Suburban Schools.* New Haven: Yale University Press, 1997.

West, Cornel. *Race Matters.* Boston: Beacon Press, 1993.

Western, Bruce. *Punishment and Inequality in America.* New York: Russell Sage Foundation, 2007.

Whitehead, Jack, and Jean McNiff. *Action Research: Living Theory.* Thousand Oaks, Calif.: Sage, 2006.

Whyte, William Foote. "On the Evolution of *Street Corner Society.*" Pp. 9–73 in *Journeys through Ethnography: Realistic Accounts of Fieldwork,* edited by Annette Lareau and Jeffrey Shultz. Boulder, Colo.: Westview Press, 1996.

———. *Street Corner Society: The Social Structure of an Italian Slum,* 4th ed. Chicago: University of Chicago Press, 1993; orig. pub. 1943.

Willis, Paul E. *Learning to Labour: How Working Class Kids Get Working Class Jobs.* Farnborough, Eng.: Saxon House, 1977.

Wills, Eric. "Parent Trap." *Chronicle of Higher Education* 51, 46 (2005): A4.

Wolf, Diane L., ed. *Feminist Dilemmas in Fieldwork.* Boulder, Colo.: Westview Press, 1996.

Wolf, Margery. *A Thrice-Told Tale: Feminism, Postmodernism, and Ethnographic Responsibility.* Stanford, Calif.: Stanford University Press, 1992.

Wright, Erik Olin. *Class, Crisis, and the State.* London: New Left Books, 1978.

———. "The Conceptual Status of Class Structure in Class Analysis." Pp. 17–38 in *Bringing Class Back In,* edited by Scott G. McNall, Rhonda F. Levine, and Rick Fantasia. Boulder, Colo.: Westview Press, 1991.

———. "Rethinking, Once Again, the Concept of Class Structure." Pp. 41–72 in *Reworking Class,* edited by John R. Hall. Ithaca, N.Y.: Cornell University Press, 1997.

———, ed. *Approaches to Class Analysis.* Cambridge, Eng.: Cambridge University Press, 2005.

Wrigley, Julia. "Do Young Children Need Intellectual Stimulation? Experts' Advice to Parents, 1900–1985." *History of Education Quarterly* 29, 1 (1989): 41–75.

———. *Other People's Children.* New York: Basic Books, 1995.

Young, Alford A., Jr. *The Minds of Marginalized Black Men.* Princeton, N.J.: Princeton University Press, 2004.

Zelizer, Viviana. *Pricing the Priceless Child: The Changing Social Value of Children.* New York: Basic Books, 1985.

CHAPTER 9

GENDER AND DISCRIMINATION IN EDUCATION

Consider the following questions as you read this chapter.

QUESTIONS TO CONSIDER

1   The author states that there is discrimination against black males in the education system. How does he support this claim? Give some of the data here.

2   What were some of the personal experiences related by black males about their experience of gender discrimination in an educational setting?

3   Most people reading this are college students. Have you witnessed people being treated differently in K–12 or college due to their gender? Their race?

4   Are the stratification systems of gender and race distinct and separate, or do they intersect? Discuss, relating to this article.

5   What is the author's main point?

KEY TERMS

the black gender gap

GENDER AND DISCRIMINATION IN EDUCATION

BY TERENCE FITZGERALD

As mentioned earlier, part of my research for this book involved interviewing dozens of Black men about their experiences with the
education system. One theme that recurred throughout these interviews
was the observable differences in experiences between Black males and
Black females. Of all the topics of conversation, this issue proved to be the
most stressful and at times contentious area of discussion. This chapter
offers evidence of the gender gap in Black education and the ways in
which Black males are faced with specific struggles as they pursue their
schooling.

An examination of the educational differences between Black males and
Black females is an important one. The effects of their distinct treatment
are evident in everything from the disproportionalities seen in white-collar
employment trends and academic attainment to murder rates and involvement within the criminal justice system. Further, differences in treatment
are seen in the "helping professions" such as social work. In general, this
profession does little to nothing in regard to Black heterosexual males
in comparison to its involvement with issues of those overseas, US immigrants, homosexual and transgendered populations, and females. In an
earlier piece in *Dilemmas of Black Faculty at U.S. Predominantly White
Institutions: Issues in the Post-Multicultural Era*, I spotlight the way in which
social work education and the profession, despite their publicized doctrine
of social justice, operate within a style speaking to racial oppression toward
Black males.[1] For a particular population that is socially and academically at

risk, I find their avoidance of the population very telling. Their blindness and disregard of the well-being of Black males is simply a mirror of society's in general.

How and why do these gender differences exist? What are the effects of them? Even talking about Black male versus Black female issues can be a contentious undertaking. But my position of reporting on and exploring this topic in terms of data presented and the narratives is simply to shed light on a sensitive subject that few have really thought about. Moreover, by exploring the topic of gender difference, I am hoping to begin a process that will alleviate a degree of social conflict occurring between the two groups. For example, in Great Britain the increase of females in the areas of education and employment has called many to call males "tomorrow's second sex."[2] The increase of females within these spaces, coupled with the overall lacking male education and employment trends, has begun to have critical ramifications upon their social interactions.[3] The British government and representatives in the field of education have begun to take public notice of this socially critical situation.

In order to alleviate this from occurring within the United States, the subject must be openly investigated and discussed with rigor. We as a nation must not shy away from such subjects in order to avoid the thorny side of gender debate, for the societal stakes are too high. Given the strength of the sentiments expressed within the conversations I have collected, I hope those among us who are steadfastly pursuing constructive social change will be open-minded to the issue at hand. Next, I hope they further explore the validity of difference through the utilization of a larger sample of people. Therefore, if differences are continuously noted as documented within these pages, the internal effect of these differences must be courageously investigated in context of treatment within the domain of education, regardless of the difficult debate the issues will inevitably bring forth.

Gender difference was a fascinating area to discuss with the males I interviewed. Within these interactions I received some thought-provoking responses. All of the men unanimously affirmed they witnessed and were relatively conscious of some of the major obstacles Black girls and women confront in both public and higher education. Alex, Al, David, and many others noted a kinship with their female counterparts in regard to the prevalence and effects of a Black racist ideology within the world. Despite age or level of education, many were aware that being a male meant they could not understand the totality of what it means to be a Black female within a society rooted in White supremacy. They were very aware that the struggle Black females have and currently endure was more complex than they could imagine.

At the same time, their experiences made them believe that being Black and male subjected them to difficulties that were unique to them as men. This was true within the discussions pertaining not only to education but society in general.

THE BLACK GENDER GAP

The gender disparities across all racial groups within institutions of higher education are not uncommon findings. But the severity of and consequences for Blacks are exceptionally noteworthy. The National Center for Education Statistics (NCES) revealed in 2004 a 28.6 percent gender gap for Black students in postsecondary enrollment in comparison with the 1976 rate of 8.7 percent.[4] This gender gap results in Black females outnumbering males by a ratio of 2:1. For Whites, Asians, and Latinos during the same time span, the difference was 11.8 percent, 7.5 percent, and 17.1 percent in 2004 and 4.7 percent, 8.6 percent, and 7.6 percent in 1976, respectively. In 2008, out of the fifteen million undergraduate students attending postsecondary institutions, only 5 percent were Black males.[5]

The American Council on Higher Education (ACE), in March 2011, released its *Annual Status Report on Minorities in Higher Education*. It confirmed that the rate of Black males attending and graduating from college and university campuses had declined significantly.[6] It has been estimated that twenty years ago, approximately 30 percent of all Black males attempted to attain some form of higher education, while Black females attended at a rate of 28 percent. Today, the ACE reports campuses are experiencing a 37 percent attendance rate for Black males and a 42 percent rate for Black females. The difference between the two groups shows that Black males are dropping out while Black females stay in school and graduate. Between 1999 and the 2000 academic school year, there were 55,314 associate degrees earned by Blacks (66.2 percent by females).[7] In 2007–2008, there were 95,702 associate degrees earned by Blacks (68.6 percent to females). There were 98,251 (64.9 percent to females) and 152,457 (65.7 percent to females) bachelor degrees earned respectively for 1998–1999 and 2007–2008. Black females earned 68.0 percent of the master's degrees in 1997–1998 and 71.8 percent in 2007–2008. For doctorates, 60.1 percent and 66.4 percent of degrees were awarded respectively for the 1998–1999 and 2007–2008 academic years. This trend is not specific only to predominantly White campuses, as one might assume; even at historically Black colleges and universities (HBCU), in 2007 the rates of Black males and females graduating were estimated at 28.5 percent and 43.1 percent, respectively.

Dr. Boyce Watkins, an educator for over seventeen years, attempted to answer the riddle as to why the trend exists in an interview on CNN.[8] He affirmed that the environment on college campuses systematically does not provide role models within the classroom (professors). In addition, the overall system of public education has not adequately prepared and supported Black males for life after their formal education. In a web article, he wrote,

> I was angry during the interview because the lack of educational and economic achievement of the black male, along with mass

incarceration, has continuously threatened the strength and stability of the African American family. I was angry because most of us, as Americans, have not had a sense of urgency when it comes to resolving these disparities. Some black men are too busy learning how to become thugs, and white America is too busy perpetuating racially imbalanced institutions that keep Jim Crow alive. Many black women are busy blaming every social ill on black men, which is equally problematic. At the end of the day, all of us are wrong, and we all have the ability to work together to solve this problem.[9]

I interviewed many educational professionals while doing research [...]. Those who work within these institutions of higher education, such as Jerry, Aaron, and Matt, who have taught and held administrative positions for the past fifteen to twenty years, provided me with an interesting perspective on institutional pursuits. They all talked about the need for not only connecting with the students on a personal level, but also considering the social dynamics of their lives and how they have affected their stance on college campuses before creating initiatives that focus on Black male achievement, recruitment, and retention. Jerry, who happened to be at the time an academic advisor and administrator at a research university in Illinois, noted, "The sisters know what questions to ask when on campus. They establish relationships early with professors, peers, and administrators. They take advantage of the resources, even if they do not need them. Brothers just don't ... for whatever reason."

GENDER DISCRIMINATION IN THE PUBLIC SCHOOL AND BEYOND

Some evidence has indicated Black males and females experience the same amount of racial discrimination during the middle school years.[10] Black males, however, in addition to experiencing racial discrimination must also deal with gender discrimination.[11] Although women of all races must contend with gender discrimination, the combination of Blackness and maleness produces serious problems for young Black male students.

This was evident from the comments by people like Alex and Russ during our interviews. Alex, a high school science teacher, discussed an incident in public school that exemplified gender discrimination: "Being a Black male in school, I always had to be sweet [pause] ... never demonstrative [pause] ... I had to always be nice. I could not be emotional. If I did, I was considered the Angry Black male! That always bothered me." I asked if he ever noticed gender discrimination in public school. He responded,

> I remember a debate where I was showing that I knew my stuff and I was getting very passionate about the subject. And I remember my speech teacher stopped the debate and said, "It sounds like you are getting upset here. Just calm down and take a couple of breaths ... she is not attacking you." I remember thinking I know she is not attacking me. I am whipping her ass in this debate here. I was only responding to the subject. At that time in education, you never challenged a teacher. So I just ate it. I ended up getting a B. She said it was due to my emotions displayed during the debate. I was taking it personal? I needed to remove myself from the debate? Interesting ... the topic was nothing personal to me.

When Russ, a laid-off field service engineer, was asked about the issue of gender discrimination, he said this:

> All the sisters I graduated college with have a masters or PhD. The brothers on the other hand either dropped out of school [paused] ... maybe got bachelors. Why? [short pause] Because it is not encouraged with us. There are subtle undertones ... so subtle that we are not encouraged ... . The bottom line is this [pause] ... the message to all of us, even from Black women, is that the Black male ain't nothing. If the Black woman wants something, they gotta get it on your own. That is what the Black woman is taught and what they do. To a degree, the world allows this due to their gender. Now, I am not saying all Black women are granted the golden ticket. I am saying that Whites, especially White men in charge, look at them as women. Their sexist mindset does not see them as much of a threat as a Black man.

Jerry, a university administrator, had similar experiences:

> Black females and in particular White females had better treatment than we did where I came from. I remember, getting ready for state exams, the teachers pulled the girls out of the room and give them test prep. The Black boys, we were inside playing checkers or the paper football game. We were not considered valuable enough to

be given these tips on how to take these state exams. I blew that test off for the first time that year.

The men I interviewed also offered examples of Black male gender discrimination in the areas of special education and discipline. Astin, a forty-year-old high school science teacher, discussed in great detail the manner in which discipline is disproportionately doled out to Black males. He mentioned his fellow teachers were more likely to seek a punitive solution to remedy Black male disruptive behavior than for all others in his school. He explained, "There are lots of examples of discipline not being equally dealt out. White boys get away with more than the Black males. The little sisters get it, but we gotta [get] them little Black boys first [said in a ridiculing tone]." Cole, a twenty-nine-year-old teacher and graduate student in Illinois, said he noticed a difference in discipline from an early age:

> First grade was the first time I noticed Blacks were treated differently. I was mischievous as all kids are…. I was put on top of the heater in front of the whole class by the school principal due to an early altercation where a kid and me fell into a big puddle in the school yard. He belittled me in front of the class. The white student received no such treatment. Then I knew something was not right.

Romello, a single father who graduated from an inner-city and all-Black public school system, took notice of the treatment of his mostly Black female staff. He affirmed that his experience of being raised in a large family with brothers, sisters, and cousins helped him to see this occurrence. When asked about observations of gender discrimination, he explained,

> I think cause I had so many siblings and nieces and nephews, I noticed the discipline in school. Boys just got it the worse. I think it is a physical thing. The fighting. But then again we had some girls beatin' up on the boys. They never got the paddling the boys got, though. Sometimes you could feel that we as Black males in high school were seen as more of a physical threat.

In regard to perception and gender differences, Cole, who attended HBCU and PWCI for his undergraduate and graduate education, respectively, was quite aware of the perceptions and gender discrimination on both campuses. While attending undergraduate, he explained he did not see incidences of gender discrimination until his junior year of college. Cole affirmed, "At Central State I remember the administration at the college of education always had their favorites. It was apparent to all of us. Female deans and professors always mentored the Black females. I didn't have one myself." While pursuing a doctoral degree in a well-known college of education, Cole was confronted with many examples of gender discrimination. At first these incidences were difficult to comprehend because most of the administrators, professors, and instructors within his specific department were people of color, which is an example of Collins's matrix of domination—the oppressed becoming the oppressors:

> When I came to the [program], the difference between males and females was apparent. I would not think this would happen [when] the majority of staff were people of color. They should know better. It is a struggle everyday here. It is a struggle to get fellowships or word of fellowships, [teacher assistant] offers … just the money is rough. You see females getting most of the money and opportunities. They are getting the majority of resources and mentorship. I try not to think about it. Once I remember applying for an internal grant and another Black male student in the main office of the department told me as I turned it in that, you know, you are not a female. You are not gonna even get it, so do not waste your time.

I proceeded and asked him if he was aware of other males openly complaining about this observation. He explained he had seen no one openly complaining within his department. Then I proposed, "What if the department was 90 percent male and this population was receiving all the resources and attention? What do you think the female students would do about it?" He answered, "They would raise hell and changes would be made." I asked Cole why he thought gender discrimination existed within his department.

> I would assume that females think that cause we are males, we automatically have privileges. The same White males have, the exact same, which is not the case. A lot think this. I have called sisters out in my program before about this. They seemed to have a sense that Black females' struggle is different and that the Black male is not really on the same page because our privileges are equal to White males. If you are a heterosexual male who is assertive, you are viewed as a type of privileged male. They see you as more threatening as well.

He then broached the topic of difference in terms of sexuality. Cole alleged, "The gay males are seen in a better light. Females are more welcoming to them. They share information with them. [pause] In fact I have never worked with another female on a project. They do not share as they do with homosexual males. I really believe the females go out of their way to work together and avoid us."

Given the experiences of my interviewees and current research, it is hard not to conclude that Black male issues of concern do not sincerely matter in our culture. It is difficult to think otherwise when people like Christina Hoff Sommers, author of *The War against Boys: How Misguided Feminism Is Harming Our Young Men*, discuss incidences that support this argument. She notes the remarks of Rudy Crew, then chancellor of the all-girl Young Women's Leadership School, located in the eastern portion of Harlem in New York City.[12] Due to the school's success in enhancing the academic and social lives of a poor and an almost all Black and Latino female student body, the *New York Times* advocated for the creation of an equivalent school for their male counterparts. Chancellor Crew discarded the idea and responded by expounding, "This is a case where the existence of the all-girls school makes an important statement about the viable education of girls. I want to continue to make that statement."[13] It is hard to see why building a school dedicated to the excellence of a population of mostly poor males of color would hinder that statement. This sort of anti–Black and Latino male attitude sends a strong message to marginalized males that they do not matter. This observation was clear in Alex and Kevin's conversations. In fact, it was established in a number of other conversations as well. Alex explained:

> The system needs to shut down Black males. If you want to keep any race under your thumb, you control the male population. You want to keep people under your thumb economically, socially, and psychologically? The Black male is the key to that [pause]. The man is the key. If you destroy the Black male, you destroy the race … or at least control it. This can be done in education. We do not give a damn about [Black and Latino males] in education … . White people in control are thinking, I am not afraid of females … . I do not think the system of oppression really pays as close attention to the rise of women as it does men.

Kevin also discussed the issue of Black male social control and the overall purpose of it in education:

> One with power is not gonna teach those he oppresses to take away power. The major threat to White men is Black men. We are a threat. How do you take away the power of Black males? Well, if you could turn a kid off to education, if you could get a kid to

believe that education is not the ticket or get him to believe that his success is up to him, you got a slave. If you take away his model in life and make the predominate teachers White … no Black males in the home … if he goes to the church and sees none, but goes to the community he sees a bunch of males who are not role models or represent real men … he becomes that male on the streets. What do you expect of them in school when they do not see the positive models who have gone through the process and come out successful?

THE RESISTANCE TO ADDRESSING BLACK GENDER DISCRIMINATION

There is clearly a gender problem when it comes to Black students in secondary and university education. But the resistance to addressing it is strong. One interviewee, Cole, told about a meeting he attended in grad school to plan a conference on perceptions and Black gender discrimination:

> Once I was in a group of Black males and we were preparing to write a proposal for a conference on oppression of the Black males on HBCU campuses. As we were discussing the issue a sister came in and listened while we were discussing our narratives and experiences. Later she left and I did not think anything of it. She then told other females about it, and they were really upset. They confronted us as we were exiting the building. We asked, Why can't we talk about our narrative, our stories? One said she found it interesting that we did not talk about Black females. I was like, Is it like that? I was sad cause it showed that Black males cannot or should not talk about what is going on in our lives as oppression affects us specifically. The females basically felt that Black females could not be left out. They told us that it was uncalled for to only talk about Black males and what we [were] attempting to do was not right.

This resistance is common. The few forward-thinking programs that have tried to address the problem have been met with their share of public opposition. For example, the City University of New York created the Black Male Initiative in 2004 and met resistance toward their efforts.[14] And at the time of writing this chapter, the New York Civil Rights Coalition, which opposes racially separated programs, filed a complaint that was still pending with the US Education Department's Office for Civil Rights. They claim that singling out Black males for specific support violates federal civil rights laws (Title VI of the 1964 Civil Rights Act and Title IX of the 1972 educational amendments).

HOW TO CLOSE THE GENDER GAP

Although the statistics regarding the Black gender gap are daunting, the situation is not hopeless. There are important ways that institutions and individuals alike can work to close the achievement gap.

On the institutional level, a handful of universities have begun to seriously study Black male status in higher education, and some have even developed programs to address the problem on their individual campuses. The Ohio State University's Todd Anthony Bell National Resource Center on the African American Male and several other programs reach out to Black freshman males in an effort to help reduce barriers and negative experiences influencing their academic careers.[15] Due to the fact the overall graduation rate at Ohio State was estimated at approximately 92.8 percent, while Black males ranged within the area of 80.7 percent, the university realized their overall emphasis should be to effectively increase the retention and success rate of this student population. A select few collegiate institutions focusing on the Black male retention rate are the University System of Georgia, the National Association for Equal Opportunity in Higher Education, and Georgia Southwestern State University.[16]

Many of the interviewees emphasized the role of mentoring as well. For example, Jerry conveyed his opinion in regard to why Black males are academically falling behind their black counterparts in college:

> Why sisters are excelling? I think that from the Brothers I talked to and what I see is a lot of them have realized they have to let go of home. They are caught between two worlds ... their persona on the block and their persona on campus. The block [short pause] ... academics is not celebrated. Here on campus [short pause] ... the thug is not celebrated. So it is a matter of them learning how to navigate and code switch and be able to speak both languages. That is one of the major struggles I see.

Aaron continued this theme:

> Trust is huge … it is about relationships. If you establish it with one dude, he will bring four or five of his buddies to the next meeting you have with him. I see it happen all the time. It is not what I get paid to do. When I articulate my efforts to my supervisor in lieu of what they have me assigned to do, they get upset. They convey the message that relationships is not my job…. I keep doing it anyway.

Those institutions that step out on the ledge of creative thinking and make investments founded in social justice should be commended instead of condemned. One such institution is the Urban Prep Academy in Chicago, a high school whose efforts deserve close attention. Not only did the graduating class of 2010 graduate 100 percent of their senior class but its entire cohort of 107 students reported to the building principal that they planned on attending college.[17]

CONCLUSION

A small number of people like Chris displayed an uneasiness and disconcerting sentiments about the topic of gender discrimination. But I observed this when I pressed them on the issue: when they were made to feel comfortable discussing the matter due to examples I provided from my life or others I previously talked to, their tension subsided and they all began to state examples within their lives where this was displayed.

It is important to note that studies do exist that examine both gender and racial discrimination in education. But they are small in numbers. Relying upon them fully would be a case of overgeneralizing. However, these outcomes illustrate dissimilarities between Black male and female experiences concerning racism within the area of education. This is definitely counter to those studies that suggest that Black women face more gender discrimination than Black males.[18] More research is clearly needed regarding this issue with students.

It is encouraging that some universities are proactively addressing the issue through research and mentoring programs. In the next chapter, we look at another way that mentoring and community support can bolster the opportunities and success of young Black students.

NOTES

1 Terence Fitzgerald, "Is Social Work Education Beyond the Grips of the White Racial Frame? Historical and Present Examples of Oppression within the Discipline of Social Work," in *Dilemmas of Black Faculty at U.S. Predominantly White Institutions: Issues in the Post-Multicultural Era*, ed. Rudolph Alexander, Anthony J. Lemelle, and Sharon E. Moore (Lewiston, NY: Edwin Mellen Press, 2010).

2 Christina Hoff Sommers, *The War against Boys: How Misguided Feminism Is Harming Our Young Men* (New York: Simon and Schuster, 2000), 33–44.

3 Sommers, *The War against Boys*, 33–44.

4 National Center for Education Statistics, *Status and Trends in the Education of Racial and Ethnic Minorities* (Washington, DC: National Center for Education Statistics, July 2007).

5 Terrell L. Strayhom, "The Role of Supportive Relationships in Supporting African American Males' Success in College," *Journal of Student Affairs Research and Practice* 45 (2008): 26–48.

6 *The State of Black America*, available at http://www.blackamericaweb.com/?q=articles/news/the_state_of_black_america_news/17673.

7 U.S. Department of Education, National Center for Education Statistics, "Condition of Education 2010," available at http://nces.ed.gov/fastfacts/display.asp?id=72.

8 "Boyce Watkins Talks College Enrollment Rates for African American Males on CNN's HLN," available at HLN at http://blip.tv/file/3715241.

9 Boyce Watkins, "Black Voices, CNN Asks Why Black Men Are Not Graduating from College," available at http://blogs.blackvoices.com/2010/06/05/why-black-men-are-not-graduating-from-college/.

10 Courtney D. Cogburn, Tabbye M. Chavous, and Tiffany M. Griffin, "School-Based Racial and Gender Discrimination among African American Adolescents: Exploring Gender Variation in Frequency and Implications for Adjustment," *Race and Social Problems* 3 (2011): 25–37.

11 Cogburn, Chavous, and Griffin, "School-Based Racial and Gender Discrimination."

12 Sommers, *The War against Boys*, 39.

13 Sommers, *The War against Boys*, 39.

14 Peter Schmidt, "Colleges Seek Key to Success of Black Men in Classroom," *Chronicle of Higher Education*, October 10, 2008, 55, A1–A25.

15 Howard Feintuch, "Black Male Rising," *Diverse Issues in Higher Education* 27 (2010): 18–19.

16 Schmidt, "Colleges Seek Key to Success."

17 Boyce Watkins, "Black Male School in Inner City Has 100 Percent College Attendance," available at http://www.bvblackspin.com/2010/05/27/black-males-in-college/.

18 Michael T. Schmitt, Nyla R. Branscombe, Diane Kobrynowicz, and Susan Owen, "Perceiving Discrimination against One's Gender Group Has Different Implications for Well-Being in Women and Men," *Society for Personality and Social Psychology* 28 (2002): 197–210.

CHAPTER 10

A LATE CAPITALIST WORLD

Consider the following questions as you read this chapter.

QUESTIONS TO CONSIDER

1 How is the creation of value related to the exploitation of labor?

2 What is it about capitalism that makes it an unstable system?

3 What characterizes advanced capitalism?

4 The author discusses political involvement of the population. How involved is he saying people should be? How involved are you? Do you plan to be politically involved? How?

5 What is the author's main point?

KEY TERMS

capitalism
private profit
commodity production
wage labor
use value
exchange value
surplus value
labor theory of value
advanced capitalism
rationality crisis

A LATE CAPITALIST WORLD

BY STEVEN M. BUECHLER

READING 10

For critical sociology, capitalism is the dominant force in the modern world. Its corporations dwarf the social landscape. Its pursuit of profit shapes all social priorities. Its logic saturates our culture. Without understanding capitalism, we can't know where we came from, what we are doing, or where we are going.

We begin with Marx, followed by an analysis of the advanced capitalism that matured in the twentieth century and is expanding globally in the twenty-first century. We then explore potential crises that might emerge in advanced capitalism and conclude with some economic trends shaping our world as the new century unfolds.

MARX'S ANALYSIS OF CAPITALISM

Marx saw capitalism as a historically specific economic system. It is not eternal. It was preceded by other economic systems and will be followed by still others. It is distinguished by three elements. First, it is devoted to the realization of profit. Second, this occurs through the production and sale of commodities. Third, these commodities are produced by wage-labor. This combination of private profit, commodity production, and wage-labor sets capitalism apart from all other economic systems.

LABOR THEORY OF VALUE

Marx begins with a seemingly simple question: Where do profits come from? How is it possible for a capitalist to invest in resources, labor, and technology to create products whose sale results in more money than was there at the beginning? Not every business succeeds, but there is a systematic quality to the accumulation of capital as a whole. How does this happen?

Any commodity has two types of economic value. It has use-value because it meets some human need. This use-value is realized when someone consumes the commodity. Commodities also have exchange-value. One commodity can be exchanged for another commodity. The exchange-value of a commodity is realized when someone trades it for another. This raises another question: How is the exchange-value of a commodity determined? Why are some more valuable than others?

Mainstream economics points to supply and demand, but this is merely a theory of price fluctuation. Low supply and high demand increase prices, whereas high supply and low demand decrease prices. But what is the "real" value of a commodity when supply and demand are in balance? The question is difficult because the use-values of commodities are qualitatively different. You can't wear a cheeseburger to stay warm or eat a stocking cap to relieve hunger. So why do cheeseburgers, stocking caps, and every other commodity in the world have a specific exchange-value?

There is only one common feature of all commodities: they are products of human labor. From this, Marx advocated the labor theory of value: Commodities have economic value because they are the products of human labor. Moreover, the amount of exchange-value that any commodity has is based on the amount of labor that goes into its production. The more labor that goes into the production of a commodity, the greater its exchange-value. Some commodities are more valuable than others because more labor went into their production.

Another defining feature of capitalism is wage-labor. Workers sell labor-power (their ability to work) to capitalists for a wage. In other words, capitalism turns labor-power into a commodity that is bought and sold. As with any commodity, the price of labor fluctuates with changes in supply and demand. But what is the "real" value of labor-power when supply and demand are in balance?

Marx's logic is consistent. If labor-power is a commodity, then its value is determined by the amount of labor that goes into its production. Because labor-power is embodied in a person, the production of labor-power really means the survival of the person. People must consume a variety of commodities to sustain themselves and their ability to labor. So the value of labor-power is equal to the value of all the commodities people need to survive at a culturally acceptable level. If capitalists buy labor-power at its real value, they pay workers wages that allow them to survive and reproduce their labor-power.

The labor theory of value explains the exchange-value of all commodities in terms of the single baseline of human labor. It is the only common element in the production of every commodity, including labor-power itself.

SURPLUS VALUE AND EXPLOITATION

If we assume that all commodities exchange at their true values, we still have the question: How is profit possible? Where does the "extra" value come from? It turns out that labor-power is the only commodity that can create new value greater than its own value. The more productively it is organized, the greater the surplus that will result.

Consider a simple example. A small capitalist spends $1,000 each on raw materials, means of production, and labor-power to make pencils. Her total investment is $3,000. She then sells her pencils for $6,000 and makes $3,000 in the process. Where does the extra three grand come from? If labor-power is the only commodity that can create a surplus, then it must come from labor. The raw materials and means of production do not create new value. Their value is simply transferred to the pencils in the production process. The new value comes from labor and its unique capacity to produce a surplus. The question can now be answered. Profits come from labor.

Starting from a symmetrical situation where all commodities exchange at their value, we arrive at an asymmetrical outcome. Our capitalist created no new value but received a $6,000 return on a $3,000 investment. Workers create this new value, but they only receive a portion of it back to reproduce their labor-power. The remaining value created by labor goes to capital. When workers create all the new value and capitalists take a portion of it, that is exploitation. Capitalists exploit workers by taking advantage of labor-power's unique capacity to produce a surplus.

This exploitation is obscured by how workers are paid. Consider economic production on a large scale. Every day some commodities are completely consumed and others are partially consumed. Survival requires that a certain amount of production occur every day simply to replace what is used up. Call this necessary labor. A society could hypothetically do only this much labor and survive. However, there would be no surplus and no growth. In reality, all societies produce some surplus. Put differently, they engage in surplus labor above and beyond the necessary labor needed to ensure survival.

We can thus hypothetically divide a workday into two components. The first is necessary labor required for survival. The second is surplus labor beyond that minimum.

The value created during necessary labor comes back to workers as wages. It must, if they are to survive by buying commodities to reproduce their labor-power. The value created during surplus labor goes to the capitalists as surplus value, or profits.

It's as if workers work part of the day for themselves and part of the day for capitalists. If the day were really divided this way, logical workers would go home after necessary labor with all their wages and leave capitalists without any income. The wage form prevents this. It takes the money workers need and spreads it out over the entire workday, so they must work a full shift to receive their wages.

Imagine that workers produce eight hours of new value and get four hours back as wages, and capitalists take the other four hours as surplus value. This ratio is the rate of surplus value; it expresses what capitalists get relative to workers. It is also the rate of exploitation; it reveals what workers get relative to their contributions. Such exploitation is inherent in capitalism; it makes profits possible.

It gets worse. Capitalism systematically increases exploitation in two ways. One is by lengthening the working day. If workers can be forced to work twelve hours rather than eight, the rate of surplus value increases dramatically: four hours for workers and eight for capitalists. The other method is to increase the productivity of labor. If workers double their output, necessary labor (and workers' wages) shrinks from four to two hours and surplus labor (and capitalists' profits) expands from four to six hours. In both cases, workers still create all new value, but their share shrinks to an ever-smaller proportion of the total, and capitalists' share expands.

Capitalism increases exploitation because capitalists compete amongst themselves. As powerful as they are, even capitalists are subject to the laws of competition. The primary strategy in the competitive struggle between capitalists is to maximize surplus value by exploiting workers more extensively than rival capitalists. Over the long run, capitalism becomes more competitive between capitalists and more exploitative of workers.

Marx recognized the revolutionary power of capitalism to develop the forces of production. But he was highly critical of the price workers paid for such advances. Capitalism inevitably creates increasingly exploitative and antagonistic relations between a wealthy minority and the vast majority of the population. Marx's ultimate target was not capitalists but rather capitalism, because it deforms human relations.

This deformation includes alienating workers from their product, their work, their potential, and other people. It includes commodity fetishism where commodities become more important than people. Even though people are required to create them, commodities often acquire a life of their own, and we "forget" their origins. Marx punctured these illusions by referring to commodities as "dead labor," reminding us that they would not exist without the past efforts of workers. In a similar fashion, the socialist slogan that "property is theft" reminds us that what exists now as private property was once the creation of laborers who could not own what they produced. And most generally, Marx insisted that capital is not a thing but a social relationship. It comes into existence through the productive efforts of workers. Its ownership by others should not blind us to how it was created or to who was exploited in the process.

CONTRADICTIONS AND CRISES

Capitalism is a dynamic, unstable system because of capitalist competition and worker resistance. Its instability goes even deeper because capitalism rests on contradictions. Some contradictions develop into major economic crises that threaten capitalism's survival.

One contradiction is between social production and private appropriation. Capitalist production is socially organized; it requires the coordinated activity of many people. Appropriation, however, is private and individual. Resources that are socially produced are privately owned. As a result, capitalism is good at producing private commodities but bad at producing public goods. Capitalism produces lots of cars but not efficient mass transit. It produces lots of drugs but not affordable health care. It produces countless products to clean your house but can't sustain clean air and water. The contradiction between social production and private appropriation contributes to capitalist instability.

Another contradiction is between internal organization and market anarchy. Internal organization occurs within the corporation, which becomes a highly rational and bureaucratic firm seeking to control and predict its environment in pursuit of profits. In sharp contrast, there is economic anarchy in the larger society. There is little economic coordination, no overall plan for using scarce resources wisely, and little regulation of rapid fluctuations in commodity and labor markets. The revenues for essential services like health, education, and welfare thus become highly unpredictable. Although the wealthy can survive such instability, it threatens the livelihood of many ordinary citizens.

A third contradiction is the polarization of wealth and poverty. Because capital is concentrated in fewer hands, the rich become richer. Even when workers' living standards improve, capitalist standards often improve more rapidly, creating a relative polarization of wealth and poverty. When measured on a global scale, the polarization between rich and poor nations is staggering. Such extreme inequality creates further instability.

A fourth contradiction is that capitalism produces for profit and not for use. Imagine two circles that partially overlap. One circle represents products people need. The other represents products that are profitable. Capitalism responds to the second circle. It produces some things that are needed—but it does so because they are profitable and not because they are needed. It also produces some things that are profitable but not really needed (visit any shopping mall for examples). Finally, it does not produce things that are needed but not profitable; affordable housing is one of many examples. Production for profit and not use creates further instability by allowing the extreme affluence of some to coexist with the unmet needs of others.

Some contradictions become major economic crises. Consider how overproduction or under-consumption occurs because capitalism produces more than can be sold at an acceptable profit. Recall that workers produce more value than they receive back as wages, so they don't have the purchasing power to buy all the commodities they produce. Even when capitalist consumption is added to the equation, there is a tendency toward overproduction or under-consumption that becomes an economic crisis. On the production side, profits shrink, investment slows, production declines, inventories accumulate, and productive capacity goes unused. Stagnation, recession, or even depression can result. On the consumption side, firms seek new markets, destroy surplus products, tap government as a consumer of last resort, advertise more heavily, and extend consumer credit, so that even people without money can buy.

Another crisis tendency involves a falling rate of profit as capitalists invest in new technology to stay competitive. This means their investment in labor becomes a smaller portion of their total investment. Because labor is the only source of new value, it becomes increasingly difficult to sustain profits. Again, various strategies come into play. Capitalists can increase exploitation or depress wages to counter a falling rate of profit. In the long term, they must cheapen the cost of new technology to sustain acceptable profits. Unless they can do so fast enough, profits remain low and the entire economy experiences stagnation.

These contradictions and crisis tendencies cannot be eliminated. What capitalists and their political allies try to do is minimize and redirect their most harmful effects. The value of this crisis theory is not that it predicts an inevitable downfall of capitalism; it is rather that it identifies powerful economic tendencies that trigger certain responses. The dance of crisis tendencies and counterstrategies offers important insights into capitalist economies.

Capitalism is a system in which labor's ability to produce a surplus is turned against a majority of the population. Rather than shared abundance, surplus becomes profit for a tiny minority. Moreover, capitalists must maximize exploitation to survive in a system increasingly subject to inherent contradictions and crisis tendencies. Marx is a vocal critic of capitalism, but capitalism is really its own critic. Every unmet need in a context of affluence reveals how far capitalism remains from a rational society in which production would be organized to meet the needs of all before the wealth of a few.

FROM LIBERAL TO ADVANCED CAPITALISM

Capitalism has obviously changed over the past 150 years. A critical sociology for our time retains Marx's core insights while updating his crisis theory of capitalism. This is precisely the strategy of Habermas's *Legitimation Crisis* (1975): to analyze new crisis tendencies deriving from the dominant institution of our time.

Consider the notion of crisis. In medicine, a crisis occurs when a patient faces a grave threat to survival with the possibility of recovery. A social crisis poses an equally grave threat while also allowing for recovery and transformation. A genuine social crisis occurs on two levels. It threatens *system* integration by undermining the production and distribution of material goods needed for physical survival. It simultaneously threatens *social* integration by weakening the social norms, cultural values, and personal identities that hold society together. It is when *both* system and social integration are imperiled that societies face a real crisis.

This logic fits Marx's crisis theory. In the liberal capitalism of the nineteenth century, the market provided system integration by coordinating the production and distribution of material goods. It also provided social integration by providing norms, values, and identities that reinforced people's economic motivation. These included beliefs about upward mobility, equal opportunity, the work ethic, and the belief that hard work would be economically rewarded.

Because the market provided both types of integration, liberal capitalism was very fragile. It was predisposed to crisis. The instant the market faltered, system integration was imperiled by its inability to produce and deliver material goods. At the same time, social integration was imperiled because the market's failure demonstrated that mobility, opportunity, and rewards for hard work could be illusions. Problems on either level quickly translated into problems on both levels. Liberal capitalism was thus highly prone to crisis.

Marx was right: liberal capitalism experienced a major crisis. But unlike medical patients, societies have possibilities other than death or recovery. Capitalist societies underwent a transformation from a market-based, liberal capitalism to a corporate-dominated, advanced capitalism. This advanced capitalism has two distinguishing features. First, it is dominated by large corporations and multinationals that can monopolize production, set prices, and manipulate demand. As a result, the free market benefits of competition, price reduction, and the rest have evaporated in many sectors of advanced capitalism.

The second distinguishing feature of advanced capitalism is the high degree of state intervention into the economy. This intervention was, in part, a response to the crisis of liberal capitalism. That system failed when the market became overburdened and could no longer provide system and social integration. State intervention was like a lifeguard coming to the rescue by supplementing a faltering market. It provided needed but unprofitable goods and services; maintained the infrastructure; subsidized education and training for workers; put people back to work; provided social insurance for the unemployed, disabled, or retired; met the social costs of capitalist production by repairing environmental damage; and much more. The crisis of liberal capitalism triggered massive state intervention that, in turn, acted like a midwife in the birth of advanced capitalism.

Consider a historical example. The 1929 stock-market crash in the United States led to the Great Depression, which threatened the survival of capitalism in the United States. The only way to save the capitalist "patient" in crisis was a massive transfusion of state intervention into the economy. The New Deal promoted recovery. It reduced unemployment through federally subsidized jobs. It provided a system of social security for those unable to work. It increased government's role as a regulator of economic activity through monetary, fiscal, and tax policies. The New Deal helped the patient survive. The economic stimulus of World War II helped the patient thrive. By mid-century, the patient seemed cured. But from this point forward, a steady dose of state intervention remained necessary for ongoing economic health.

In advanced capitalism, markets are subordinated to large corporations and partially replaced or supplemented by state intervention. This raises a basic question: Has advanced capitalism achieved real stability, or is it still subject to crisis?

CRISIS TENDENCIES IN ADVANCED CAPITALISM

To answer this question, we must examine four institutions in advanced capitalism: its economic system, its administrative system, its legitimation system, and its class structure.

The economic system has three sectors. The private, monopoly sector consists of capital-intensive enterprises like corporate businesses. The private, competitive sector consists of labor-intensive enterprises like small businesses. The public, monopoly sector involves state-supported production through government contracts. The rise of this sector is yet another expression of state intervention into the economy.

The administrative system is the federal government that intervenes in the economy in several ways. It does limited planning to regulate economic cycles. It channels capital by offering tax incentives to bring investment to socially needed areas. It supplements or replaces the market as described previously. This intervention has an important consequence. By intervening, the state acknowledges that markets no longer organize economic production efficiently on their own. However, whereas markets were seen as natural forces beyond human control, states are supposed to represent citizens and act on their behalf. When states fail, they can be blamed in ways that markets rarely are.

The legitimation system emerges because the market no longer provides legitimation by itself. The purpose of this system is to gather diffuse support for elite decisions while deflecting any real input that might interfere with elite priorities. This is done in several ways. Formal democracy reduces politics to elections and limits citizens to voting for elite candidates. Technocratic decision making favors specialized experts over ordinary citizens. Finally, a lifestyle of civic privatism encourages people to focus on careers, families, consumption, and leisure while avoiding any larger role in the public sphere. The legitimation system thereby provides diffuse support for elite priorities with little meaningful role for citizens.

The class structure of advanced capitalism involves a partial class compromise. The working class has become a highly differentiated group in terms of skills, security, wages, and benefits. This has promoted a partial breakdown of class identity and a fragmentation of class consciousness. It has allowed better-off workers to enjoy good jobs, decent compensation, and fringe benefits in exchange for not challenging capitalist priorities. It has also allowed the state to shift negative economic consequences to the least powerful groups in society. Although class conflict still occurs, it is episodic and limited rather than persistent and broad.

Advanced capitalism is thus a more complex social formation that becomes prone to new crisis tendencies. In liberal capitalism, crises were clearly economic. In advanced capitalism, there are multiple crisis tendencies and a logic of crisis displacement from one sector of society to another.

ECONOMIC CRISIS TENDENCIES

There were numerous sources of economic crisis in liberal capitalism. The question is whether they continue to provoke crises in advanced capitalism.

The answer hinges on the effect of state intervention into the economy. Consider some examples. Because the state supplements the market, small problems might not be allowed to develop into a full-blown crisis. Fluctuations in interest rates or inflation that might spin out of control are now moderated by monetary and fiscal policy. Large corporations whose bankruptcy might destabilize entire industries are now rescued by government bailouts because they are "too big to fail." Unused capacity is now activated as government becomes a consumer, creates economic demand, and mitigates under-consumption problems. Think of a nautical metaphor. Unregulated markets are like huge ships at sea that can tip over when seas are rough. State intervention is like adding stabilizers that minimize tipping and keep the ship on an even keel.

State intervention goes deeper. It is heavily invested in educating and training the workforce and in underwriting research and development. This means that capitalists don't pay for the full value of labor-power or means of production. These savings can counteract the tendency of profits to fall. The state is also involved in regulating the contracts of workers who engage in collective bargaining. This means that the cost of labor-power is no longer set in a purely economic fashion but rather is influenced by political processes.

Advanced capitalism remains exploitative and prone to crisis. Because of state intervention, however, the likelihood of a purely economic crisis, while not impossible, becomes more remote. In real-world terms, economies like the United States are less likely to experience a Great Depression again, because government is committed to doing everything in its considerable power to prevent it.

Although a purely economic crisis might have been averted, this is just the beginning of the story. The same intervention that prevents an economic crisis displaces the crisis from the economy to the state. Hence, we must follow the trail of potential crises from the economic world of commodity markets to the political realm of government institutions.

RATIONALITY CRISIS TENDENCIES

State intervention creates new obligations for government. It pushes state resources beyond their limits. The outcome might be a rationality crisis. This means that the state is unable to generate and rationally distribute enough revenue to fully offset economic crises. A rationality crisis is evident when chronic problems in monetary inflation, interest rates, federal deficits, public debts, and budgetary shortfalls cannot be managed effectively. Hence, the price paid for averting an economic crisis is to transfer the crisis to the polity.

Rationality crises are likely in advanced capitalism because the state must respond to the two contradictory needs of accumulation and legitimation. Accumulation means that the state must do everything in its power to make capitalism as profitable as possible to avoid an economic crisis. This means maintaining infrastructure, subsidizing corporations, training workers, reducing regulations, cutting taxes, and much more. The state pays high costs to foster accumulation.

At the same time, state power is severely limited by property rights in capitalism. The state can never dictate how or where capitalist investments are made. It can merely seek to create a climate in which capitalists will invest capital. Moreover, when the state does this, it is really siding with capitalist interests in profits. But the state is supposed to represent all citizens and not just a particular class. When the state acts to enhance capitalist accumulation, it risks legitimation problems with the rest of the population who might resent the class bias of this state intervention.

The state must therefore be concerned with legitimation as well as accumulation. This entails costs that undermine accumulation. To gain legitimation, the state provides needed but unprofitable goods and services as well as social welfare programs for various recipients. It monitors consumer rights, worker safety, and environmental protection. It underwrites the cost of education and health care. As the state fulfills at least some of the genuine needs of its citizens, it earns legitimacy by creating the appearance that government works for everyone.

The legitimation role of government creates its own tensions. The mere fact of state intervention creates a potential trap for the state. People may accept a market crisis like a natural disaster that is unfortunate but no one's fault. But when state intervention is the norm, people are more likely to hold political leaders accountable when things go bad. In addition, every time the state creates a new program, it creates new constituencies and expectations about continued governmental support.

The net effect leaves the state in a very difficult position. It must promote accumulation, but this is costly and state power is limited. It must sustain legitimation, but this is also costly, and doing so raises expectations. Fostering accumulation and maintaining legitimacy are thus contradictory and yet both are necessary. Caught in this cross fire, the state is often reduced to crisis management, responding to the most urgent problems with little capacity for long-term solutions. Hence, the result of avoiding an economic crisis through state intervention is to transfer the crisis from the economy to the state.

This theoretical logic articulated in Germany in the mid-1970s (Habermas 1975) was vividly exemplified by the "Great Recession" in 2007. As a complex result of a housing bubble, speculative investments, and the financialization of the economy, the United States experienced a major economic downturn in 2007 (Antonio forthcoming; Smith et al. 2011). Had this occurred in liberal capitalism with minimal state intervention, it may well have led to another Great Depression and perhaps a fundamental breakdown of the world's leading capitalist economy.

Because it happened in advanced capitalism with a considerable history of state intervention, the immediate reaction was to seek a variety of government-sponsored remedies. Thus, the federal government orchestrated the demise of some financial firms while subsidizing the survival of many more through a massive taxpayer subsidy.

While the economy was in free fall, the state provided a safety net that protected crucial assets, limited the damage, and facilitated the survival and stabilization of an economy in severe crisis. If Habermas's theory was the "prediction," the events of 2007–2008 were a fulfillment of that prediction. A purely economic crisis was managed in a way that transferred the locus of the crisis from the economy to the state.

But there is more to the story. While it is evident that the system integration of the economy and polity experienced a severe crisis, we must examine whether this translated into a crisis of social integration as well. To explore this possibility, we must turn from the economic and political dynamics of the system to the legitimation and motivational processes of the lifeworld.

LEGITIMATION CRISIS TENDENCIES

Legitimation is especially important in advanced capitalism. One might think that political elites want strong legitimation where the vast majority of people actively support their decisions and policies. But this might not be the case. If ordinary people become active in politics, there is always the danger that such activism could turn against the current leadership. For this reason, leaders might prefer a weaker form of legitimation in which people provide shallow, diffuse support for leaders without becoming too involved in the political process. Following this logic, political elites benefit whenever people support the system as a whole while minimizing their actual involvement in political decision making. Elites thus prefer a passive population providing vague support to one that is actively engaged in politics and could turn against them. A politically passive population reduces legitimation pressures on elites and minimizes the chance that chronic rationality problems will translate into legitimation difficulties.

Several aspects of advanced capitalism produce exactly this result. In each case, they reinforce political passivity and reduce legitimation pressures. Collectively, they become a blank check allowing political leaders great latitude to act with very little accountability. This makes it easier for elites to promote accumulation for capitalists without suffering legitimation deficits vis-à-vis citizens.

Consider technocratic decision making. Its premise is that some issues are too complicated for ordinary people to understand because they lack specialized knowledge. Hence, they should leave the issues to experts and trust their supposedly better judgment. There is thus a tension between technocratic and democratic decision making.

If people accept the premise of technocratic decision making, they effectively disenfranchise themselves from meaningful input into many political decisions. By forfeiting their right to decide, they also reduce legitimation pressures on the state.

Technocratic decision making thus contributes to a politically passive populace. Such a situation is dangerous in several ways. Technical experts are narrowly trained and might not be in the best position to assess wider risks concerning nuclear energy, genetic engineering, tax policy, or drug safety. Technical experts might be biased or corrupted by power holders. And when experts are wrong, it is ordinary citizens who live with the harmful consequences. Nevertheless, a politically pacified population offers little resistance to technocratic decision making, and it thereby lessens the likelihood of a legitimation crisis.

Another aspect of legitimation is material goods. In principle, state action must be justifiable to citizens based on legitimate reasons. In reality, citizens might be willing to "trade" legitimate reasons for material goods. Put bluntly, as long as the system delivers the goods, citizens might accept government action that is unjustifiable or even corrupt. Put even more bluntly, people might accept any foreign policy or environmental damage that keeps gasoline prices within acceptable limits. Such a trade-off reduces legitimation pressures, because people no longer hold government accountable to any principle other than maintaining their lifestyle.

Although this can be a viable short-term strategy for elites, there are reasons to doubt its long-term effectiveness. First, it is questionable whether people would permanently set aside moral, ethical, and religious principles for material gain. Although capitalist cultures are materialistic, they also experience waves of reaction that reintroduce other principles into public discussion that could raise legitimation pressures. Second, the ability of the system to deliver material goods might itself be limited. Living standards are increasingly dependent on public goods like health care, quality education, and sustainable environments. Even if people are willing to trade legitimation for material rewards, the system's ability to provide them is limited by capitalism's historic difficulty in providing public goods. Nevertheless, if the public makes this bargain, it reinforces political passivity and reduces legitimation pressures.

A third aspect of the legitimation system is electoral politics and the idea that voting is the ultimate political act for citizens. This amounts to a very impoverished notion of democracy. A "rich" notion of democracy would emphasize much broader citizen participation, including ongoing political education, robust voluntary associations, and active social movements. This would approximate participatory democracy in which everyone affected by a decision has meaningful input into that decision. Measured against these possibilities, the idea that democracy is about voting once every four years is an impoverished notion indeed.

Another term for this impoverished version is *elite democracy*. It implies that otherwise-passive citizens choose every four years between preselected candidates. This model of elite democracy is constantly reinforced by media coverage of politics. While speaking in reverential tones about the power of voters, media rarely recognize any other form of political action or explore how candidates are preselected on the basis of money long before they are elected on the basis of votes. Elite democracy reduces politics to elections that are easily controlled by powerful interests. To the extent that citizens accept this reduction and see voting as their only political act, their political passivity again reduces legitimation problems.

A final aspect of the legitimation system involves "civic privatism." In simpler language, this means that people seek their greatest satisfactions in private life rather than public engagement. Civic privatism emphasizes family life, interpersonal relations, and personal gratifications. It encourages people to focus on what they can get as consumers or clients as opposed to what they can do as producers and citizens. This mind-set reflects another trade-off. Civic privatism basically says that because public activities are unfulfilling and alienating, then personal life is where we should focus our psychic energies.

The problem is not that these are false pleasures. Intimate relations can be deeply satisfying, and material consumption can be quite enjoyable. The problem is that civic privatism implies that these are the only possible pleasures. It also implies that we should see them as compensation for the alienation of the larger social world. When people embrace civic privatism, they lower their expectations of what is possible in social life and the public sphere. Lowered expectations reinforce passivity and reduce the likelihood of legitimation pressures that might otherwise occur.

To sum up, advanced capitalism is unstable because when the state intervenes to prevent an economic crisis, the crisis shifts to the state. It is very difficult for the state to simultaneously foster accumulation for capitalists and retain legitimation by citizens. Advanced capitalism thus relies on a legitimation system to manage this problem. To whatever extent people leave decisions to experts, accept material goods in exchange for legitimation, limit political activity to voting, and embrace civic privatism, they become a passive population. This reduces legitimation pressures, offsets crisis tendencies, and allows an unequal, unjust, and exploitative society to persist.

Legitimation pressures increase when the above scenarios are reversed. Whenever citizens question the right of experts to make decisions for them, they challenge technocratic decision making. Whenever citizens demand political accountability in addition to material rewards, they are refusing to be bought off. Whenever citizens engage in political activity above and beyond the simple act of voting, they are challenging elite democracy. And whenever citizens step outside the cocoon of civic privatism into the public sphere, they seek collective fulfillment above private pleasures. Legitimation difficulties can thus be either contained or heightened, depending on how these scenarios play out.

This analysis illuminates many political issues. Recall that the legitimation increasingly found in advanced capitalism is not detailed support for specific policies but rather broad and diffuse approval of political leaders. Now consider how often leaders create or capitalize on fears about crime, drugs, immigration, or terrorism to gain such legitimation. By "standing up to the threat," the symbolism of their stance often means more than the substance of their policies in gaining legitimation. When leaders commit troops to war, "supporting the troops" displaces questions about the logic or even the truth of the war's rationale. When leaders appeal to religious values, the validation felt by true believers overrides consideration of whether government policies actually contradict those values.

Sometimes leaders retain significant support even though a majority of the population disagrees with most of their policies. When this occurs, it means that diffuse, symbolic, and uncritical support has become the primary form of legitimation. This turns political leadership into a spectacle that rewards those who can effectively manipulate the symbols required to elicit this legitimation. This diffuse support, in turn, gives politicians great latitude to implement even unpopular policies.

Consider another example. In the mid-1970s, much concern was expressed about a "crisis of democracy" in the United States. From the perspective of state managers, the "crisis" was that too many people had too much influence over political decisions, making it difficult for elites to pursue their objectives. This prompted attacks on "big government" that persist to this day. The strategy is to lower people's expectations about what government will, can, and should do for its citizens. Whether expressed through fearful portrayals of big government running amok or through uplifting pleas for personal responsibility, the message is the same: people must lower their expectations about what government can do.

This strategy makes perfect sense as a legitimation struggle. Rationality and legitimation crises emerge in part because people develop high expectations about government. Elites can reduce the likelihood and severity of such crises if they alter what people expect from government. Lowered expectations take the heat off the state and allow it to do less for ordinary people while continuing to serve elite interests. They lessen the tension between fostering accumulation and maintaining legitimation by reducing the need for the latter. When elites can reduce the need for legitimation and frame it as broad symbolic support, they maintain power while ignoring genuine needs. This is the kind of political domination that long interested the Frankfurt School.

If lowering expectations is the strategy, cutting taxes is the tactic. Economic elites have been the major beneficiaries of the tax cuts undertaken by conservative governments of the past three decades. The long-term goal is reducing and eventually eliminating all taxes on wealth and investment, so that taxes on the wages of ordinary people become the main source of government revenue. Reduced government revenue forces the state to reduce expenditures as well. These reductions undermine state funding for education, health care, housing, and social welfare. Finally, it will be difficult to maintain or restore these programs as the tax burden shifts to the middle and working classes, who thus have reason to oppose them. The combined reduction and shift in the tax burden means that the state will do less for ordinary people at the same time that its strategy of lowered expectations gets people to accept less without withdrawing their legitimation.

Both the type and the degree of legitimation required by government and provided by citizens thus become a chronic tension in advanced capitalism. Legitimation difficulties can also appear in a more acute form in response to severe problems of system integration. The economic and political crisis of 2007–2008 provides a final example of such difficulties.

The state intervention that arguably saved advanced capitalism in 2007–2008 was widely criticized as a wasteful government "bailout." For differing reasons, these policies were massively unpopular across the political spectrum. While probably necessary to restore capital accumulation, the federal government lost considerable legitimacy in implementing this response.

From the right, the Tea Party emerged as an amalgamation of elite funding and populist fury that attacked specific government policies but also the very idea that government could play a productive role in such a crisis. There are several ironies here. Whereas Habermas's argument anticipates progressive legitimation challenges, the Tea Party voiced perhaps the most strident challenge to legitimation in recent memory from the right rather than the left. Moreover, if the state were reduced to the minor, tangential role envisioned by right-wing ideology, it would have been incapable of responding to the economic crisis in a way that actually salvaged advanced capitalism as a whole.

From the left, the Occupy Wall Street movement represented a further challenge to the legitimation of advanced capitalism. Whereas the Tea Party short-circuited its analysis by obsessing about big government and ignoring the corporate economy, Occupy Wall Street recognized the state as a junior partner in an advanced capitalism whose fundamental inequities arose from the corporate economy itself. As a democratic challenge to the capitalist domination of social life, Occupy Wall Street was, however briefly, a compelling example of Habermas's vision of a new social movement emerging out of the lifeworld to challenge the colonization of society by elite economic and political interests.

These examples underscore the centrality of legitimation issues in contemporary society. They are the logical culmination of state efforts to contain the instabilities that remain endemic in a capitalist society. There is, however, yet another dimension of the lifeworld that can also feed back into legitimation difficulties.

MOTIVATION CRISIS TENDENCIES

Social integration involves values, beliefs, norms, and identities. When these are undermined, social integration is jeopardized. When political beliefs break down, legitimation crises can emerge. When cultural values lose relevance, motivational crises can emerge because people no longer find compelling reasons to conform to social expectations. Motivational problems can also raise questions about political authority that heightens legitimation difficulties.

The big issue is how people find meaning, purpose, and motivation in life. Throughout most of human history, people found these things through religious beliefs that made sense of their world and their place within it. When modernity emerged, secular beliefs challenged religious beliefs, and traditional sources of meaning and motivation lost some of their power.

Even so, the early days of liberal capitalism still relied on religious motivations. Weber's (1904) analysis of the Protestant ethic showed that early entrepreneurs were driven more by religious than economic motives, because the accumulation of wealth was believed to signify moral worthiness in God's eyes. Even today, there is no shortage of religious belief. But in many respects, late modern societies have moved in secular, scientific directions. As secular views displace religious ones, the question becomes acute: What meanings and motivations replace religious ones in a secularizing world?

This question returns us to the lifeworld where the rise of communicative rationality has displaced blind obedience to authority with the idea that actions must be justified by reasons. Modern, child-centered socialization practices incorporate communicative rationality by promoting autonomy and self-direction as children mature into adults. The same goals are increasingly evident in the educational system with its emphasis on "critical thinking." As this occurs, younger generations internalize norms of communicative rationality for which actions and decisions need clear and compelling justifications. If actions and decisions fail this test, people socialized to these standards might reject them.

In the late modern world, the lifeworld and system are on a collision course. On one hand, new generations are socialized to value autonomy and rational justifications. On the other hand, the occupational roles of the economic system and the bureaucratic organizations of the political system operate through instrumental rationality; they are "steered" by the imperatives of money and power. The economy and polity still expect compliance and obedience from recent generations schooled in autonomy and self-direction. Put differently, while the cultural lifeworld has encouraged people to question authority, the system requires people to conform. The mismatch between socialized expectations and institutional realities sows the seeds of a motivation crisis.

A motivation crisis is expressed in alienation and anomie in modern society. A common thread is the inability to coherently link meanings, purposes, values, and identities. This condition might be particularly acute for younger generations, because identity formation is crucial in this stage of the life cycle. Possible responses to motivation crises are withdrawal, social isolation, destructive behavior, or compulsive attachments. Whatever the response, these signify the fraying of social integration.

Like legitimation difficulties, motivation crises may take both chronic and acute forms. The growing problem of student debt is becoming an acute indicator of motivation crisis tendencies. When college expenses were lower, debts were smaller, and occupational niches more predictable, taking out loans to pay for higher education was a wise investment. As the cost of college has increased, total student debt has risen to over a trillion dollars, and occupational prospects have dimmed, the links between acquiring educational credentials and successful occupational placement have been seriously compromised (Antonio forthcoming). This, in turn, has undermined traditional beliefs about work, mobility, identity, family, and the rhythm of the life cycle itself.

The sociologically intriguing question is when motivational problems will lead people to question the legitimacy of social arrangements. Such transitions depend on political and historical context. Consider the contrast between two periods of foreign military intervention. During the Vietnam War, the draft symbolized the power of the system over people in the lifeworld and it became a catalyst for resistance to war. During more recent conflicts in Iraq and Afghanistan, the "volunteer" army has eliminated that catalyst and muted antiwar activism.

But no one can anticipate which issues will provide such catalysts, so motivational crises retain the potential to spill over into legitimation crises. The aforementioned example of Occupy Wall Street illustrates how legitimation difficulties are "fed" from two directions. The rationality crisis of the state dovetailed with motivational pressures within the culture to undermine the legitimation of a system increasingly unable to justify intensifying inequality and its associated injustices. While this specific movement may be short-lived, the pressures that created it are endemic to advanced capitalism.

To sum up, capitalist societies are prone to crisis because of inherent contradictions and conflicts built into them. Advanced capitalist societies respond to this threat with massive state intervention. This has displaced the crisis from economy to state. Chronic rationality problems in the state are the price of avoiding economic crisis. Under certain conditions, problems of state intervention trigger legitimation difficulties. Meanwhile, motivational problems have also become chronic features of modern societies, which also have the potential to translate into legitimation difficulties.

Legitimation is the most vulnerable aspect of advanced capitalism because it operates under the double pressure of a state that cannot rationally make decisions and a culture that cannot convincingly provide meaning. When rationality problems of system integration combine with legitimation problems of social integration, a genuine crisis occurs. Although such a crisis could be resolved in many ways, the optimal response would be transformation toward a rational society less dominated by instrumental rationality and more grounded in communicative rationality.

CAPITALISM UNBOUND

Advanced capitalism remains a dynamic, complex, and contradictory system. Since the 1970s, several trends are especially prominent. They can be summarized as "capitalism unbound," because each involves an expansion of capitalism or the removal of limits on how it operates. Each is a response to prior economic difficulties as capitalism sought to maintain or enhance profits. At the same time, each can provide only temporary respite while fostering more serious problems down the road.

One trend is globalization. Capitalism has always been a global system, but the globalization of national economies has accelerated since the 1970s. This was a response to an unusual combination of economic problems including energy costs, rampant inflation, chronic stagnation, and declining profits. In the advanced capitalist countries, capitalism was "unbound" in geographical terms as capital flight, runaway shops, and deindustrialization shifted a great deal of economic activity outside core countries. Better-paying manufacturing jobs declined, and lesser-paying service jobs increased. The net effect was to undermine the living standards of working people and leave many communities with permanent economic stagnation and high unemployment. Such aggressive, cost-cutting strategies harmed many workers while restoring profits for corporate capital. Although ordinary people paid the price, the globalization strategy at least temporarily revived many national economies.

Another trend is commodification. Whereas capitalism was unbound externally through globalization, it was unbound internally through commodification. Capitalism has always promoted commodification, but the strategy has intensified recently. It is yet another response to stagnant profits that seeks new avenues for higher returns on investment. Commodification turns social resources into private products for profitable sale. The fast-food industry is one example; it replaces use-values for direct consumption (home-cooked meals) with exchange-values for corporate profit (burgers and fries). Commodification also substitutes private products for declining public goods. Think of bottled water. Or think of highly polluted cities where clean air is scarce but you can buy ten-minute doses of pure oxygen as a private commodity from street-side vendors. Whether the issue is housing, policing, health, welfare, education, prisons, or the military, commodification puts profitability before quality, utility, or service. Accelerated commodification of social resources is yet another response to problems of profit realization. Although it has boosted profits, it is doubtful that these problems have been permanently averted.

A third trend is privatization. Capitalism has also become unbound from forms of state intervention that impede profit making. In some ways, privatization is another expression of commodification. But the term *privatization* accentuates the reversal of long-standing governmental regulation of economic processes. With the philosophy of neoliberalism, the strategy of reducing government, and the tactic of deregulation, governments have abandoned much of their role as defenders of the public interest. Whether the issue is worker safety, environmental protection, or unemployment compensation, privatization displaces government safety nets with the logic of the marketplace. Debates over Social Security in the United States illustrate the trend. For more than half a century, the system was so popular and successful that no politician dared to challenge it. Under the banner of privatization, conservatives have sought to convert a cost-efficient, publicly administered, social insurance program into millions of highly profitable, privately owned investment accounts. Like globalization and commodification, privatization is yet another capitalist strategy to sustain profitability.

A final factor crucial to the future of global society is ecological sustainability. Globalization, commodification, and privatization are all designed to enhance short-term profitability rather than long-term sustainability. These capitalist strategies mean we will reach many ecological limits sooner rather than later. As fossil fuels continue to be depleted, their costs will increase as they become more difficult to locate and extract. Anthropogenic climate change is also creating long-term consequences that may become devastating for capitalist profitability if not human survival itself. Taken together, these trends suggest that the growth imperative inherent in neoliberal, advanced capitalism is moving ever closer to the limits of the "ecological wall" (Antonio forthcoming). As new capitalist strategies are implemented, their environmental consequences loom large as a source of future crises.

An "unbound" capitalism has intriguing implications for social stability. Globalization, commodification, and privatization each shift power from the public sphere of citizens to the private economy of corporations. They heighten the tension between capitalism and democracy. In political terms, they are designed to repeal the New Deal. That is, they seek to reduce or eliminate the very kinds of state intervention that were necessary to rescue liberal capitalism from a catastrophic economic crisis. These moves might be necessary to sustain short-term profitability, but they might simultaneously increase legitimation pressures for the system as a whole. As advanced capitalism follows this trajectory, the question of whether it can retain legitimacy will be essential to the prospects for progressive social change.

REFERENCES

Antonio, Robert. Forthcoming. "Plundering the Commons: The Growth Imperative in Neoliberal Times." In *Sociologies of Moderation: Problems of Democracy, Expertise, and the Media*, ed. Alexander Smith. Cambridge: Cambridge University Press.

————. 1975. *Legitimation Crisis*. Boston: Beacon.

Smith, David, Brock Ternes, James P. Ordner, Russell Schloemer, Gabriela Moran, Chris Goode, Joshua Homan, Anna Kern, Lucas Keefer, Nathan Moser, Kevin McCannon, Kaela Byers, Daniel Sullivan, and Rachel Craft. 2011. "Mapping the Great Recession: A Reader's Guide to the First Crisis of 21st Century Capitalism." *New Political Science* 33(4):577–601.

Weber, Max. 1904/1958. *The Protestant Ethic and the Spirit of Capitalism*. New York: Charles Scribner's Sons.

CHAPTER 11

DO RELIGIOUS CHILDREN CARE MORE AND PROVIDE MORE CARE FOR OLDER PARENTS?

Consider the following questions as you read this chapter.

QUESTIONS TO CONSIDER

1. What questions were the authors trying to answer in their study?

2. What research design did they use: sample, design, data sources?

3. What did they find out about the relationship between how religious someone is and how likely he or she is to care for his or her aging parents?

4. What is the authors' main point?

KEY TERMS

religiosity
intergenerational support

DO RELIGIOUS CHILDREN CARE MORE AND PROVIDE MORE CARE FOR OLDER PARENTS?

A STUDY OF FILIAL NORMS AND BEHAVIORS ACROSS FIVE NATIONS

BY DAPHNE GANS, MERRIL SILVERSTEIN, AND ARIELA LOWENSTAIN

INTRODUCTION

Much of the literature on the normative obligation to provide care to older parents centers on its role in motivating supportive behavior. However, most studies find that the relationship between norms and behavior in the domain of parent care is weak or holds true only under particular circumstances (Silverstein, Gans & Yang, 2006; Silverstein, Parrott, & Bengtson, 1995). While previous studies have noted the complexity of the relationship between filial norms and filial behavior, little is known about the societal and religious contexts within which normative obligations are enacted into

Daphne Gans, Merril Silverstein, and Ariela Lowenstein, "Do Religious Children Care More and Provide More Care for Older Parents? A Study of Filial Norms and Behaviors across Five Nations," *Journal of Comparative Family Studies*, vol. 40, no. 2, pp. 187-201. Copyright © 2009 by University of Calgary, Department of Sociology. Reprinted with permission. Provided by ProQuest LLC. All rights reserved.

actual support. This investigation examines the correspondence between filial norms and supportive behavior of adult children toward their older parents in four European countries (Norway, England, Spain, and Germany) and Israel, emphasizing the role of religiosity in the development and enactment of filial norms in those national contexts.

Despite recent gains in the longevity of older adults, many of the years added to life are accompanied by chronic conditions and experienced with frailty (Freedman, Schoeni, Martin, & Cornman, 2007). As a result, adult children are likely to spend prolonged periods of time assisting aging parents. However, increasing demand for eldercare is not matched by an increasing supply of potential family caregivers as a result of declining fertility, delayed parenthood, elevated rates of divorce and remarriage, and increased labor force participation of women (Easterlin, Schaeffer, & Macunovich, 1993). In such an environment, it is imperative to understand the ideological and structural conditions that promote or inhibit the development of normative obligations to support aging parents, as well as the conditions that encourage or impede the translation of such commitment into actual support.

RELIGIOSITY AND INTERGENERATIONAL SUPPORT

Despite growing evidence of the importance of religion in family life (Chatters & Taylor, 2005; Mahoney, Pargament, Tarakeshwar & Swank, 2001) and its obvious relevance as a normative factor in family decision-making, only few papers have addressed the role of religiosity in intergenerational relationships.

From the somewhat sparse literature on this topic, three general aspects of religion that are likely to shape intergenerational supportive relationships emerge: religious doctrines that prescribe appropriate behavior toward older parents; religious values emphasizing compassion and reinforcing helping behaviors; and institutional structures as well as religious rituals reinforcing strong intergenerational bonds and commitment to family members.

Doctrinal aspects of religion are best summarized by the dictate of the Old Testament to honor one's father and mother, a filial prescription made in various forms by virtually all religions of the world. Individuals who are more involved in practicing religion through both the public sphere (participation in religious services) and the private sphere (family prayers, personal salience of religion) are more likely to be exposed to messages that promote strong family commitment (Pearce & Axinn, 1998). Moreover, co-religionists can reinforce positive adherence and performance of desired family norms as well as provide role models for preferred family behaviors and place informal sanctions on those deviating from desired norms (Chatters & Taylor, 2005; Ellison, 1997).

Religious teachings also inculcate collectivistic values that encourage service to the most vulnerable members of society (Ellison, 1997; Myers, 2004). Dollahite and Marks (2005) suggest that religion creates a sense of community supportiveness from which evolves "deep and abiding caring relationships" (p. 537). It is likely that individuals who are so influenced by their religious orientations are more inclined to provide support to needy parents. Additionally, some religious organizations provide formal education programs such as family life education, which explicitly promote and support desired family behaviors including care for frail parents (Chatters & Taylor, 2005). Such programs may indicate that religious commitment to helping other family members may be even stronger than the commitment to help other individuals.

Finally, most religious groups endorse strong family relationships (Myers, 2004). In the public sphere, religious institutions typically provide opportunities for family activities including family camps and retreats, which promote stronger intergenerational family bonds (Pearce & Axinn, 1998; Chatters & Taylor, 2005). In the private sphere, celebration of Holidays, as well as various religious rituals, provides opportunities for bringing families together, emphasizing the importance of families, and making individuals more aware of their role within the generational structure of the family (Chatters &Taylor, 2005). Pearce and Axinn (1998) demonstrated that religiosity had a significant positive effect on the quality of parent-child relationships by strengthening the affective bond between them. Given the strong relationship between affective ties and support provided to parents (Cicirelli, 1983; Rossi & Rossi, 1990), it is likely that religiosity indirectly enhances supportive behavior by strengthening intergenerational cohesion.

Taken together, it is clear that religiosity is a useful vantage point from which to study filial commitment and filial behavior.

In addition, religion and religious institutions are likely to attract adherents and congregants who already adhere to an ideology that emphasizes selflessness and providing for others. Thus, religiosity may be selective with respect to characteristics that predispose individuals to help their aging parents.

A host of factors beyond religious values are important in motivating adult children to provide care for their aging parents or inhibiting them from doing so. Previous articles (see Gans & Silverstein, 2006; Silverstein, Gans & Yang, 2006; Silverstein, Conroy, & Gans, 2008) provided extensive literature reviews of these factors and we summarize them briefly here. These factors typically divide into three main groups: parental needs, intergenerational relationship quality, and adult child availability. Prime among the factors is parental need for support, typically manifest by physical and cognitive impairments, or widowhood (Silverstein, Gans & Yang, 2006). Another factor facilitating supportive behavior is having an emotionally close and engaged relationship with parents (Rossi & Rossi, 1990; Silverstein, Parrott, & Bengtson, 1995). Finally, competing demands such having minor children in the household may serve as a barrier to provision of support by imposing barriers on adult children's availability and resources (e.g., time, money, energy). Normative orientations inconsistently predict whether supportive roles are enacted, but as discussed earlier, the expression of filial values by supportive behavior is highly contingent on these aforementioned factors. Other characteristics of children and parents may further be important. For example, Myers (2004) found that the relationship between religiosity and parental assistance was conditioned on gender of the child and the marital status of the parent, with more religious adult daughters providing higher levels of support to continuously married parents compared to provider sons and recipient divorced parents.

The political economy and family culture have increasingly been considered as important contextual factors in structuring how intergenerational relations of the elderly are maintained. The availability of internationally comparative data across European nations has been especially useful for studying how national context influences micro-family interactions (Glaser, Tomassini, & Grubndy, 2004; Hank, 2007; Lowenstein, Katz & Daatland, 2005). These investigations generally find that the salience of intergenerational relations—as measured by proximity, frequency of contact, and provisions of support—tends to be more common in nations with less generous social welfare regimes and more familistic cultures. For the most part, these differences follow a north-south divide. Collectivistic cultures tend to thrive in the south compared to individualist traditions of the north (Reher 1998), while the public sector is more developed in the social welfare regimes of the north compared to the more restricted system in the south (Epsing-Andersen 1990,1999; Ferrera 1996).

The goals of the current study are to: (1) examine the degree of consistency between filial norms and support—the gap between what adult children believe they should do to support aging parents and their actual supportive actions; (2) identify how national context shapes the consistency between norms and behavior by examining the norms-support relationship across five countries with varying political economies, family cultures, and religious compositions; and (3) explore the role of religiosity in whether filial norms and support are consistent or inconsistent. It is hypothesized that more strongly religious adult children and those from more familistic national cultures will be more likely to be congruent in their norms and support. They will be more likely to express strong filial values toward older parents as well as more likely to act on those values.

METHODS

SAMPLE

Data from the five-nation study known as OASIS (Old Age and Autonomy: The Role of Service Systems and Intergenerational Family Solidarity) are used. OASIS includes data collected in Norway, England, Germany, Spain, and Israel, each nation representing a unique welfare regime and familial culture. Data were collected using face-to-face structured interviews with random samples of about 1,200 adults aged 21 and older from each country, totaling 6,100 respondents (see Lowenstein and Ogg [2003] for a full description of the OASIS design and methodology). Over-samples were drawn of individuals aged 75 and older. As the data do not include weights, it was impossible to recalibrate the data for sampling distortions related to non-response, design effects, or disproportionate sampling. However, refusal rates were low in each nation (Lowenstein & Ogg, 2003) and focusing on the younger portion of the sample renders inconsequential the over-sampling of aged individuals. The sub-sample for this analysis is comprised of 2,327 adult children from the five countries, who have at least one surviving parent. Table 1 shows the descriptive characteristics of the subsample. The sample is slightly more educated than the general sample, likely due to the inclusion of respondents with living parents. It is possible that there is a selection effect of healthier families who are likely to be more educated and possibly wealthier.

The five countries considered in the current study can be ranked along several dimensions that roughly follow a north-south divide. Spain has weak welfare institutions, and along with Germany imposes legal obligations on adult children to support their older parents. The mixed Israeli model is characterized by legal family obligations and strong collectivist orientation, but also has high service levels. Norway, and to a lesser degree England, has strong social care policies, and no legal obligations between generations. Roughly, we predict stronger congruence between elder-care norms and behavior in Spain, followed by Israel, Germany, England, and Norway. As religiosity is a key variable of interest, it is useful to note that in the five sub-samples Catholics form a plurality in Spain (59.7%), Jews are the large majority in Israel (98.5% given that only the Jewish population was surveyed), and Protestants are a plurality in Norway (73.3%). In England and Germany large portions of respondents reported no religious denomination (42.6% in England and 34.39% in Germany). The next largest faction was Protestant in England (28.3%) and Catholics (29.8 %) in Germany.

MEASURES

FILIAL NORMS AND FILIAL BEHAVIOR

The dimensions used for classification are filial norms and filial behavior, each assessed with respect to two domains or content areas: geographic proximity and instrumental support. Parallel measures allow us to match the norm to the corresponding behavior in the two domains.

The first domain relates to *geographic proximity*. Filial norms in this domain were measured by level of agreement with the following statement: *"Adult children should live close to their older parents so they can help them if needed."* Responses were dichotomized whereby "1" represents strong endorsement of this filial norm (agree or strongly agree), and "0" represents weak endorsement (neither disagree nor agree, disagree, or strongly disagree.) Filial behavior in the domain of proximity was measured using response to the following question: *"how long does it take you to travel to parent(s)?"* Responses were dichotomized whereby "1" represents a travel time of 29 minutes or less, and "0" indicates longer travel time.

The second domain relates to *Instrumental support*. Filial norms in this domain were measured using the level of agreement with the following statement: *"Older parents*

Table 11.1 Descriptive characteristics of the sample (N = 2,364)

	NORWAY N = 546	ENGLAND N = 372	GERMANY N = 417	SPAIN N = 468	ISRAEL N = 561	OVERALL N = 2,364
	M(SD)/%	M(SD)/%	M(SD)/%	M(SD)/%	M(SD)/%	M(SD)/%
Age	38.8 (10.1)	41.8 (10.2)	40.6 (9.9)	38.5 (10.3)	38.4 (10.9)	39.4 (10.4)
Female	55.7	62.2	49.5	52.2	63.5	56.8
Married	63.2	68.5	69.3	61.2	66.9	65.6
Has Minor children	51.2	66.0	51.5	43.9	59.1	53.9
College Education+	34.1	7.2	18.0	17.5	11.9	18.5
Very Religious	4.1	7.8	4.6	4.5	1.7	4.3
Not-At-All Religious	38.3	43.3	33.9	28.5	60.8	42.1
Age of Parent	67.9 (11.4)	69.8 (10.2)	67.6 (9.8)	68.9 (10.7)	67.5 (10.9)	68.3 (10.7)
Closeness with parents[1]	4.4 (.9)	4.5 (1.2)	4.3 (.8)	4.5 (.9)	4.7 (.9)	4.5 (.9)
Contact with parents[2]	3.9 (1.5)	4.2 (1.8)	3.5 (1.6)	4.5 (1.6)	5.1 (1.5)	4.3 (1.6)

1 Closeness to parents is measured on a scale of 1-6 with 1 indicating the most distant and 6 indicating the closest relationship.

2 Contact with parents is measured on a scale from 0-6 with 0 indicating once per year or less and 6 indicating daily or more often contact

should be able to depend on their adult children to help them do the things they need to do." Responses were dichotomized whereby "1" represents strong endorsement of this norm (agree or strongly agree with the statement), and "0" represents weak endorsement (neither disagree nor agree, disagree, or strongly disagree). Filial behavior was measured using the response to following question: *"During the last 12 months, have you provided any of the following kinds of help, assistance or support to any of your parents?"* We considered only the following tasks that were deemed to be instrumental in nature: house repair or gardening; transportation or shopping, help with household chores, and personal care. Affirmative responses were dichotomized whereby "1" represents provision of at least one supportive instrumental task, and "0" indicates that no instrumental support was provided.

PREDICTOR VARIABLES

SUBJECTIVE RELIGIOSITY

Respondents were presented with a single item question asking *"Do you consider yourself to be not-at-all religious, somewhat religious, moderately religious, or very religious?"* In this analysis we are especially interested in the extreme cases, those *not-at-all religious* and those who are *very religious*. Two dichotomous variables were created to represent the two extreme responses, leaving the middle group of those defining themselves as somewhat or moderately religious as the reference group.

Parental needs were measured using a dichotomous variable whereby "1" indicated parents older than 75 years of age and "0" indicated a younger parent. Advanced age is used as a proxy for parental health status. The data do not present with an objective health measure for the parents and about 24% of the subsample had missing data on the subjective measure of health (asking whether one's parent needs help). Additionally, a variable measuring marital status of the parent was included whereby "1" represents widowed parent and "0" represents other marital status.

Relationship quality was measured using the mean score of responses to three questions measuring affectual solidarity—the emotional closeness between the child and the parent (Bengtson & Mangen, 1988). These items were: (1) *How close do you feel to your parent?*; (2) *How good is your communication with your parent?*; and (3) *How do you and your parent get along?* Responses to each item were scored on a six-point Likert scale, ranging from "not-at-all well" to "extremely well." Frequency of contact with parents was measured by a continuous variable indicating the highest frequency of contact (via email, phone or in person) with a parent. This variable ranged from 0 to 6 where 1 = once a year or less to 6 = daily or more often.

Competing demands of adult children were measured using two variables: marital status (1 = married or living in partnership; 0 = any other marital status) and the presence of young children (1 = has at least one minor child aged 21 or younger; 0 = has no minor children). Other variables included in the model were gender (1 = female; 0 = male), age in years and a squared age term, and education level (1 = university degree and beyond; 0 = lower levels of education).

PROCEDURE

In the first stage of the analysis, a model that defines adult children based on the congruence between their filial norms and their filial behavior is developed. To do this, we use latent class analysis (LCA), an exploratory method for classifying individuals into unobserved or latent classes based on the association among observed variables (Vermunt & Magidson, 2000; Clogg, 1995). A key assumption of the technique is that the latent classes account for the true covariation among the measured variables. Model selection is based on progressively adding latent classes until a good fit to the observed data is achieved, using the following statistics to evaluate model fit: (1) chi-square likelihood test (L^2), where a non-significant L^2 indicates that the predictions of the theoretical model fit the observed data, (2) Baysian Information Criterion (*BIC*) statistic indicates the relative fit of competing models, with lower values indicating a better fit (Raftery, 1986), and (3) classification error rate indicates the percent of misallocated cases in a specific model, where lower errors are preferable. Whereas the L^2 is prone to showing poor fit in large samples, BIC and classification error statistics are not sensitive to sample size.

Once a best-fitting model is identified and assignments to the classes are made, two sets of probabilities are examined to interpret the meaning and identify the prevalence of the classes: (1) Conditional latent class probabilities describe the distribution of observed indicators within each class and are used to label the classes. These are analogous to factor loadings and describe the measurement model. Nationality is included as a nominal covariate in the latent class analysis such that the measurement model is considered invariant across nations. (2) Latent class probabilities signify the distribution of sample members across classes, and describe the prevalence of each class in the population. These probabilities are free to vary across national contexts.

In the second stage of the analysis, we use *logistic regression analysis* to predict the likelihood of belonging to specific latent classes. The dependent variable at this point is nominal class membership based on assignments made by the LCA best-fitting model. Four dichotomous country indicators are included as predictors in the logistic regression with Israel (representing a unique mixed model) treated as the reference category.

RESULTS

CLASSIFICATION OF INDIVIDUALS BASED ON FILIAL NORMS AND FILIAL BEHAVIOR

The goodness-of-fit statistics for latent class models ranging from one to six classes is presented. The one-class model, which assumes that there are no relationships between the four measured items, fits poorly with the data. Successive addition of latent classes reveals that the L^2 of each is statistically significant and not until the six-class model does the model fit the observed data. In choosing between competing models we dismiss the L^2 as an absolute indicator of model fit due to the large sample size and rely on the other indicators. The BIC statistic reaches a generally similar minimum for the three-class, four-class, and five-class models. Among these, the three-class model has the lowest classification error at 17%, a rate somewhat higher than desired, but in keeping with those found in other applications of LCA (Vermunt & Magidson, 2003). Thus, we select the three-class model as the best-fitting model to our data.

Table 11.3 represents the latent class conditional probabilities associated with each class in the selected three-class model. We use these to profile the classes. Those assigned to the first class are defined by high probabilities of endorsing filial norms and engaging in filial behaviors in both domains, a group we label the *committed supporters*. Their actions are consistent with their normative commitment in both domains. The second group has low probabilities of endorsing filial norms and relatively low probabilities of engaging in filial behaviors of either type, a group we label as

Table 11.2 Latent Class Models of Intergenerational Relationships Using Four Dichotomous Indicators of Filial Behavior and Norms.

	L²(DF)	P-VALUE	BIC	CLASSIFICATION ERROR RATE
One class–complete independence	699.75 (71)	4.2e−104	−149.34	0
Two class	330.99 (62)	2.2e−38	−149.65	.05
Three-class	218.60 (53)	5.4e−22	−192.22	.17
Four-class	146.88 (44)	5.3e−13	−194.22	.22
Five-class	79.76 (35)	2.4e−5	−191.57	.30
Six-class	43.52 (26)	0.017	−158.03	31

Table 11.3 Conditional Latent Class Probabilities for Constrained Three-Class Model.

MEASURE	CONDITIONAL LATENT CLASS PROBABILITIES		
	COMMITTED SUPPORTERS	INDEPENDENT	LONG DISTANCE SUPPORTERS
Filial Norms			
Should live close to parent	**.74**	.01	.38
Should be dependable	**.73**	.19	**.76**
Filial Behavior			
Lives close to parent	**.70**	.48	.40
Provides instrumental support	**.53**	.41	**.67**

Note: Probabilities greater than .5 are shown in bold.

independent. Finally, the third group favors the domain of support over that of geographic proximity in both norms and behavior, and are labeled *long-distance supporters.* They tended to endorse the norm of being a dependable support provider and actually provide support, but tend not to endorse a norm of proximity, nor do they live close to their parents. In general, the types can be characterized as consistent in norms and behavior within each content domain.

In Table 11.4 the latent class distributions across the total sample as well as by country are presented. The class described as *committed supporters* represented slightly less than half (46%) of all respondents. The group termed *independent* was the next most frequently occurring class, describing about 31% of respondents. The remaining 23% of respondents fell into the class of *long distance supporters*. Striking differences emerge in the latent class distribution when examined by country. These figures are shown in Table 11.4 and shown graphically in Figure 11.1. Norway is unique in that almost three-quarters (72%) of its respondents in the *long-distance supporters* class and very few (2%) in the *committed supporters* class. Spain and Israel are the mirror image of Norway with very few (3% and 1% respectively) of its respondents in the *long-distance supporters* class and almost three-quarters (71% and 74% respectively) in the *committed supporters* class. Germany came closest to the mirroring the distribution for the total sample with about one-third of its respondents in each of the three classes. England was notable for its high representation (45%) in the *independent* class, more than half (53%) in the *committed supporters* class, and very few (1%) in the *long distance supporters* class, reflecting a polarization in the class assignments made in that nation.

Table 11.4 Latent Class Probabilities for the Three-Class Model: Total and by Country

COUNTRY	COMMITTED SUPPORTERS	INDEPENDENT	LONG DISTANCE SUPPORTERS
Norway	.02	.26	.72
Spain	.71	.26	.03
England	.53	.46	.01
Israel	.74	.25	.01
Germany	.34	.34	.32
Total	.46	.31	.23

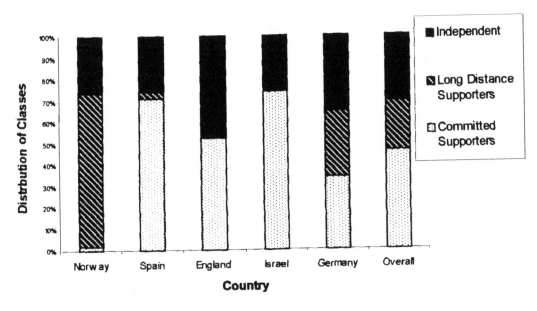

Figure 11.1 Distribution of classes across countries

PREDICTORS OF CLASS MEMBERSHIP

As discussed, the distribution of classes varies markedly across the five nations considered. Because four out the five nations were sparsely represented in at least one class, multivariate estimation predicting membership across the three classes is not feasible with covariates indicating national membership. Therefore, we collapse the *committed supporters* and the *long-distance supporters* to form a single class that is differentiated from the *independent* class. Aside from being methodological convenience, this also provides a meaningful contrast of those who have weak normative commitment and are unlikely to be support providers with those who have moderate to strong normative commitment and tend to provide support at least in one of the two domains (instrumental support).

The results of the logistic regression are presented in Table 11.5. The analyses were performed using the combined *committed supporters* and *long-distance supporters*

Table 11.5 Logistic Regression Analysis Predicting Independent Compared to Combined Committed Supporters and Long-distance Supporters[a].

PREDICTOR	E^x	SE
Religiosity[b]		
Not-at-all religious	1.31**	.14
Very religious	.47**	.13
Parental need		
Parent aged 75+	.98	.14
Widowed parent	1.09	.13
Relationship Quality		
Closeness to parents	.81***	.04
Frequency of contact	.93*	.03
Competing Demands		
Married	1.07	.12
Has minor children	.85	.10
Age	1.04	.04
Age squared	.99	.01
Female	1.20	.12
College education +	1.22	.16
Country indicators[c]		
Norway	1.32	.20
England	2.64***	.43
Spain	.98	.15
Germany	1.32	.20
Pseudo R^2		.043
χ^2 (df)		109.02(17)

*p < .05. **p < .01. ***p < .001.
[a] Results are presented as oddsratios.
[b] Reference group consists of those somewhat or moderately religious.
[c] The reference group is Israel.

as the reference category. Odds ratios are reported. As expected, those defining themselves as not-at-all religious were 30% more likely (OR = 1.3) to be in the *independent* group than in the other more committed and more involved group. Moreover, those defining themselves as very religious were about half as likely (OR = .47) to be *independent*.

Other variables also predicted likelihood of class membership. In terms of national contrasts, respondents in England were more than 2.5 times likely to be *independent* than their counterparts in Israel. When effect coding rather than dummy coding is used for national context (not shown) results show that England is exceptional in this regard compared to all countries taken together.

Relationship factors also had an influence on class membership. Quality of relationship and frequency of contact with parents were significant in the equation. Those with stronger emotional ties with parents and those with more frequent contact with them were less likely to be *independent*. Competing demands in the forms of having a spouse or having a young child at home did not affect the likelihood of class membership.

DISCUSSION

Our first goal in this investigation was to understand the relationship between what respondents think the role of children should be with respect to aging parents and what they actually do to support their parents. To investigate this issue we created a typology based on filial norms and filial behavior. The results indicate that most respondents across the countries studied are congruent with regard to norms and behavior in the domains of geographic proximity and instrumental support. Little evidence of cognitive dissonance in the sample was found, as there were few respondents whose commitment was strong but unfulfilled, or weak despite their involvement. To what degree, this correspondence reflects filial norms as an attribution or a motivation of behavior will await longitudinal research on this topic. Nevertheless, these results help resolve discrepancies in the literature regarding the relationship between norms and behaviors in intergenerational relationships. The strength of our findings could be due in part to innovations in the design and method used in the study such as matching norms and behaviors in specific domains of involvement, using classification analysis as tool to categorize individuals based on several dimensions simultaneously, and examining the issue from the child's rather than the parent's perspective.

Our second goal was to examine the representation of classes in the pooled sample and by national context. The largest group—about half of the pooled sample—consisted of adult children who expressed strong normative commitment and were engaged with their older parents in terms of living close and providing support. About a third did not feel strongly about the role of children nor did they live close or provide support to their parents. The third class was the most variegated, with strong commitment to and enactment of support, but little intent and realization of living in close proximity to their parents. Although these respondents provided support and did so from afar, they were congruent in their norms and behavior within each domain. In other previous research we found that long-distance care providers had extraordinarily strong normative commitment to withstand the costs of negotiating care at a distance (Silverstein, Conroy & Gans, 2008). The consequences of such support arrangements—in terms of caregiver stress and the quality of distant care—require further research.

There is wide variation across countries in the distribution of the three identified types. As expected, national differences followed a north–south divide with more committed supporters in the more familistic nations of Spain and Israel, and greater independence in England and (geographically) in Norway. Germany, the nation in the middle of the north–south axis is equally distributed across the three types. The large proportion of long-distance supporters in Norway is consistent with research showing that intergenerational proximity is not a strong goal in Norwegian families and that multigenerational households are extremely rare (Daatland, Herlofson, 2003; Daatland & Lowenstein, 2005). In part, the generosity of formal services and universal access to services allows Norwegian children to be involved in ways that are less onerous and demanding such that they may not need to live close to their parents in order to exchange support (Daatland, 1997).

Both in the cross-classification and logistic regression analysis England was unique in its over-representation in the *independent* class. While this finding is somewhat difficult to interpret in light of the findings in Norway, it is possible that England represents a mixed system in which nationalized health care comes with increasingly strict eligibility requirements. Thus, adult children may be more likely to prefer formal arrangements but often face the prospect of parent care given restrictions in the public system (explaining why over half were in the *committed-supporters* class). While it possible that cultural factors are also at play we are reluctant to speculate about this at present without additional evidence.

The third goal of this paper was to examine the role religiosity plays in developing normative obligations and enacting parent-care roles. The current results indicate that religiosity plays a part in how adult children are involved in the support and care of their older parents. Further, the findings suggest a linear trend rather than a threshold effect, whereby the least religious are *most* likely and the most religious *least* likely to be independent of their parents. In other words, the religious extremes represent distinct groups with respect to the outcome variable, with religiosity following a dose-response pattern with respect to commitment and enactment of support to older parents.

These results demonstrate that religiosity is an important context within which filial norms are developed and are enacted. However, the means by which religiosity exerts its influence is not identified by this analysis. As discussed earlier, most religions proclaim it a virtue to take care of older people—particularly older parents—reflecting their concern for supporting the more vulnerable of society and for preserving the sanctity of family life. Religious activities instill values of collectivism that encourage caring behaviors to others and provide a context that promotes both informal and formal venues for helping others, all of which may promote a strong sense of family cohesiveness and commitment leading to higher levels of commitment and support to one's family members (Chatters and Taylor, 2005; Ellison, 1997).

Given that this study is cross-sectional, one cannot state with certainty that religiosity predicts the development of filial norms and their enactment into actual support, nor can one propose that religiosity promotes congruence between norms and behavior. One cannot rule out the possibility that other factors such as cultural conservatism are in fact explaining both religiosity and caring commitment and behavior. That said, the results indicate that religiosity is indeed significantly associated with filial norms and parental care across five different national contexts. As such, the study contributes to the literature and opens the door for future investigations. Future research should utilize longitudinal data to address the temporal relationship between the development of religiosity, filial norms and actual supportive behavior towards parents. Future research in the area of religiosity and exchange of intergenerational support in other societies and cultures will further be needed to establish whether the relationship between religiosity and filial norms and behavior is universal.

We recognize that a multidimensional approach to measuring religious belief, practice, and identification, along the lines suggested by Levin, Taylor, & Chatters (1995), will best shed light on the pathways by which religion promotes familistic attitudes and behaviors in later life families. From the current study one can only speculate how the world-view and institutional structures provided by religions collude to reinforce altruistic motivations and enable actions of adult children toward their aging parents in need.

REFERENCES

Attias-Donfut, C. & Wolff, F.C. (2005). Generational memory and family relationships. In M.L. Johnson, V.L. Bengtson, P. Coleman & T. Kirkwood (Eds.), *The Cambridge Handbook of Age and Ageing* (pp. 443–454). Cambridge: Cambridge University Press.

Chatters, L.M., & Taylor, R. J. (2005). Religion and Families. In V.L. Bengtson, A. Acock, K. Allen, P. Dilworth-Anderson, & D. Klein (Eds.) *Sourcebook of Family Theory and Research* (pp. 517–530). Thousand Oaks, CA: Sage.

Cicirelli, V. G. (1983). A comparison of helping behavior to elderly parents of adult children with intact and disrupted marriages. *The Gerontologist, 23,* 619–625.

Clogg, C.C. (1995). Latent class models. In G. Arminger, C.C. Clogg, And M.E. Sobel (Eds.), *Handbook of statistical modeling for the social and behavioral science* (pp. 311–360). New York: Plenum Press.

Daatland, S.O. (1997). Family solidarity, popular opinion, and the elderly: perspectives from Norway. *Ageing International, 1,* 51–62.

Daatland, S.O., & Herlofson, K. (2003). 'Lost solidarity' or 'changed solidarity': a comparative European view of normative family solidarity. *Ageing Society, 23,* 537–560.

Daatland, S.O., & Lowenstein, A. (2005). Intergenerational solidarity and the family-welfare state balance. *European Journal on Ageing, 2,* 174–182.

Dollahite, D.C., & Marks, L.D. (2005). How highly religious families strive to fulfill sacred purposes? In V.L. Bengtson, A. Acock, K. Allen, P. Dilworth-Anderson, & D. Klein (Eds.) *Sourcebook of Family Theory and Research* (pp. 533–537). Thousand Oaks, CA: Sage.

Easterlin, R., Schaeffer, C., & Macunovich, D. (1993). Will the baby boomers be less well-off than their parents? Income, wealth, and family circumstances over the life cycle. *Population and Development Review, 19(3),* 497–522.

Ellison, C.G (1997). Religious involvement and the subjective quality of life among African Americans. In R.J. Taylor, J.S. Jackson, & L.M. Chatters (Eds.), *Family life in Black America* (pp. 117–131). Thousand Oaks, CA: Sage.

Esping-Andersen, G. (1990). *The three worlds of welfare capitalism.* Princeton: Princeton University Press.

Esping-Andersen, G. (1999). *Social foundations of post-industrial economies.* Oxford: Oxford University Press.

Ferrera, M. (1996). The 'southern model' of welfare in social Europe. *Journal of European Social Policy, 6,1,* 17–37.

Freedman, V.A., Schoeni, R.F., Martin, L.G, & Cornman, J.C. (2007). Chronic conditions and the decline in late-life disability. *Demography, 44,* 459–477.

Gans, D., & Silverstein, M. (2006). Norms of filial responsibility for aging parents across time and generations. *Journal of Marriage and Family, 68,* 961–976.

Glaser, K., Tomassini, C., & Grubndy, E. (2004). Revisiting convergence and divergence: Support for older people in Europe. *European Journal of Ageing, 1,* 64–72.

Hank, K. (2007). Proximity and contacts between older parents and their children: A European comparison. *Journal of Marriage and Family, 65,* 584–596.

Levin, J.S., Taylor, R.J., & Shatters, L. (1995). A multidimensional measure of religious involvement for African Americans. *The Sociological Quarterly, 36 (1),* 157–173.

Lowenstein, A. Katz, R., & Daatland, S.O. (2004). Filial norms and intergenerational support in European and Israeli comparative perspective. In M. Silverstein (Ed.), *Annual Review of Gerontology and Geriatrics,* Volume 24: *Intergenerational Relations Across Time and Place* (pp. 200–223). New York: Springer Publishing Company.

Lowenstein, A., & Ogg, J. (2003). *OASIS Final Report.* Centre for Research and Study of Ageing, University of Haifa, Haifa, Israel. Available online at: http://oasis.haifa.ac.il/downloads/oasis-final-report.pdf

Mahoney, A., Pargament, K., Tarakeshwar, N., & Swank, A.B. (2001). Religion in the home in the 1980s and 1990s: A meta-analytic review and conceptual analysis of links between religion, marriage, and parenting: Families and religion. *Journal of Family Psychology, 15,*559–596.

Myers, S. M. (2004). Religion and intergenerational assistance: Distinct differences by adult children's gender and parent's marital status. Sociological Quarterly, 45 (1), 67–89.

Pearce, L.D., & Axinn, W.G. (1998). The impact of family religious life on the quality of mother-child relations. *American Sociological Review, 63,* 810–828.

Raftery, A.E. (1986). Choosing models for cross-classifications. *American Sociological Review, 51,* 145–146.

Reher, D.S. (1998). Family ties in Western Europe: Persistent contrasts. *Population and Development Review, 24, 2,* 203–234.

Rossi, A. S., & Rossi, P. H. (1990). *Of human bonding: Parent-children relationship across the life course.* New York: Aldine de Gruyter.

Silverstein, M., Conroy, S., & Gans, D. (2008). Commitment to Caring: Filial Responsibility and the Allocation of Support by Adult Children to Older Mothers. In M. Szinovacz, & A. Davey (Eds.). *Caregiving Contexts: Cultural, Familial, and Societal Contexts.* New York: Springer Publishing.

Silverstein, M., Gans, D., & Yang, F.M. (2006) *Filial Support to Aging Parents: The Role of Norms and Needs. Journal of Family Issues, 27,* 1068–1084.

Silverstein, M., Parrott, T.M., & Bengtson, V.L. (1995). Factors That Predispose Middle-Aged Sons and Daughters to Provide Social Support to Older Parents. *Journal of Marriage and the Family, 57:* 465–476.

Vermunt, J.K., & Magidson, J. (2000). *Latent Gold user guide.* Belmont, Mass: Statistical Innovations Inc.

Vermunt, J. K. & Magidson, J. (2003). Latent class models for classification. *Computational Statistics & Data Analysis, 41,* 531–537.

CONCLUSION

You are on your way! Whether your next step is to take more courses in sociology or this is the only exposure you will have to the field of sociology, once you have successfully completed the material in this book, you should be in a position to apply sociological concepts to your everyday life. This can be an important part of understanding how the world works and why people act in the ways that they do.

Having an understanding of how living in a society affects people can help you in many aspects of your future life and career. Whether you become a social worker or work in business, this understanding can help you work with people better and better understand "where they come from." Sociology can help you make sense of the world, which is why I titled this book *Making Sociological Sense*!